"The story of the Meserete Kristos Church in Ethiopia bears witness to the fact that God is planting his church today through faithful people, prayer, demonstrations of power, and severe persecution. Stories like this inspire and give meaning to our work, and challenge our own complacencies.

"Beyond Our Prayers is not the story of human efforts, but of God's power working through his people to plant churches in difficult settings. It testifies to the fact that God can and is doing his work through ordinary people faithful to his calling."
—*Paul G. Hiebert, Trinity Evangelical Divinity School*

"The quickening work of the Spirit of the Lord is always surprising, refreshing, and life-changing. *Beyond Our Prayers* takes the reader inside the Meserete Kristos Church to experience the transforming power of God in the face of daunting opposition. A faith-building book for our time."
—*Donald R. Jacobs, Mennonite Missiologist*

"A well-told story of creative mission, a steadfast and suffering church, imaginative leadership, and remarkable growth. An important contribution to understanding the Christian movement in Africa."
—*John A. Lapp, Executive Secretary Emeritus, Mennonite Central Committee*

"Hege documents God's faithfulness in calling North Americans to varied witness in Ethiopia. We see struggles of an emerging church, the energizing power of spiritual renewal, trials under Marxist ideology, and creative vision of contemporary leadership. One cannot read this book without reverently acknowledging God's surprises beyond our prayers."
—*Calvin Shenk, Eastern Mennonite University*

—*Other endorsements appear on the back cover.*

D1218584

Beyond Our Prayers

Anabaptist Church Growth in Ethiopia, 1948-1998

Nathan B. Hege

Herald
Press

Scottdale, Pennsylvania
Waterloo, Ontario

Library of Congress Cataloging-in-Publication Data

Hege, Nathan B., 1927-
    Beyond our prayers : Anabaptist church growth in
Ethiopia, 1948-1998 / Nathan B. Hege.
      p.   cm.
    "The story of the Meserete Kristos Church (MKC) in Ethiopia will
hold a special niche in the annals of Mennonite history"—Pref.
    Includes bibliographical references and index.
    ISBN 0-8361-9085-8 (alk. paper)
    1. Meserete Kristos Church (Ethiopia) 2. Mennonites—Ethiopia—
History—20th century. 3. Mennonites—Missions—Ethiopia.
4. Persecution—Ethiopia—History—20th century. 5. Ethiopia—
Church history—20th century.   I. Title.
BX8119.E8H34 1998
289.7'63—dc21   98-13888

The paper used in this publication is recycled and meets the minimum
requirements of American National Standard for Information Sciences—
Permanence of Paper for Printed Library Materials, ANSI Z39.48-1984.

07 06 05 04 03 02 01 00 99 98 10 9 8 7 6 5 4 3 2 1

*To the memory of
Kelifa Ali and Kiros Bihon.
Imprisoned because of their faith and
leadership in the Meserete Kristos Church,
they followed the Master obediently and
faced with courage the disappointment
of illness and early death.*

Contents

Foreword

The power of God's reign to overcome persecution is dramatically illustrated by this record of the Meserete Kristos Church (MKC) in Ethiopia. Leaders decided that home cell groups were their only alternative when a Communist regime sealed the doors of their churches. Secretly slipping into their home groups and worshiping together, the underground cells grew from five thousand people to over fifty thousand in a period of ten years!

The priesthood of all believers is the foundation for the success of this home cell movement. Removed from the traditional role of pastors who cared for them, these brothers and sisters discovered they could minister to one another through Christ's empowerment. Even more, they discovered that evangelism no longer meant attending a meeting in an auditorium. The massive conversions within this persecuted church far outstripped previous harvesting using traditional forms of evangelism! The increase came as believers personally shared their faith with others.

The MKC, like the sixteenth-century Anabaptists of central Europe, has discovered the joy and empowerment that believers experience as they meet in small-group fellowship around Christ and the Scriptures. In the midst of severe persecution, the Anabaptists planted five hundred churches within the first five years of the movement (1525-30). The MKC has experienced similar growth in the last five years (1992-97).

We must not underestimate the importance of this event as we enter a time of growing persecution of the church, the bride of Christ. As Hong Kong reverts to the ownership of China, a cell-based fraternity of over 150 churches there has circulated the videotape about the Meserete Kristos Church. They have received encouragement from what God did during the persecution in Ethiopia. Someone asked one of their key leaders if he expected that persecution would come to the Christians of Hong Kong. He replied, "I certainly hope so!" This Ethiopian church model has given them courage to face what might happen there, and an awareness that toughness in personal faith grows in adverse conditions.

The Russian government has been trying to pass a law that would close all churches which have developed since *perestroika* began in 1987. Some have predicted that the Ukraine will also try to outlaw new churches in that nation. If these restrictions are enacted, the example of the church in Ethiopia will bring great encouragement to the tens of thousands of believers who face the possible closing of their churches, whether in Russia, the Ukraine, China, the Sudan, or elsewhere.

Within the Islamic nations, the underground cell groups have become the primary means for evangelical Christians to worship. The spread of cell groups in the nations that oppress Christians is significant. Those brothers and sisters are finding inspiration from the faith and courage of believers in Ethiopia.

After freedom returned, the leaders of the Meserete Kristos Church did not revert to the previous traditional forms of church life. The cell structure was preserved, and the continued growth demonstrates the need for all churches around the world to be "two-winged," having the large group *and* the small group, to allow the body of Christ to soar into the heavens and experience the presence of God in wonderful ways.

It is my prayer that this stirring account of God's people discovering God's power will help us all to see that church cells are a global activity of the Holy Spirit in these last days. Throughout the earth, this movement spreads, even though it has never been organized or structured.

The book of Acts describes the multiplication of house churches. Around the world today, Christians are freshly discovering the Acts experience of multiplying growth groups. May the account you are about to read further move you to a necessary paradigm shift: we must abandon traditions smothering the community-based forms of church life that God desires for his children!

—*Dr. Ralph W. Neighbour Jr.*
TOUCH Outreach Ministries
Houston, Texas

Preface

The story of the Meserete Kristos Church (MKC) in Ethiopia will hold a special niche in the annals of Mennonite history. In many ways, it repeats on the African continent the Anabaptist experience of the sixteenth century in Europe—the emergence of a free church in a state-church society.

In the Amharic language, MKC means "Christ Foundation Church." Thus in its very name it picks up Menno Simons' theme from 1 Corinthians 3:11, that Jesus Christ is the one and only foundation. This serves to give identity to more than a hundred thousand evangelical believers scattered in all fourteen regions of Ethiopia.

The MKC's phenomenal growth during the decades of the 1980s and the 1990s is similar to the scope and spread of Anabaptists in Germany, Switzerland, and Holland during Reformation times. In a country ten times the size of Pennsylvania, MKC members had established 192 congregations by 1997. They are committed to spreading the gospel to every part of Ethiopia, and beyond.

This book tells two stories: the outreach of Lancaster Mennonite Conference into Ethiopia beginning in 1948, and how the MKC developed out of those mission efforts. The early chapters note that Mennonites first went to Ethiopia in 1945 as medical workers appointed by the Relief and Service Committee of Mennonite Board of Missions, Elkhart, Indiana; and Mennonite Central Committee, Akron, Pennsylvania. In 1948 the government of Ethiopia granted mission status to Eastern Mennonite Board of Missions and Charities, Salunga, Pennsylvania. This beginning leads to the fifty-year celebration in 1998.

The MKC commends Lancaster Conference Mennonites

for putting into place, even in the early days, a systematic plan for transferring administrative responsibilities to Ethiopians. Lancaster Conference is deeply grateful to be related to a church that has modeled faith and faithfulness in the face of persecution and difficulties of many kinds. Lancaster Mennonites and the MKC members thank God for a relationship in Christ that has matured and grown richer through the years.

God used a group of inexperienced missionaries and many Ethiopian believers to begin a movement that grew far beyond their expectations and prayers. God has surprised us all. May the name of the Lord be praised!

—*Nathan B. Hege*

Acknowledgments

In a book of this size, it is impossible to give individual recognition to the hundreds of people who have made significant contributions to the development of MKC in Ethiopia. The few people mentioned here are representative of many more—people who taught students and treated patients, who loved and prayed, who suffered for their witness, who deprived themselves for the sake of the gospel, and who allowed the Holy Spirit to direct their lives in serving the Lord by serving others.

Tilahun Beyene, currently writing the MKC story in Amharic, has shepherded this writing project from its beginning. Bedru Hussein, executive secretary of MKC, and Alemu Checole, member of the executive committee, facilitated the research. Yeshitela Mengistu developed the book's outline. Dr. Tesfatsion Dalellew, former executive secretary of MKC, read and commented on the chapters as they were being written. Chester Wenger, Janet Kreider, Herb and Sharon Kraybill, Shawle Wehibe, Nevin Horst, Paul T. and Daisy Yoder, and Peg Groff Engle also read and gave helpful comments on early drafts. Other reviewers of the manuscript include Calvin and Marie Shenk, Sinait Abebe, Carol Wert, Paul and Ann Gingrich, John A. and Alice Lapp, Jerry and Ann King-Grosh, Million Belete, Negash Kebede, Solomon Kebede, Mulugeta Zewdie, Pastor Kassa Agafari, Pastor Seyoum Gebretsadik, Girma Teklu, and Simon Badi.

Jewel Showalter and Allen Brubaker, who served on the MKC History Committee, gave valuable editorial guidance. Alice Snyder and Anna Frederick assisted in the research and checking of details. Eloise Thomas Plank helped in transcribing the interviews. Janet Kreider served as photo editor. My son, Harold Wharton-Hege, programmed my computer. My wife, Arlene, assisted with the interviews and was constantly by my side providing counsel and perspective. The "we" in this book includes her.

I am also indebted to more than a hundred missionaries and MKC members who graciously consented to be interviewed and to record their memories on tape. May God bless them for sharing their stories!

Finally, I am deeply grateful for the initiative Meserete Kristos Church took in preparing this fifty-year history and for the gracious way Eastern Mennonite Missions authorized and undergirded the publication of this book.

—*Nathan B. Hege*

1

The Day the Church Was Closed

Night had fallen that Sunday evening over Addis Ababa, the mile-high capital of Ethiopia. A dozen men, some of them armed, entered the gate of the enclosure around a little church where hundreds of people gathered to worship each Sunday. It was January 24, 1982. A total of 1,500 people had worshiped at three services that day. That afternoon there had been a wedding, and throughout the week instruction classes for new believers and prayer meetings were constantly in progress. Adjacent to the building was the church's elementary school where 150 pupils attended. A guesthouse and a central office for the Meserete Kristos Church of Ethiopia were nearby.

The leader of the guards glued strips of paper across each door frame of the chapel and the school. Now no one could enter without leaving evidence of a broken seal. The Marxist government of Ethiopia (Provisional Military Administrative Council), known as the *Derg*, had decided that the Meserete Kristos Church (MKC) with its fourteen congregations was a deterrent to the Marxist Revolution, now eight years in the making. Government leaders reasoned that people who would worship God instead of attending Marxist indoctrination meetings were not loyal to the socialist principles the government was trying to enforce. They assumed that the church was simply a front to harbor anti-revolutionaries.

Next the *kebele*[1] leaders, backed by armed guards, went to the church's guesthouse to close it as well. Here they opened the door without knocking and told Arlene Kreider, guest-house hostess, to order all the guests out of their rooms. A missionary of fifteen years, Arlene had determined to remain in Ethiopia after the Marxists took over in 1974. She had worked at Menno Bookstore in Addis Ababa and had weathered the difficult negotiations of relinquishing that store to government control when labor problems made it impossible to continue operating under the church. Now, as an elementary schoolteacher in the school next door and as hostess of the guesthouse, she had decided that she would not run from the country even though the government might make it difficult for missionaries to function.

Arlene stood there, her knees trembling in fear. She took deep breaths and prayed that God would help her remember the things she had been practicing to say to government officials if they ever took over the church.2

Nationalization of private property by the Marxist government was not new. Soon after the Marxists took over the government in 1974, people who owned more than one dwelling had to surrender the extra ones to the government. They could choose and retain only one house to live in. The officials took over businesses without apology, and they often blamed businessmen for taking too much profit from the people. Unreasonable fines for supposed failure to pay enough income taxes in previous years were slapped on businessmen. People who had no experience in governing were threatening everyone who seemed to be successful or who had any wealth at all. The revolution, though based on the slogan, "Land to the tiller," did not provide for private ownership of land. In the cities people waited in long lines for hours to buy their monthly allotment of grain and sugar.

On this night the guesthouse was filled with Ethiopian young people who had come to the city for a seminar with the Christophel Blinden Mission on how to grind eyeglasses for the visually impaired. A few of them were MKC members.

The foremost kebele leader, Comrade Kebede (not his real name), wore a jacket and hood, leaving only his face and

Above: The congregation at worship inside the Bole church before it was closed in 1982. Although the church was built to seat 250 people, about 500 gathered for worship services held on Sundays at 6:00 a.m., 8:30 a.m., and 11:00 a.m. *Lower corner:* Bole church (now called Kebena), Addis Ababa, was built in 1961 by Daniel Sensenig and Allen Byler. Three services were held here each Sunday at the time it was closed by the Marxist government in January, 1982. Today it is used by one of the 15 congregations in Addis Ababa.

big brown eyes visible. Arlene greeted them, but they would not talk in Amharic. They also did not accept her offer to shake hands.

"These are human beings," she thought, "and no matter what, I'll respect them. But I see I'm not dealing with *warm* human beings." It looked as though Arlene would not have a chance to prepare her guests for this invasion of their privacy.

Marxism was indeed destroying Ethiopian civility, making gruff legalists out of a gentle and polite people. Under the guise of equalizing wealth, the leaders that had bought the Marxist line were making everybody suspicious of everyone else. Government informants roamed the city and country-side, making it unsafe to talk freely. Nationalization of businesses and institutions under a corrupt bureaucracy was just one of the disrupting actions of leaders ill-trained to rule.

"As of this moment, this building, the car, everything on this compound—they all belong to the government," Kebede announced. "There will be no discussion, and you have no permission to make any phone calls. You will go through this house and tell people to come out of their rooms and go with us. Inform them that this building now belongs to the government."

It was a command similar to one that the government would issue in the following weeks and months to church leaders at all fourteen congregations.

The statement took Arlene by surprise. She was not prepared for her guests to be taken off to prison. Her biggest concern that night was that *they* might go to prison but *she* would be free. The guards had promised that no harm would come to her.

"What if they go to prison and I am free?" Arlene ago-

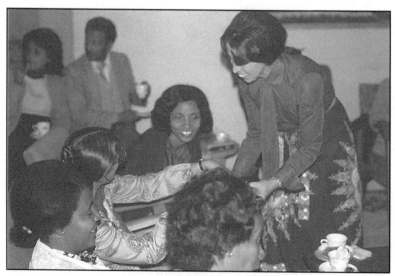

Arlene Kreider serving food to guests in the guesthouse, Addis Ababa.
Herb Kraybill photo.

nized as she walked from room to room. "Why am I taking comfort in their promise that no expatriate will be harmed? Should I just tell the kebele leaders to take me too?"

The men with their guns followed Arlene as she roused her guests, but strangely she felt no fear. When she reached the room of a girl who was a deaf mute, Arlene turned to the kebele leader and spoke with authority. "You will *not* take this girl with you. She will stay with me in my apartment. She does not understand what is going on. She cannot speak or hear."

The officials did not object. They told Arlene to inform Kelifa Ali, executive secretary of MKC, that he should appear at the higher kebele[3] office the next morning. Then they rounded up the rest of the guests and detained them at the police station for questioning for 24 hours.

Membership of MKC in its 14 congregations reached about 5,000 by 1982. Growth had been slow in the early years through the 1950s and 1960s when the Mennonite Mission in Ethiopia was establishing clinics, schools, and hospitals. During the Marxist rule, however, people began to take faith more seriously. They met in large numbers on Sundays for animated worship, testimonies, singing, clapping, and praising the Lord. In Addis Ababa, the Bole congregation held three services, the first one starting at 6:00 a.m. Even then the overflow had to sit in shelters built on two sides of the church building. The other 13 churches were located in a 300-mile stretch east of Addis Ababa; they reported similar growth. Every Sunday new people declared their intention to follow the Lord.

Marxist rule in Ethiopia was a fearful time. Anyone considered a threat to the revolution, especially during the "Red Terror" of the late 70s, might be found dead in the morning by the roadside. Student demonstrators protesting for any reason were loaded into trucks and hauled off to prison, without a hearing or trial. The government launched the Red Terror to uproot the EPRP (Ethiopia People's Revolutionary Party). That underground political party had ideas for its own type of revolution and tried to overthrow the government. Innocent people were often caught in the crossfire. The population was terrorized by seeing bodies in the streets each morning, and families were not allowed to bury their dead.

However, the churches had kept on worshiping openly during this fearful time. The many people coming and going on Sunday mornings at the Bole church tended to block traffic on the street, another irritation to the community. Officials attended church meetings to see who was there and to observe everything that was done. Persons carrying Bibles to church were sometimes detained. Evangelicals were derisively called "Pentes," based on the word *Pentecostal.*

Local kebele leaders in the Bole area of Addis Ababa were irritated that MKC members were frequently absent from the compulsory meetings for Marxist indoctrination. They deliberately held these sessions on Sunday mornings to conflict with churchgoing. Kebele leaders didn't know how to cope with people who boldly said that the Lord they served was above everything. The revolution was not the final authority, as its leaders tried to make them vow. "Why do the youth go to church and not come to us?" the kebele leaders asked.

At the kebele meetings near Bole Church, a few people sat stiffly and looked bored by the endless droning of the speaker as he recited the Marxist line. In contrast, worshipers repeatedly filled the Bole church. The crowd waiting to enter would move as one mass into the east door while those who had finished worship moved out the west side. People going to and coming from the chapel filled the streets all morning long.

Arlene slept little that night. Five guards outside her window laughed and talked. Sometimes their guns would bang against the wall. Comrade Kebede had told her that he was responsible for her welfare.

The next morning at six o'clock, Kelifa Ali went to the higher kebele office number 18. For him, it was the beginning of four years in prison without a hearing and without trial.

Months before, Kelifa would often have a distant look in his eyes, but he did not discuss the problem with Yakuta, his wife, except to say that he needed prayer. Sometimes he would say, "Things are getting worse. We may have to pay the price for what we believe. Yakuta, it's time for you to prepare, too." Kelifa and Yakuta, former Muslims, had already paid dearly for their faith. The community had opposed them when they had declared themselves followers of Christ. Now rejection was coming from the Marxist government. When Yakuta received the word of Kelifa's imprisonment, she knelt beside the phone and thanked God that he gave them the privilege of suffering for him. Then she prepared food and took it with a blanket to her husband, but she was not allowed to see him.

In the days following Kelifa's arrest, many Christians came to Yakuta's house to offer condolence. Mixed among them were government agents intent on getting more information about the family's connections. They tried to find out who was caring for her needs. With God-given wisdom, Yakuta answered simply, "My Father is caring for me."[4]

Also on the government's list for arrest were Kiros Bihon and Abebe Gorfe, pastors of the Bole congregation in Addis Ababa. Kiros had started early with the mission, working first in the Dire Dawa bookstore and serving as an evangelist. He often spent his lunch hour witnessing at the local prison. Later he transferred to Addis, where he served many years as cashier in Menno Bookstore. Kiros eventually opened his own bookstore near the railroad station in Addis to support his family of five children. He spent all his spare time serving the church. Security guards took him on Monday for questioning. His wife, Kelemwa, had to learn to manage the bookstore for four years without him.

Abebe Gorfe, an employee of the Commercial Bank of Ethiopia, was a man with eight children and an impeccable record. He had given faithful service to the bank and to the church for many years. In 1972 a special vision from God had led him and his wife, Tsehai, to go to the MKC congregation in Nazareth and make a commitment to evangelical faith. They were especially gifted with counseling skills and pastoral ministry.[5]

Security guards took Abebe from his office and jailed him for over four years, also without trial. It was no surprise for Abebe. It had been revealed to him in a dream that he would be taken to prison. During that time he never knew whether he would be released or executed. Prison guards seemed to enjoy keeping the prisoners guessing about their fate.[6]

Several days later, Shamsudin Abdo, the former chairman of MKC, was taken into custody. When guards came to his home, he told his wife, Miskie, and children, "I don't know where I'm being taken. I may come back this evening. Maybe in a week's time. Maybe in a month or a year, or maybe never. The Lord will take care of you." His family started to weep. He kissed them and left.

An official gave him a long questionnaire, asking him about his vocation, background, family, work experience, church, and Christian life. Shamsudin answered everything, writing out the answers clearly and hiding nothing. Nevertheless, the official said, "We know that you are an agent of the CIA; we have proof in our files."[7]

During the 1970s the Eastern Mennonite Board of Missions had corresponded with MKC about their loan funds through Church Investment Associates and often referred to this fund with the letters CIA. Missionaries previously had alerted the home office that the name of this organization would have to be changed because these initials could be incriminating. The name was eventually changed, but the old correspondence was still in the files. The government confiscated those files a few days after they closed the church's central office on that first night. Now they accused the former MKC chairman of having political connections with the American government. They would not listen to his explanation of their misinterpretation.

Shamsudin did achieve one breakthrough. During the interrogation, he had noticed that the official had a list of seventeen MKC members the government was planning to arrest. He told them that he would answer any questions about the church they wanted to know, and that if he was unable to do so, he'd call someone who could. "You don't need anyone else," he said.

The official looked at Shamsudin and said, "We work under government authority. They tell us what to do, and we don't take orders from you."

Shamsudin replied, "I made a suggestion; I did not give an order. If my suggestion doesn't work, use the method you wish, but you will find all the answers you want from me."

The official scratched off sixteen names, keeping the name of Tilahun Beyene, treasurer of MKC and chairman of the Addis Ababa congregation.

Shamsudin was pushed into a crowded dark room less than thirteen feet square with thirty-five other prisoners. Here they sat, ate, and slept on the floor. At night they were crowded tightly against each other, alternating head to feet. They could turn from one side to the other only when they could get the permission of the whole row to turn at the same time.

Tilahun Beyene, chairman of the Addis Ababa congregation and treasurer of MKC, was arrested one week after the Bole church was closed. Officials came to the Ethiopian Airlines office where he worked and asked to see him. He gave his keys to his secretary, who wondered why he was doing this. He simply said, "In case I don't come back."[8]

For some months Tilahun had known that the government was focusing an investigation on MKC. He had even been warned to keep low, that the name of MKC was being discussed in the regular kebele meetings. Several days before the church closing, the grapevine carried the word that MKC funds were being frozen at the bank, although the bank would not confirm this. The general church fund had a balance of about $120,000 U.S. In addition, the Addis Ababa congregation had accumulated close to $50,000 in anticipation of enlarging their building. Other accounts—the Bible Academy, Development Board, Elementary Education, and pension funds—had a total of about $50,000.

On Wednesday, two days after the closing, a man in a VW stopped at the Bible Academy in Nazareth, sixty miles east of Addis Ababa, under the pretense of wanting to enroll a stu-

Negash Kebede, chairman of MKC at the time it was closed, was director of the Bible Academy, Nazareth, from 1979 to 1982. During 1977-78 Negash served as Africa Director at Eastern Mennonite Missions, Salunga, Pa.

dent. He asked for the director, Negash Kebede, who was also the new MKC chairman. The dean notified Negash. Suspecting the ruse, Negash left for Addis Ababa, driving out of the campus right past the man waiting to see him.[9]

Negash stayed in Addis Ababa for ten days while he consulted with church leaders about the best course to take. Eventually they decided that Negash should present himself to the police station and inquire whether they were looking for him. They were. By phone, Negash tried to explain to his four-year-old daughter that his "work" would keep him away from home for a long time. As it turned out, he was not present for the birth of his son six weeks later. He was imprisoned with the others for four years.

Neither Negash, nor any of the other five leaders, ever made an attempt to escape from what they almost certainly knew might be their fate. None of them had violated any known law of their government. They were obedient citizens, even under a Marxist regime.

Other leaders were called for interrogation and later released. Among these was Dr. Tesfatsion Dalellew, once executive secretary for MKC and at this time employed by World Vision. The weekend the church was closed, he was speaking at a spiritual life conference in Sidamo. When officials came to his house, the family reported Tesfa to be away on a trip. Authorities guarded his house with army jeeps and machine guns, ready to arrest him on his return. Alerted by his wife, Amsale, Tesfa phoned the Ministry of National

Security and told them he would be happy to appear for an interview. Three hours of interrogation followed. Tesfa was relaxed, but he matched the interrogator's forceful approach. Finally the officer said he had not found a reason to arrest him and told him to go home, do his job, and not be angry.[10]

Yohannes Germamo, once vice chairperson of MKC and at the time working with the Wonji Sugar Company, was approached by security men through the company's head office. Yohannes was interrogated for about three hours and released after being given a strict warning not to preach or be involved in any religious activities.

By 1982 MKC was hoping it had weathered the storm, that after eight years the worst terror of the Marxist regime was over. However, apparently the government until this time had been preoccupied with conflicts in the north and with Somalia on the east. In keeping with Marxist policy to stamp out all religion, the government was just now getting around to attacking the church. Officials regarded an evangelical church as a good place to start. Evangelicals were accused of following a foreign religion and were not well liked by the Orthodox Church. Records that came to light after the Marxist ouster revealed that the government intended eventually to attack all faiths, including Muslims.

Meanwhile Arlene Kreider, still living at the empty guesthouse, went in and out between armed guards. Comrade Kebede was becoming quite friendly. It was obvious that he was simply following orders and not opposing church or missionaries. Arlene made tea for the guards, which they would drink unless they were expecting other officials to arrive. They did not want to be seen drinking tea with an American "CIA." Sometimes Kebede wanted to talk outside the house because he thought the guesthouse was bugged. Once he confided that he had gone to a mission school and that he knew the Bible. With tears in his sorrow-filled eyes, he said, "Now my job is to get rid of Christians and to get rid of God."

On Saturday, five days after the first arrests began, the Nazareth church building was closed and sealed as well as the Wonji and Shoa churches six miles south of Nazareth. The Dire Dawa church was closed on February 17 and the Awash Valley churches—Abadir, Awaramelka, and Metahara—on March 12. Then Deder was closed on May 8, Melkawerer, Algetta, and Melkesedi on August 14, and Asebeteferi on August 16, all in 1982.

Buildings once used for worship now became indoctrination centers for Marxist propaganda. Kebele leaders expected someone from each family to be present for these harangues. They intentionally planned the sessions for Sunday mornings, to discourage Christians from attending churches still open. Believers persistently absent from these propaganda meetings could be ridiculed by kebele leaders or even imprisoned.

Now that the churches were being closed, MKC members and missionaries wondered whether the Bible Academy at Nazareth would also be seized. If so, would the missionary teachers have to leave the country? The 305 academy students tried to pursue their secondary education amid the upheavals of a society undergoing drastic change. Thirty-four seniors were hoping to sit for their matriculation exams in four months. Now their director was suddenly absent, and no one would tell them for sure what happened. In whispers, students and faculty speculated about what might happen to the chairman of a church accused of promoting a "foreigner's" religion. Their director, a respected church leader, had been herded into prison along with other "criminals."

For weeks the academy staff negotiated with government officials about keeping the Bible Academy open. The Ministry of Education wanted it to continue operating. They considered it as a model school, a place of stability amid frequent unrest plaguing the public system. However, it was not to be so. Church schools, political leaders well knew, did not promote the ideology of a Marxist government. That government, called the *Derg*, said it would take over the academy when the spring term ended in 1982. Expatriate teachers were expected to find employment elsewhere or to leave the country.

Meanwhile, MKC leaders asked God to show them how to lead a church when public worship was outlawed, how to be faithful under oppression and persecution, and how to work and plan when trust at every level of society had broken down.

Other evangelical churches in Ethiopia grappled with these same questions throughout the 1980s, although the central government officially closed only a few as denominations. Through those years a miracle of God's grace unfolded in a scope vastly beyond the prayers and expectations of anyone.

2

How Christianity Came to Ethiopia

"What are you missionaries doing in Ethiopia, where they already have a strong Christian church?" The U.S. police officer spoke with contempt as he processed my paperwork for a Pennsylvania driver's license. Mine had expired during our first term in Ethiopia.

It was 1956, and most Americans knew little about Ethiopia, let alone the Ethiopian Orthodox Church. However, here was one person who saw the country as Christian. My reply was weak: "We are assisting the government in its attempt to establish schools in rural areas." This way I avoided a discussion which was much over my head in the 1950s.

Indeed, what were Christian missionaries doing in this country on the Horn of Africa? Ethiopia had heard the Christian gospel centuries before Luther nailed his ninety-five theses on the Wittenberg church door, and long before the followers of Menno Simons were known in the world. While our barbarian forebears were fighting each other and drinking wine from the skulls of those they killed, Ethiopians were chanting the Psalms and worshiping the Lord God. Before dawn on Sundays, they assembled with deep respect and reverence at their octagonal churches.

Even today, worshipers often stand outside their church buildings, not considering themselves worthy to enter such a holy place. A replica of the ancient Ark of the Covenant (*Tabot*) resides in every church. It is a holy moment when, on special holidays, a priest emerges from the church, carrying the ark on his head. A joy cry, *ililta*,[1] rings out from the gathered people as they celebrate this singular event practiced only by the Ethiopian brand of Orthodoxy.

According to historical record, Christianity came to Ethiopia in the fourth century (A.D. 335) through the teaching of two Syrian monks, Frumentius and Aedesius. En route to India, according to the story, their ship stopped at a Red Sea port for food and water. Local inhabitants massacred the crew but spared the monks and took them two hundred miles inland to the cool capital of Axum, six thousand feet above the sea. Here at the king's court, Frumentius became treasurer and Aedesius was cupbearer. After the king's death, the monks taught and converted the son, Ezana, to the Christian faith.

Aedesius then returned to Tyre, but Frumentius went to Alexandria, where he requested Patriarch Athanasius to appoint a bishop to Axum. Instead, the patriarch consecrated Frumentius himself, later known as *Abba Salama*, who returned to Ethiopia to spread the gospel. It was A.D. 346.[2] Here, isolated from the rest of the world, a church grew, mixing together teachings from Jewish, Christian, and even local traditions. By the time Mennonites arrived in 1945, Ethiopian Orthodox Christians numbered about ten million in a country that estimated its population to be twenty million, including Muslims, animists, Roman Catholics, and Protestants.

Orthodox Ethiopians are deeply religious. Each morning the devout scatter a handful of roasted grain around their homes to ward off evil. They call on the angels Gabriel and Michael as well as saints to protect them in times of danger. They thank God for their health every time someone greets them with "Good morning." Their respect for Jesus is so great that they are taught not to call on him directly but approach him with reverence through the mediation of revered saints and angels and the holy virgin Mary. In some churches, angel faces with big eyes painted on the ceiling look down on the worshipers in artwork so cleverly done that one can never move out of their gaze.

Orthodox Church buildings are typically eight-sided, and each church contains a miniature replica of the Old Testament ark of the covenant. *Arlene Hege photo.*

While Europe was building its cathedrals in the twelfth century, Orthodox Ethiopians were hewing thirteen churches out of solid sandstone rock at Lalibela to assure themselves that the faith would never die out. When Anabaptist leaders in the sixteenth century were dying as martyrs for the freedom of conscience, the Ethiopian faithful were giving their lives to stop the onslaught of invading Muslims. In the nineteenth century, their king Theodore (Teodros, reigning 1856-1868) called Ethiopia an island of Christianity in a sea of Islam.

It certainly was an island of Christianity, not only because of surrounding Muslims, but also because of its isolation from the rest of Christendom. That isolation set the stage for Ethiopian believers to develop practices found in no other Christian churches, Orthodox included.

Ethiopia is reputed to be custodian of the original Ark of the Covenant of ancient Israel. One tradition has it that Menelik I (900 B.C.), legendary son of King Solomon and the Queen of Sheba, visited Israel and took the ark with him when he returned to his homeland.

A more credible tradition says the ark first was taken to

Egypt by faithful priests, probably when King Manasseh desecrated the temple in the seventh century B.C. Many people believe it resided for several hundred years in a special temple made for it at Aswan, after which it was eventually taken to Axum in Ethiopia.[3] Tradition claims that it is secretly kept by faithful monks at the church of Saint Mary, at Axum. No one is allowed to see it. No one has been able to verify the truth of the traditions. No one knows how and when it passed from the custody of the black Ethiopian Jews to the care of the Orthodox Church.

The Ethiopian Orthodox Bible with the Apocrypha has eighty-one books. In addition to this, priests and monks also study many other books written about the saints and angels. The people tell stories of the miraculous protection of the Scriptures when infidels tried to commit their ancient parchments to the flames. Those early books are in the Ge'ez language, and today Bible scholars study their ancient texts along with Greek and Hebrew. Ge'ez and the modern Amharic and Tigrinia are Semitic languages related to Hebrew. Certainly Ethiopians had contact with Israel long before the advent of the Christian era.

Some say the Ethiopian eunuch (Acts 8) must have carried the gospel to Ethiopia. Actually, he served Queen Candace, who ruled at Meroe in present-day Sudan (part of Ethiopia at the time), over 1,600 miles upstream from the mouth of the Nile. Meroe is just 200 miles below Khartoum, where the White Nile joins the Blue Nile. On the banks of this great river, the faithful eunuch would have shared his Christian faith. What would keep a man with such vision from sending evangelists up the Blue Nile to the isolated part of his country? Historians tell us that, before the days of Ezana, some form of Christianity may have existed within the political boundaries of present-day Ethiopia. At least one ancient historian claims that the eunuch did establish churches.[4]

We know that the eunuch had access to a scroll of Isaiah, that he could read, that he was a man of wealth and influence. Any man who would travel two thousand miles by chariot all the way through Egypt to worship at the temple in Jerusalem would have the zeal to spread the gospel beyond the confines of his own area. If he danced in his chariot with joy because of his new-found faith, he would not have kept his testimony to himself upon arriving back in his country.

There are many other stories of those ancient times. One is that the apostle Matthew traveled as far as Axum and spread the gospel there within the first century A.D. Did the eunuch know Matthew? Did they together develop a plan to evangelize among the hills and valleys of that mountain fortress? As the eunuch read from Isaiah about the "land the rivers have spoiled" (Isa. 18:2), did the Spirit urge him to proclaim the resurrection there, so that the people would not be spoiled, also? What Isaiah said about the land is true. In the rainy season, the rushing Blue Nile is chocolate colored with the silt it carries from the volcanic soil of the Ethiopian highlands. Acts 8 has the eunuch reading the part of Isaiah (53:8) that asks, "Who shall declare his generation?" The story shows a man so changed that he would certainly want Jesus and himself to have faith descendants, not only in his own area but in the regions beyond.

Ethiopia is a land rich in Christian history!

However obscure its early beginnings, we know that the ancient Ethiopian church developed traditions peculiar to itself. Relating mainly—and almost exclusively—to the Coptic Orthodox Church of Egypt, the Ethiopian body became highly skeptical of other Christian traditions. There is good reason for this attitude.

In the 1500s Portugal came to assist the country in its fight against Muslim invasions. Catholic missionaries, who taught the two natures of Christ instead of the monophysite view, stayed on and worked to bring the church under the umbrella of Rome.[5] Ethiopians took this as a great insult and affront to their identity. As late as 1950, four hundred years after the Portuguese and others attempted to Romanize the church, Mennonites discovered that people of the countryside still called any foreigner, themselves included, a *catolic*. The military occupation of the country by Italy, 1936-1941, also a Catholic country, only reinforced their suspicion of foreigners.

Memory lives long in Ethiopia. It took years for foreign missionaries to convince people of the countryside that they had no political motives as they pursued their task of teaching the gospel.

However, did the missionaries of the twentieth century pause long enough to really appreciate the faithfulness of this people? For more than a thousand years, they had kept alive the resurrection story amid the onslaught of Muslim and pagan invasions and limited contacts with Christians of other nations.

Some recognized that faithfulness. Others, in their rush to establish a mission, seemed to forget the early faithful Orthodox monks who painstakingly translated and copied the holy Scriptures from Syriac and Greek into their own living Geez (Ethiopic) language. These were actually the only Sub-Saharan Africans in the first millennium to translate the Scriptures into their native tongue. In all of North Africa, only Ethiopian churches were not subjugated during the Muslim expansions of the sixth and seventh centuries. This was the only country ruled by Christian kings.

To trace the struggles of the Orthodox Church through the centuries is beyond the scope of this book. However, anyone who pursues such a study will be amazed at the diligence put forth by a persistent people to preserve the Christian faith. The Ethiopian Orthodox Church endured theological disputes from within and military conflicts from without. It experienced golden ages when literature, music, art, and architecture flourished, as in the fifth and again in the thirteenth centuries.

The Nine Saints, for example, who came from the Eastern Roman Empire to Axum in about A.D. 480, were active in evangelizing. They brought renewal that lasted for two hundred years. The Nine Saints were persecuted in their homelands for being non-Chalcedonian, since they rejected the two-nature theory and believed Christ had but one nature, a fusion of the human and divine. They developed monaster-

To celebrate Orthodox Church holidays, a priest carries the ark on his head as the people follow in procession. *Herb Kraybill photo.*

ies that became learning centers for the development of Orthodox liturgies and Bible translations. This period is known as the golden age of the Ethiopian Orthodox Church.[6]

However, from the seventh through the twelfth centuries, the church also had its dark ages, about which little is known. Politically, Axum declined and Lasta or Lalibela became the new capital. Next was Gondar, and finally, at the end of the nineteenth century, Addis Ababa (new flower) became the center of power. As the capitals moved southward, so did the Christian faith. Small Orthodox communities built their churches among people of many languages and non-Christian traditions. As historians trace this long and arduous history, they develop the compelling conviction that Ethiopian orthodoxy is unparalleled in its ability to survive.

The modern era of Ethiopia coincides with the coming of Protestant missionaries to the country. In 1866, Swedish missionaries landed at Massawa and began work among the Kunama people. In 1872, they contacted the clergy of St.

Giorgis, serving the Orthodox Church in Eritrea. These leaders had become interested in the biblical teaching on salvation when they found an Amharic Bible in a niche of their church wall. They "tried to convince their parishioners that legends of saints and martyrs stand no comparison with the pure word of God." [7] Orthodox monks opposed this reform movement, and so it became part of the beginnings of the Evangelical Church of Eritrea. Later, these ideas also helped give rise to the Evangelical Church Mekane Yesus (Lutheran) in Ethiopia.

Eventually, Lutherans from three other European countries and the United States joined them. Today, Mekane Yesus people are in every region of the country and number well over two million.

In 1918 the United Presbyterian Church of America opened a station among the Oromo people of Wollega province in western Ethiopia, and in 1923 they began a hospital in Addis Ababa. Churches growing out of these efforts formed the Bethel Evangelical Church, which later united with the Mekane Yesus Church under a separate synod.

The Sudan Interior Mission (SIM) opened its first stations 200 miles south of Addis Ababa in 1928, under the direction of the famous Dr. Thomas Lambie, who had previously worked in Sudan. The first company of seven missionaries traveled from Addis Ababa in a caravan a quarter mile long, with 26 mules, 20 donkeys, 9 horses, and 25 head carriers. There were no roads, only trails, and maps that were not reliable. Headed for Jimma in Kaffa province in the west, they ended up to the south, at Hossana and Wolaytta Soddo, and began work among the Wolaytta people.

By the time of the Italian occupation in 1936, when all the missionaries left, the SIM had established 15 stations, and about 30 people believed their evangelical message. The church grew rapidly during the 5-year absence of the missionaries, who returned to find 20,000 believers worshiping in over 100 congregations. They had copied by hand two Gospels, translated into Wolaytta, so each church could have a copy.[8]

Today the Kale Heywet churches growing out of SIM's work have spread to many tribes and are scattered over many parts of Ethiopia. They have a membership close to three million people.

Other missions dating from before the Italian occupation are the Bible Churchman's Missionary Society (Anglican) in 1934, and the Seventh-Day Adventists. After the occupation, Mennonites, General Conference Baptists, Southern Baptists, and various other groups joined the increasing number of Protestant organizations working in the country.

Ethiopians have endured unpleasant experiences with foreigners who had political and religious designs on the country. Thus, it is a marvel that they have welcomed foreign missions at all. Emperor Haile Selassie wrote to the League of Nations in 1926 that "Ethiopians have seldom met with foreigners who did not desire to possess themselves of Abyssinian territory and to destroy their independence. . . . For this reason, prudence is needed when we have to convince our people that foreigners . . . are genuinely innocent of concealed political aims."[9]

Evangelical missions have profited greatly by the prudence of Emperor Haile Selassie I, who often came to their rescue in difficult circumstances. Problems did arise. Although some missions focused on reviving the Orthodox Church, others felt it necessary to break away from its centuries-old traditions and start new churches based on the evangelical tradition of personal commitment to faith.

The mission scene in Ethiopia in 1945, when Mennonites first arrived, was one of comity. The government gave each mission its own area so as not to overlap with others, and one church would not proselytize the members of another. Roman Catholics, who have been engaged in mission in Ethiopia since the sixteenth century, are noted for developing well-managed schools in population centers. Lutherans developed churches largely in the north and west, and SIM developed them in the south.

Still, amid the more than fifty language groups in the country, enough areas remained for others to establish missions: Presbyterians began mission projects in the west in 1919; Mennonites worked mostly in the east; Baptists and Pentecostals came, too. Throughout the 1950s, evangelical Christians in all groups totaled between 200,000 and 300,000.[10] By 1995, among a total Ethiopian population estimated at 56 million, evangelicals were estimated to be 6 million. Roman Catholics were estimated at 500,000, and Orthodox Christians at 30 million. The rest of the population is composed of Muslims, estimated at 16 million, and a few followers of traditional religions.

The government urged missions to be holistic in their approach and not just to focus on evangelism. For the most part, mission agencies respected these guidelines, providing clinics and hospitals, schools and literacy programs, agriculture and community development. For the most part, the government allowed them to develop their programs according to their own mission policies so long as they did not proselytize Orthodox Christians or criticize the mother church. The government directive was that any mission schools including Orthodox Christians must teach only those things common to all Christian groups.

Mennonites first arrived in 1945, when Ethiopia was busy with reconstruction after the Italian occupation. They brought with them a shipment of relief goods—clothing and foodstuffs—and opened a hospital in Nazareth, 60 miles east of the capital city, Addis Ababa. In this town of 12,000, they set about renovating an old cotton gin building to accommodate 40 beds and a primitive operating room.

The Mennonite Relief Committee, Elkhart, Indiana, and Mennonite Central Committee, Akron, Pennsylvania, sent short-term workers—doctors, nurses, administrators. They treated patients and trained medical assistants (dressers) to work in hospitals and open rural clinics. By 1950 the transfer from MRC to Eastern Mennonite Board of Missions was complete, and the government granted the mission permission to expand beyond relief and medical services and include education and evangelism.

3

Mennonites—
Called to Ethiopia

"We had little idea what to expect when in 1947 we boarded the *Marine Carp* at New York for our first trip to Ethiopia," recalls Blanche Sensenig. She, her husband, Dan, and young daughter Janice were the first missionaries appointed by Eastern Mennonite Board of Missions to serve in that country. In the hold of the 12,000 ton U.S. troop ship was a four-wheel-drive Dodge Power Wagon equipped with a winch. It was supposed to be tough enough to take them over the roughest and muddiest roads.[1]

In a "land the rivers have spoiled," as the prophet Isaiah described it (18:2), some Ethiopian roads in 1947 were little better than dry streambeds and would require the most rugged vehicle available to negotiate. Dan Sensenig had heard of the rough terrain and wanted to be prepared. He insisted on a Dodge Power Wagon, a vehicle developed by the U. S. Army during World War II to transport military equipment where roads did not exist. His own brother, A. R. Sensenig, bought it and donated it to the Mission Board for Dan's use.

Dan knew how to choose the proper vehicle; he had worked with his brother in car sales for several years. However, it was not only for his business knowledge that Dan Sensenig was chosen to be the first director to lead in opening mission work in Ethiopia. Dan had administrative skills, and he was a preacher. Ordained to the ministry by the New Holland, Pennsylvania, congregation in 1941, he was known as a spiritual man. At sixteen, employed by his brother, he was sent to repair Delco generators on farms not yet electrified. "I didn't know how to fix those motors," he confided once to Blanche, "but I'd pray, and somehow they got fixed." In Ethiopia, he once commented that he did not consider himself a mystic, and yet on occasion he prayed over a balky carburetor when his tinkering failed to start a motor. Dan could adjust an engine in his Sunday clothes and not get them soiled.

More important than mechanical and administrative abilities was the fact that Dan was loyal to the church's disciplines. The Bishop Board of his conference was careful in their selection of missionaries for Ethiopia, because they had already started to have misgivings about the workers in Tanganyika. By this time the Mennonite missionaries in that country had begun to criticize the Mennonite church in North America after they had experienced spiritual renewal and joined what was called the East Africa Revival. Critical feedback from African missionaries was not generally appreciated stateside. Loyal Lancaster Conference Mennonites did not like to be told by a missionary on furlough that they needed to repent. Dan and Blanche, they believed, would never be critical.

The Sensenigs were sensitive to the Spirit's call. "I had a feeling that something was coming," recalls Blanche, "just like I had a feeling that Dan would become a minister even before he was chosen." On their long journey to Israel, where they disembarked, they tried to imagine how long it might take to plant a church in Ethiopia. Orie O. Miller, secretary of Eastern Mennonite Board of Missions, had told them that they were to help to *start* the mission; the board would recruit others for the long haul. Because additional recruits were slow in coming, Dan and Blanche faced the possibility of serving in Ethiopia for a long time.

On board the *Marine Carp*, the Sensenig family—Dan and Blanche and their ten-year-old daughter, Janice—had to bunk separately. The ship had been adapted to transport troops during World War II and had not yet been restored for

Daniel and Blanche Sensenig with their daughter, Janice, arrived in Ethiopia in December, 1947. Dan was the first director of the Mennonite Mission in Ethiopia.

civilian use. On that rough Atlantic crossing in early December 1947, the family gathered each morning in one of the lounges to pray. The backdrop for their petitions was the prayer chanting of Jews quartered on a lower deck en route to Israel: they were imploring God that their homeland might at long last gain independence.

The Sensenigs studied the Scriptures for direction. They talked with other missionary families traveling back to their assignments in Africa. They felt overwhelmed among the experienced missionaries serving with the Sudan Interior Mission (SIM) and the United Presbyterians. The only specialized training the Sensenigs had was six weeks at the Summer Institute of Linguistics in Oklahoma, where they tried to shape their lips to make the sounds they would encounter when studying the Semitic tongue, Amharic, the national language of the ancient empire. Neither of them had completed high school or attended college. Dan sat in the eighth grade for three years until he was sixteen because his community did not believe in "higher" education.

"When we were first asked to go," Blanche recalls, "I was certain that all God wanted was for us to be willing; I was sure God would release us like he did Abraham at the 'sacrifice' of Isaac, once he was sure we were willing to go any place. But one day the chairman of the mission board literally took hold of Dan's top button hole on his plain coat and said, 'We want you for Ethiopia.'

"We knew then that God must be serious," Blanche recalls.

"Of course, we had heard the words 'ancient Christian kingdom,' 'benevolent monarch,' 'a people eager for education.' But our only certainty was that we were trying to be faithful to God's call." At age eighty-four, Blanche remembers how that motivation gave them the courage they needed to undertake the unknown.

However, Ethiopia was not unknown to Orie Miller, secretary of Eastern Mennonite Board of Missions in Pennsylvania. In 1929 he had prompted I. E. Burkhart of the Mennonite Board of Missions, Elkhart, Indiana, to address its annual meeting on how Africa was calling the Mennonite Church. Orie had provided Burkhart with material on the subject. Later, when the board decided to postpone the discussion about Africa for another year, Orie deplored the delay. "This whole field (Abyssinia) is just opening up to mission work, and it is as yet practically unoccupied by Protestant forces." [2]

Orie had a reputation for having his morning devotions with *The New York Times* on one knee and his Bible on the other. Had Orie kept abreast of Ethiopian politics and noted that a new monarch, thought to be a progressive one, was about to come to the throne? Haile Selassie I was crowned king in 1930, after he had filled the role of regent for several years. He and Orie were the same age. Both their birthdays were in July.

By 1933 the Indiana board still had not decided to enter Africa, so Orie encouraged the Eastern Mennonite Board of Missions in Pennsylvania to accept the challenge. Tanganyika was its first field. Ethiopia would have to wait until the Italian occupation ended and it would again be possible for missionaries to travel, after World War II.

Orie lost no time in pursuing his goal once World War II was over. He arranged for Samuel A. Yoder of Goshen, Indiana, and Paul Hooley of West Liberty, Ohio, to explore the possibility of opening a hospital and clinic in Ethiopia.

They were already serving at the El Shatt Refugee Camp in Egypt. In August 1945, they arrived in Ethiopia.

Samuel and Paul visited Nazareth and Maeso to the east, and Dessie, Mekale, Gondar, and Debra Markos to the north. At each place, they assessed the medical needs of the people. After consultation with mission agencies and government advisers, they recommended to Orie that Nazareth—along the rail line and only sixty miles from Addis—be the first location. Here they found an idle cotton gin complete with staff dwellings, all built of brick. The Italians had constructed them during their occupation of the country, 1935 to 1941.

Samuel returned to the United States, but Paul stayed on for a year to renovate the factory for use as a hospital and clinic. Paul hired local artisans and laborers. Within a few months, he had moved out the ginning machinery, installed partitions, plumbing, and electrical wiring, and made it ready for Dr. Paul and Nancy Conrad, the first medical people to be appointed. Mennonites were welcomed to open a hospital. Their ability to provide an acceptable spiritual ministry would have to be tested.

In 1945, the Relief and Service Committee of Mennonite Board of Missions, Elkhart, Indiana, cooperated with Mennonite Central Committee of Akron, Pennsylvania, in sending a shipment of clothing and medicine to Nazareth, Ethiopia. The Italian occupation had disrupted the lives of many people. If Ethiopia was to be a modern society and take its place alongside other African nations, it needed everything—schools, hospitals, clinics, and technologies of every kind.

Haile Selassie I was determined to promote changes that would bring progress and prosperity for his people. He welcomed help from foreigners if those outsiders could lay aside their imperialism and work with respect for the people and the history of his ancient kingdom. The "help" his country had recently received from Italy was not appreciated. Ethiopians were not willing to learn from any foreigners out to conquer them, even though the Italians had built many factories and all-weather roads. People from abroad who offered their help would have to come as guests and servants and identify with the aspirations of the people.

"Haile Selassie prefers evangelicals," C. Gordon Beacham of SIM wrote in the *Christian Life and Times* and quoted in *Missionary Messenger* in 1946. "Can anything be done to awaken spiritually minded Christian men in America to take advantage of this golden opportunity to serve Christ through the school system of this young and growing nation?" Beacham pleaded.[3] Orie Miller would not have missed this news note.

By the time the Sensenigs flew from Lydda, Israel, to Addis Ababa in December 1947, the Haile Mariam Mamo Memorial Hospital at Nazareth was operating under the direction of the Mennonite Relief Committee (MRC) of Elkhart, Indiana, with an expatriate staff and Ethiopian helpers they had trained. "I am reasonably sure Dan will fill an important place in our unit by helping to supply the Spiritual needs," business manager Jacob R. Clemens wrote in his diary. He had just heard Dan preach his first sermon at Nazareth, on the mystery of the church. Clemens used a capital *S* for spiritual to indicate its importance and the inadequacy of social service alone.[4]

At the same time, Mennonites were also serving as teachers in government schools. In 1948 Laura Conrad, Margaret Ulrich (Strubar), and Ed Weaver began teaching in Addis Ababa on government salary. In 1949 Erma Grove and Leona Yoder (Hostetler) joined them. Later, Eastern Mennonite Missions also appointed teachers and continued this ministry until 1952.

Daniel Sensenig's first specific assignment was to petition the Ethiopian government for permission to begin a mission that included teaching the Bible with an evangelical emphasis. The only permission the government originally gave the Mennonites was to operate a hospital, along with a strict warning that they were not to proselytize in the community. The Ethiopian government had designated open areas for missions among non-Orthodox people, where missionaries could evangelize; and closed areas, where it was

Chester and Sara Jane Wenger with their three daughters, Betty, Margaret, and Jewel, arrived in Ethiopia in November 1949.

strictly forbidden to convert an Orthodox person. Relief and medical workers adhered to this directive.

However, now that an evangelistic mission was to begin, a new approach had to be hammered out—or prayed through—with the government. Dan was a man of integrity; he had to find a way to obey the king and yet be true to God's call. He and Dorsa Mishler, director of the MRC unit operating Nazareth Hospital, teamed together to explore the possibilities for mission.

Where were the open areas where Mennonites could freely proclaim the gospel? In the closed areas, would it be possible for Mennonites, separatists as they were, to teach only those doctrines common to all Christian groups? The *Negarit Gazeta*, which carried the government edicts, clearly stated that requirement.[5]

Could the medical work at Nazareth become a center for establishing a church in a land with over 1,500 years of Christian history, as well as a large Muslim population? The

Sensenigs were sent to explore that possibility.

Orie Miller was a strategist for Eastern Board in Pennsylvania, the MRC in Indiana, and Mennonite Central Committee (MCC), as well as many other institutions among Mennonites. He believed that God could use well-meaning people with little experience or specialized training to develop international missions. Recruiting many people who had not completed a college education, he had already spearheaded the opening of the mission in Tanganyika. If anyone told him it couldn't be done, he did not believe them.

Miller himself wrote to His Imperial Majesty, Haile Selassie I. He made no apologies, stating forthrightly that Mennonites wanted to "enlarge their present program to include an evangelical mission service" in the country. Would his Imperial Majesty be pleased to suggest the area?

The deterrents were frightening. All the counsel Dan and Dorsa could glean from the other mission societies was that any new mission agency not present before the Italian occupation would not be allowed to enter the country. They interviewed directors of SIM, United Presbyterian Mission, Bible Churchman's Missionary Society (BCMS), and other expatriates employed by the government. Mishler summed up the research in a letter to Orie Miller: "It will be very difficult and maybe even impossible for any new group to establish a mission in Ethiopia. . . . There is a certain influential element in the government which is definitely anti-mission. . . . Several other mission societies who asked for admittance . . . since the War . . . have been refused; . . . [an evangelical] mission will probably be impossible unless there will be a *special* opening by the Lord."

Dan and Dorsa were ready to look for that special opening: "We would like to have the home church to realize this difficulty so they will pray much in this behalf," they wrote,[6] dispatching the letter with a messenger to have it mailed to the States from Nairobi. They gave a strict warning that none of its contents should be published. Meanwhile, Dan and Dorsa asked the staff at Nazareth—J. R. and Miriam Clemens, Truman Diener, Paul and Nancy Conrad, Geneva

Alexander, Mary Byer, Mary Mishler, and Ada Showalter—to join them in prayer.

With Miller's application in hand, Dan and Dorsa wondered how to present it to the king. Dorsa's article in *Gospel Herald* told the story:

> We were at a loss to know how to proceed. . . . But it seemed well that we should wait on the Lord for another week or so and continue to ask for definite leading. Perhaps we had some degree of faith at that time, but we certainly had not imagined the dramatically definite demonstrations of God's leading in every detail that we experienced in the following weeks. Many prayers were offered asking for guidance during these days, and the answers always came at the right time, when the situations were ready, not too soon and not too late.[7]

Then, one day the emperor came to visit Nazareth hospital. This was not his first visit, but it was timely. His Majesty was quite personable for a monarch, shaking hands with American and Ethiopian staff, and asking many questions, especially about the Mennonites. He concluded his visit by inviting the relief workers to come to his palace and have an audience with him, discussing the proposed expansion of Mennonite work.

The rest, as they say, is history. The anxious waiting for the actual interview to take place, the nervousness of Dan and Dorsa as they worried about how to perform before royalty, the wondering whether the delays indicated reluctance—all these details pale in the retelling. This team had watched the government's every move, and a church in America was anxiously waiting to hear the outcome of the June 1948 audience with the emperor in Addis Ababa. The events taking place between Mennonites and Majesty were extremely significant to all of them.

Dorsa described the meeting with the emperor:

We felt reasonably well composed, but . . . meeting an Emperor in an official appointment was not an everyday experience for either of us. The secretary to the Emperor . . . gave us complete instructions concerning proper courtesies in meeting the King. . . . As we stepped in on the thickly carpeted floor, the Emperor . . . arose and greeted us with a pleasing smile. We bowed slightly and then walked to the center of the room and made very low bows together. His Majesty extended his hand and beckoned us to come. We walked to his desk and shook hands with him and then bowed slightly again. . . . The Emperor asked a few friendly questions about the work at Nazareth and then paused and smiled pleasantly, as much as to say, "All right, I am ready to hear your story."

I had memorized the points to be cleared, but when the time came, I was speechless, momentarily. . . . But after . . . explaining the two types of programs of our church—relief and mission—and before I said anything about a mission application, His Majesty assured us that he was prepared to give the Mennonites mission status under a long-term basis.[8]

Dan and Dorsa set off for Harar Province to explore Muslim areas at Dire Dawa, Deder, and Bedeno: Dire Dawa because it was on the rail line from Addis Ababa to Djibouti, Deder because it was a market center for thousands of Oromo farmers who had no hospital; and Bedeno because it had no school for its children. This area of Harar Province was called an open area. In such areas, missions could legally evangelize Muslims with the government's blessing. They could also teach—but not proselytize—even those with an Orthodox string around their necks, certifying they were already Christian. However, any teachings had to agree with doctrines shared by all Christian groups.

The first conference of the Mennonite Mission in Ethiopia, held in Dire Dawa in January 1950. Back row, from left: Daniel and Blanche Sensenig, Noah Sauder, Amos Horst, Orie Miller. Center: Dr. Walter and Mae Schlabach. Front: Chester and Sara Jane Wenger, John Lehman, Rhoda Lind, and Mary Byer.

At Deder, sixty miles into the mountains from the railroad town of Dire Dawa, Dan and Dorsa worked with the local governor in finding a site to build a mission station. That station would consist of missionary dwellings, a school building, a clinic, and a hospital. For a week they pitched their tent on the threshing floor belonging to the family of Tilahun Beyene, who one day would become treasurer of Meserete Kristos Church (MKC). As a lad of six, he came home each evening from watching the cattle and asked, "What did the foreigners do today?" The children of the village gathered round to see these strangers cook their food on a kerosene pressure burner.

Some of the children who observed the strangers in their village were the Abebe Likyelebet family. Abebe helped to construct the clinic, hospital, school, and dwellings needed for the mission program at Deder. He was aware of the wider world; he had traveled to Italy as a prisoner of war during the Italian occupation. Abebe encouraged his eight children to go to the foreigners for an education. Today, three sons have doctoral degrees and hold positions in American colleges and universities. Dr. Zenebe Abebe, vice president for multicultural education at Goshen College, credits missionaries and early Ethiopian church leaders for their mentoring, which helped keep his family related to the church.

The governor of Deder showed Dan and Dorsa an excellent twenty-acre property that belonged to the queen. It had a spring bubbling out of the hillside and was one mile out of town. They immediately made plans to lease this land.

Deder is a market center overlooking several river valleys. Rural people, most of them Muslims, bring their coffee beans there to exchange them for cloth and oil and salt. Deder is 7,500 feet above sea level. The sun sets behind the mountain soon after 4:00 p.m., and by dusk, two hours later, one reaches for a sweater to ward off the chilly temperature. On a typical day, the noon temperature of 80 degrees Fahrenheit drops to 55 degrees in the evening. Deder was the right location for a hospital. However, the first buildings were a shop, a two-room, mud-walled clinic, a one-car garage (later used as the first school), and a dwelling for the missionaries.

Here the Power Wagon came into its own. It carried them on numerous trips to provincial government offices in Harar, as they applied for permissions to occupy and develop the chosen site. Later, the Dodge would groan its way over mountain trails, hauling stone from the fields, lumber from the sawmill, supplies for the hospital, and the missionaries' steel drums of clothing and household goods.

The missionaries faced many cultural puzzles and found the Amharic language difficult to learn. Nevertheless, they did press ahead to open schools, hospitals, and clinics, and to teach the Bible. Most of them were now making commitments for five-year terms.

4

Missionaries and Culture

The missionary homemaker was expecting guests and asked her cook to buy meat in the local market. The cook reminded her that Wednesday is a fast day, so no "Christian" meat is available. On Wednesdays and Fridays, Orthodox Christians refrain from eating meat or animal products such as milk, eggs, and cheese.

"Well, then buy meat from the Muslim shop today," the homemaker told her cook. The cook, a devout Orthodox Christian, acted as though he was asked to do an impossible task. "Muslim meat?" he exclaimed. "I cannot touch it; it has not been blessed by the priest or slaughtered in the name of the Trinity. Muslims slaughter their animals in the name of Allah."

In desperation, the woman was ready to go to the market and buy the meat herself. However, her cook said he could not in good conscience prepare the dinner, for he would be working in a "defiled" kitchen. If the cook had been a Muslim and she had asked him to buy meat from the Christian shops on a Thursday, the problem would have been the same. Muslims should handle only meat slaughtered by someone of their own religion.

Missionaries constantly faced such cultural dilemmas in Ethiopia. The homemaker could have solved her problem by serving only vegetables on Wednesdays and Fridays. Yet she remembered that missionaries were there to bring Muslims also to Christ. By eating their meat sometimes, she could show that true faith does not depend on habits of diet. Meanwhile, both Orthodox Christians and Muslims were watching, amazed that the missionary did not seem to have any scruples at all.

The tensions arising out of cultural differences never went away. Missionaries always had to make decisions about whose values they would respect and whose they would ignore. They lived among Muslims, Orthodox, and Protestants, and they didn't want to offend any.

One Sunday a missionary placed his Amharic Bible in the crook of his back as he leaned against a stone wall. This happened during a lengthy conversation after the worship service. A Muslim in the group asked him how he dared to treat his holy book in such a disrespectful manner. "We Muslims would never use the Koran as a cushion to prop ourselves against," he said. The missionary's long explanation of the printed word being different from the living Word made little sense to the Muslim.

A missionary on a walk with an Ethiopian would want to walk abreast to facilitate conversation. If the other person was an employee or a student, that partner insisted on walking behind, in single file.

Missionaries puzzled over the proper use of polite and familiar forms of speech when addressing an Ethiopian. In Amharic, four words translate the English word *you*: the masculine singular, the feminine singular, the plural, and

Students at the Bedeno elementary school playing games, 1955.

polite address. The verbs also have to agree with the gender and number of the pronoun.

When does one use the familiar form to convey friendliness or the honorific form to show proper respect? One missionary was especially embarrassed while struggling with the intricacies of Amharic during his first year in Ethiopia. He let slip a feminine verb when addressing an older man.

Another missionary committed a goof in language usage that became proverbial. In one community, he introduced himself as a preacher of the gospel. Instead of using the soft *k* when pronouncing the word *preacher*, he used the explosive *k* (with a click), which means *talebearer*. A listener remarked, "We had some doubts about what he was doing here; now we know."

The calendar, too, was different. Ethiopia follows the Julian calendar, which has twelve 30-day months and one five-day month to fill out the year, ending on September 10. This year 1998, for example, is 1990 in Ethiopia. When setting appointments, one has to specify which calendar is being used.

Ethiopians refer to two weeks as fifteen days. This sum comes from counting the starting day of the week again at the end of the two weeks. It makes sense, for fifteen days are always exactly half a month.

The hours of the day are computed as they were in Bible times. People rise at 12:00, eat lunch at 6:00, supper at 12:00, and go to bed at 4:00 or 5:00. The only way to be clear is to speak Amharic when referring to Ethiopian time and to speak English when referring to Western time. Foreigners who try to use Ethiopian time when speaking English bring confusion into a conversation.

The proper respect for holidays is always puzzling to the missionary. The 12th of each month celebrates St. Michael, the 19th St. Gabriel, the 21st Mary, and the 27th The Savior of the World. Other days are assigned to various saints. It depends on the level of an Ethiopian's devotion to the Orthodox faith as to how well that person kept holidays. In rural settings, the truly devout tried to refrain from work.

Missionaries usually felt that the recognition of these days implied too much reverence for angels. They especially avoided any veneration of Mary that might suggest her as an intercessor. It did not occur to Protestant missionaries that, within the bounds of Scripture, they could have smoothed their relationships with Orthodox people more often by speaking positively of Mary's unique place in salvation history. Instead, they tended to argue about whether Mary had influence with her Son.

While missionaries were dealing with such cultural conundrums in Ethiopia, they also grappled with the customs of Pennsylvania Mennonites. According to stateside expectations, when missionary men dressed for formal occasions (which were few), they were supposed to wear their plain suits and no ties. Women wore their prayer coverings all the time. Appointees from other conferences not accustomed to these practices conformed to Lancaster Conference regulations in order to serve under the Pennsylvania board.

The instruction of the first believers included teaching on the need for women to wear a prayer veiling and against the superfluous necktie for men. However, within the first five years of the mission's beginning, it became clear that the plain coat was commonly understood to be clerical garb. The missionaries did not wish to promote a rigid division between clergy and laity. They reasoned, If it is not proper to require the plain coat for Ethiopian believers, perhaps the missionaries should not wear it either.

The matter came to a head when missionaries completed their doctrinal questionnaires for reappointment to their second terms. On one occasion, the bishops had reviewed a missionary's questionnaire and learned that he did not intend to wear a plain coat during his next term. In the men's rest room, one of the bishops announced, "Here is a ringleader whose rebellion must be nipped in the bud." The missionary in question happened to overhear the conversation. He began to make contacts with Presbyterian missionaries about returning to Ethiopia under the Presbyterian board.

A compromise was struck with the Pennsylvania bishops

when that missionary promised not to wear a tie. Even so, the mission board secretary on his next visit to Ethiopia expressed disappointment that the missionary was wearing a lapel coat (even though he wore no tie) instead of a plain coat. The missionary felt hurt, for he thought he was keeping the promise he had made.

Not all were caught in this screening, however. When the mission board secretary accompanied by a Lancaster Conference bishop made their deputation visit in 1958, they were met at the airport by men wearing lapel suits and ties. The agenda for the following week was overshadowed by this issue, considered by the visitors to be a breach of trust. The inability of the home church to bring its missionaries "into line" was a factor in the request of five bishops and a number of ministers and deacons to be released from the Lancaster Mennonite Conference in 1968. They organized the Eastern Pennsylvania Mennonite Church, with its own mission projects.

In an international setting, the plain coat also carried a political message. In 1963, Paul Erb, editor of the Mennonite weekly magazine, *Gospel Herald*, visited Ethiopia as part of a world tour. The missionary men debated how they would dress to meet him. Paul had heard that missionaries in Ethiopia were conservative and that he would probably need to carry a plain suit for his visit to that country.

Paul arrived in Addis Ababa on a plane with international observers. They were slated to attend the inauguration of the Organization for African Unity. Airline personnel whisked Paul through customs without opening his bags and into a large Buick. When the driver asked for the name of his hotel, Paul replied that there must be some mistake. He was expecting to be met by missionaries. The driver said, "Aren't you the Red China observer to the OAU meeting?" Paul replied, "No, why do you think so?" The driver inquired, "Then why are you wearing the Red Chinese uniform?" Paul finally located the missionaries, who were wearing lapel coats, some with and others without neckties.

Gradually stateside leaders came to realize that some

Family drinking coffee. *Jonathan Charles photo.*

Mennonite customs practiced at mid-century in America were not suitable for export. For example, on a visit to Ethiopia, the board treasurer was riding in the back of a pickup, running through powdery dust on an unpaved road during the dry season. He was going from Nazareth to visit an outlying church. At the end of his journey, he discovered that his black hat had now turned brown. At that church, he sat on a backless bench with people dressed simply without suits or hats.

The missionaries did teach a prayer veiling for women. They felt that such a covering had a basis in Scripture which the plain suit did not have. In the early days of the mission, this was an easy matter, because Ethiopian Orthodox women always wore a *shash*, a bandanna type of headgear that completely covered the hair. The missionaries and the first Ethiopian believers decided that this *shash* would fulfill the veiling taught in 1 Corinthians 11. By the late 1960s, many younger women in stateside Mennonite churches had stopped wearing the covering. Gradually the missionary women also dropped the practice. Some Ethiopian women still wear a veiling today. The Meserete Kristos Church (MKC) *Meserete Iminet* (Foundation of Faith) states that women during worship should have their heads covered.

Another debate between Ethiopian missionaries and the stateside church was whether the Mennonite Mission in Ethiopia could become a member of the Inter-Mission Council in Addis Ababa. This council brought together Lutherans, Presbyterians, SIM, and Baptists primarily for sharing information about each other's work. The Mennonites were invited to join. What followed was a long correspondence with the stateside office about the pros and cons of such an alliance.

The reluctance of the Pennsylvania bishops to approve membership in the Inter-Mission Council is hard to understand, from the perspective of today's ecumenism. At that time, however, the bishops believed that the only way to maintain a distinct Mennonite identity was to keep separate from all other church groups, whether they described themselves as conservatives or liberals. The stateside church did not join either the National Association of Evangelicals, including their Foreign Missions Council, or the National Council and World Council of Churches. However, someone usually attended such meetings as an observer, to hear the deliberations.

The missionaries welcomed visits to Ethiopia from the stateside church, whether by administrators from the mission board or by bishops from the Lancaster Conference. The church in Pennsylvania usually sent people who had some cross-cultural awareness. However, this was not always enough to bridge the gap between the missionary's viewpoint and the expectation of the home church.

In the summer of 1952, one Pennsylvania bishop visited Ethiopia as part of a deputation trip that included Tanganyika. He spent a good part of July in Ethiopia, including days of riding in a bouncing pickup to see the station at

Deder. He was fearful of switchbacks on mountain roads that seemed to go nowhere but up and down. He wondered why the highway department of the government had not built guardrails.

After traveling for several hours and passing through a number of towns en route from Dire Dawa to Deder, he heard that two more laborious hours of driving lay ahead. This led the bishop to question the need to press so deeply into the hinterland when opportunities for witness seemed to exist closer to good roads and the shopping town of Dire Dawa. He could hardly understand that Deder, located at the head of several valleys, was an important shopping center for thousands of people who grew coffee, oranges, and bananas in surrounding valleys.

Then there was a disagreement with mission director Dan Sensenig over whether Ethiopians should be ordained. The visiting bishop did not think it proper for laymen to perform baptisms. Dan said, "If rebaptizing Orthodox Christians is illegal, the ordination of someone to do so would be more serious." It was only the beginning of differences that would arise between what missionaries thought was good for the Ethiopian church, and expectations of Lancaster Conference. A bishop who was a strong leader stateside, pressing his conservative convictions on Pennsylvania Mennonites, found himself ill at ease, in deep culture shock, and unable to do much during his visit. Missionaries also did not feel greatly encouraged by a bishop who was frightened by travel risks they were expected to live with daily.

Probably the greatest struggle missionaries had was to learn the language. This meant learning Amharic, the official language of Ethiopia, well enough to teach and preach in it. This was a formidable task. The first project was to master the alphabet of 231 characters, an ancient script with no resemblance whatsoever to the Latin letters. Amharic is one of the few African languages with its own script. It is a Semitic tongue with a complex grammar system and sounds so foreign to the Western ear that it seemed to defy learning.

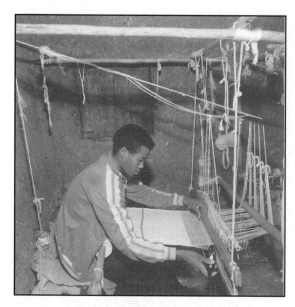

Traditional cotton weaving on a loom. *Jonathan Charles photo.*

Missionaries from Europe and America alike struggled with its complexity and sound formation. Many did not get beyond speaking halting phrases. The language is famous for its double meanings, subtleties, and abundant use of proverbs to express everyday truth.

The mission board added to the difficulty by never insisting that missionaries master the language before they began their work. Institutions were usually understaffed, and workers had to fill vacant positions immediately upon arrival in the country. The mission board promised them time to study language at a later date. For some, this time never came until a second term, and then it was often at the insistence of the missionaries themselves. They bargained to have time off for study if they were to renew their contract. These breaks for language study were usually for three or four months, but hardly anyone could learn to use Amharic meaningfully in that short time. In three months, one could not learn even enough to form a sufficient foundation for eventually developing fluent speech.

In addition, Ethiopians were eager to learn English. They studied it as a subject in elementary school and were expected to receive all their instruction in English by the time they reached high school. Consequently, most missionaries reverted to speaking English as soon as they got back to the job because Ethiopian employees wanted to improve their English by conversing with a native speaker. Missionaries often used interpreters when teaching nurse aids in the hospitals or examining patients. A few had a full year of uninterrupted study in a language school away from other responsibilities. They are the ones who did eventually learn Amharic well enough to teach and preach in it.

The couples appointed for evangelism were usually

Right: Church leaders eating in traditional Ethiopian style. From left: Fikru Zeleke, Girma Edo, Shiferaw Koyamo, Bedru Hussein. *Jonathan Charles photo. Below:* Oxen threshing *tef,* a small cereal grain. *Jonathan Charles photo.*

allowed more time for language study. However, they were often given part-time administrative responsibilities in the institutions before they completed their studies. It became almost the accepted practice for the missionary to use an interpreter when teaching Bible classes in the schools or when preaching on Sunday mornings. If the Ethiopian interpreter had a faulty understanding of English, a sermon could be hilarious. One interpreter rendered the speaker's reference to Jesus' words, "If your eye is sound, your whole body will be full of light" (Matt. 6:22, RSV), as "an eye filled with noise." The missionary speaker didn't notice. Those in the audience who did understand were too polite to laugh.

Ethiopians, though they appreciated the missionaries' attempts at conversation, did not expect them to use the language well enough for serious communication. Usually an Ethiopian, who knew English better than the missionary knew Amharic, was readily available to interpret. Rather than wait for the missionary to stumble through his sentences, it was less stressful for missionary and national alike to rely on translation. Many sermons were preached in English and translated into Amharic.

Missionaries knew that to teach the gospel, they should know the language, and most made noble attempts to learn it. Many prayers went up for those studying, that they would be given "language mercies." However, the difficulty of the language and the pressing duties of operating schools and hospitals and building programs—these all seemed to make mastery of Amharic an illusory goal. A veteran missionary from Tanzania visited once and declared, "Learning language is a spiritual matter." That statement did not help workers who already felt defeated, though they had prayed long and hard that their ears would be opened and their tongues unloosed.

Fluency in a second language, Oromo, was essential at Dire Dawa, Deder, and Bedeno if missionaries were to be serious about starting a church among these people. Yet none of the workers succeeded in learning Oromo. Instead, they taught in Amharic and used interpreters to translate for them. Government policy required that all teaching and preaching was to originate in either English or Amharic and be translated into the vernacular where that was necessary. This was an effort to unify the country by the use of common languages. All elementary schools used Amharic. Nevertheless, how could one expect a people to turn to Christ if their teachers did not even think it important enough to communicate with them in their native Oromo tongue?

The mission board, however, was serious about evangelism of the Oromo people of Hararge Region. The board arranged for Nathan Heges, Nevin Horsts, and Paul Gingrichs to take graduate studies in Islamics during their first leave, after five years of service. The missionaries soon learned that the Islam of Hararge was more deeply entrenched than in the western part of Ethiopia, where missions had been more successful in evangelizing Muslims. MKC showed its interest in Muslims by becoming a member of the Islam in Africa Project, an interdenominational agency promoting Christian-Muslim understanding. Shamsudin Abdo, for many years MKC's representative on the Islam in Africa Project, has helped evangelicals understand the dynamics of Christian-Muslim relationships.

Today, evangelism among the Oromo of Hararge Region largely remains an unfinished task. Congregations are now established at Deder, Dire Dawa, Harar, and Jigjiga. Each has many satellite fellowships. This expansion shows that MKC in the late 1990s has begun to focus on reaching into Oromo communities.

In their letters and articles of the 1950s, missionaries wrote about the joys and difficulties of planting a church in a foreign land. They told of new commitments made by believers, of their eagerness to witness to their fellow countrymen, of hospital evangelists who led patients to the Lord, of students who would spend their vacations selling Christian literature.

However, missionaries also reported disappointments—believers growing careless in their Christian walk, and forces of evil that seemed to snatch away their best efforts. Constantly, the mission team asked the church in America to intercede: "Pray that Satan be defeated, that God's Word would not return void, that Ethiopia would soon stretch out her hands to God."

Missionaries asked the home church to pray for Ethiopians who had told of their temptations and requested prayer support for them to be victorious. "Don't fail us at the throne," one missionary wrote after telling stories of people who appeared to be moved by the gospel message but who didn't "openly confess" faith in Christ.

The mission workers could not always discern when opposition was due to their own cultural blunders or to the work of Satan, who did not want a vital church planted in Ethiopia. Dr. Walter Schlabach wrote, "The enemy of souls is attacking from many angles, usually in a sinister, undercover way, by such means as false rumors, slander, and backbiting. . . . But one bright aspect of this is that the devil is being challenged or he would not be so busy."[1]

In their letters missionaries often requested prayer for their own needs. "Each one of us needs to learn daily the way of love and humility. . . . We need strength for the trials . . . of each day. We constantly need wisdom and grace to meet the needs and desires of these young believers," one wrote from Nazareth.

Missionaries also indicated answers to prayer. "We have become increasingly aware that there are those who are striving mightily in prayer with us. We have no other explanation for the increased interest among the children in the Sunday service and . . . older folks in the Bible teaching in the English classes and at Sunday worship," wrote Robert Garber from Dire Dawa. "We are often made aware of an overshadowing presence and guidance as we go through testing. I am sure your prayer and supplications to God have taken us through many deep waters."[2]

One of the deep waters for the missionary team was the death of Ellen Keener Eshleman of a stroke in May 1953. She was the daughter of Clayton and Martha Keener, who managed the school for the blind in Addis Ababa. In less than three years of missionary service, Ellen had already anticipated that the largely male group of early believers would need Christian wives. She urged greater efforts for evangelizing women. "Probably you don't know how much we appreciate your prayers," she wrote home. "Prayer makes the difference between rough and smooth days," Ellen noted after seeing twenty ill patients arrive from the Wonji Sugar Estate. They overloaded the forty-bed hospital, that now had to care for sixty patients.

Lois N. Garber (Kauffman), who taught at the school for the blind, commented on Ellen's short missionary life: "Ellen's ministry became the important ministry of an intercessor, and this influence was definitely felt in the mission program."[3] Ellen's husband, Dr. Rohrer Eshleman, asked the church at home to "take up this praying task where Ellen left off."

In their letters, missionaries repeatedly quoted Isaiah 55:11 and vowed their own firm belief that God's Word would one day surely accomplish his purposes. During the 1950s, when *Missionary Messenger* ran a bimonthly "Prayer Letter Supplement," missionaries supplied a half dozen letters for each issue. They chronicled the woes of understaffed hospitals, the headaches of government bureaucracy, the shortages of school supplies, and their own unsuccessful struggles with the language. Yet they also noted the joys of seeing students eager to learn, people who got well with just a little medical care, and blind boys making remarkable craft items for sale. Often they praised God for giving them strength to cope with the great demands made on their energies. At the same time, they reminded the home church that more workers were needed.

It was not uncommon for the hospital staffs at Nazareth and sometimes at Deder to treat over a hundred patients in a morning and deal with a spate of surgeries in the afternoons. At the same time, the hospital was training dressers to operate rural clinics. Nurses and doctors were especially overworked and on call twenty-four hours a day. Schoolrooms at Deder and Bedeno had as many as fifty children in them, often three or four crowded into a desk built for two.

The basic team of thirty-five workers served five-year terms, then took one year to recuperate in the States from the rarified air of the Ethiopian highlands. Some came back again two, three, and even four times. The basic team was supported by short-termers—builders, nurses, teachers, secretaries—who usually served for three years and ended their assignments. Short-term commitments turned into long-term service for some. A number went out single and married other missionaries or nationals in Ethiopia. Of the 194 expatriate workers who served in Ethiopia from 1945-1998, most were sent by Eastern Mennonite Missions. Mennonite Relief Committee and Mennonite Central Committee jointly appointed 34 workers between 1945 and 1950, to prepare the way for mission. After the mid 1970s, MCC again became involved and appointed 27 workers to serve in relief and development ministries. Some of these were jointly appointed by EMM.

By 1960, Eastern Mennonite Board missionaries had assisted in starting five major institutions that they helped staff until they were turned over to government management in the late 1970s.

5

Education— A Hunger to Learn

The lad appeared to be full grown. Accompanied by his father, he came one morning to the elementary school at Bedeno and asked to be admitted to the first grade. The first and second graders, listening in on the conversation, tried to stifle their reaction when the father, speaking in the Oromo language, said the boy was twenty years old. Would the director of the school admit him?

Coming from the Oromo people, the young man had never had an opportunity to learn to read his tribal language or Amharic, the official language of the country and used in all schools. Abdu, as we shall call him, would at the same time have to learn to speak Amharic. The father didn't want his son to delay another day. Abdu did not seem disturbed to sit with children as he took up his book to study the alphabet with its 231 characters. Here was a chance to learn. Abdu walked the five miles to school each morning without complaint.

It is hard for Americans who have grown up where school attendance is compulsory to understand the great thirst for education in Ethiopia during the 1950s. The emperor, Haile Selassie I, was eager to have at least an elementary school in every town and village. However, his Ministry of Education could not begin to cope with the great demand. Some communities were so remote that they had not yet awakened to the need for a school. Others, especially those within several days' walk of larger towns, wanted to copy what they saw happening in these centers.

Such communities petitioned the Ministry of Education, which then tried to send teachers to the rural areas if the communities built their own schoolhouses. The government was not always able to provide teachers to meet the demand because there were so few high schools and teacher-training institutes that could produce teachers. So the emperor welcomed expatriate teachers, especially missionary teachers, who often were supported by their mission agencies.

The Mennonite Relief and Service Committee of the Mennonite Board of Missions, Elkhart, Indiana, saw this opportunity and appointed its first teachers for government schools in Addis Ababa in 1948. When Eastern Mennonite Board of Missions, Salunga, Pennsylvania, received permission from the government in 1948 to function as the Mennonite Mission in Ethiopia, the mission director, Daniel Sensenig, planned for three teachers to teach at a government secondary school in Harar, in eastern Ethiopia. He also arranged for the mission to open elementary schools at Deder and Bedeno, in the same region.

When the governor of Bedeno, a town of two thousand, some sixty miles from the railroad city of Dire Dawa, met Daniel Sensenig and Dorsa Mishler on their first investigative trip in 1948, he wept. At last he saw hope that the children of Bedeno would have a chance to learn. He welcomed the missionaries warmly and suggested that they locate on a tract of land close to the town. That plot had an all-weather spring bubbling out of the hillside. He helped to arrange the deal.

Within a year after the contract for this land was signed, Menno and Delilah Chupp of Michigan had built a school, and Martha Wikerd (Ludwig) of Lititz, Pennsylvania, had opened grades one and two. By 1958 the school had been enlarged to four classrooms, accommodating 120 students. "A fine Ethiopian [Daniel Lemma] has come from fourth-year college to take charge of the school and help in other ways to reach the people for Christ," Chester Wenger wrote in his annual report.[1]

Bedeno elementary school students, circa 1955.

From this school have come many who went on to get further training and to serve the church in Ethiopia and abroad.

The town of Deder is a market center also sixty miles from Dire Dawa, along another mountain range. Like Bedeno, Deder is located among the eastern Oromo people in mountainous country. As the crow flies, the two towns are twenty-five miles apart, a ten-hour trek by foot or mule through the hot valleys. By road it took eight hours to cover the hundred miles in a four-wheel-drive vehicle. The government ran an elementary school at Deder. Because of the great demand, officials did not see a mission school in the same area as competitive. In the fall of 1950, soon after she arrived in the country, Mildred Heistand (Mullet) opened first grade in a garage.

The following year, ten seventh graders from the government school in Deder approached Mildred about helping them get ready for the grade-school-leaving exam, a prerequisite to enroll in high school. They felt the teachers at the Deder government school were not trained well enough to help them through this hurdle. However, Mildred had agreed, in keeping with government policy, not to accept students from the government school. So the students secured letters from their school director, stating that they were free to pursue their education wherever they chose.

On the basis of these letters, Mildred started a special class for them, alongside the grades one to three she had already started. A month later education officials from the provincial capital at Harar visited the Deder mission school. With them was the director of the Deder government school, who pointed out the students who were supposedly admitted illegally. Mildred asked the education inspector to allow these students to sit for the school-leaving exam. He said he could grant the request if she would follow the curriculum. Mildred made the necessary changes in textbooks. At the end of the school year, the students were allowed to take the exam in the name of the Deder government school—not the mission school.

One of the students, Million Belete, walked the round trip from his home, fourteen miles daily, to complete his elementary education. Twenty years later he became secretary of the Bible Society for Africa and president of Mennonite World Conference. Another student, Dr. Ingida Asfaw, took training as a cardiologist and now works in the United States. A third, Tsega Woldemariam, is a regional director for World Vision and lives in Kenya.

The mission school grew to become an elementary school offering eight grades. Beginning in 1954, it provided boarding for fifteen girls in an effort to encourage girls to obtain an education. Here Robert and Alta Garber from Mount Joy, Pennsylvania, served many years, directing the schools, teaching the Bible, and nurturing a church into being. Later, Henry and Pearl Gamber from Scottdale, Pennsylvania, directed development projects mentioned in a later chapter.

The city of Dire Dawa was well supplied with regular government schools when Daniel and Blanche Sensenig moved there in 1956. So they opened evening classes in a rented dwelling and offered English, mathematics, and Bible. These projects attracted young people. Many of them attended Bible classes, worship services, and prayer meetings. In 1957 the mission leased a plot of land for thirty years. The mission workers erected a dwelling, chapel, garage, and guesthouse. Then they added classes in Amharic and English typing and opened a small bookshop.

Dire Dawa is on the Djibouti-Addis rail line and just 3,200 feet above sea level. It was the shopping town for missionaries working at Deder and Bedeno. Here they replenished their supplies, such as flour, margarine, cement, and gasoline. The mission guesthouse provided a few days' respite for workers to get away from their pressing duties and breathe a "thicker" atmosphere than they had at their highland stations, with elevations above 7,000 feet.

The next educational endeavor was a school for the blind in Addis Ababa. In 1948 the emperor asked the Mennonites to operate a school for blind children that he would personally finance. Eye problems were common in Ethiopia because of river blindness, the failure to treat children's eyes infected with trachoma, and various kinds of accidents.

In the case of river blindness, a small black fly infects the bloodstream and kills the optic nerve of people who live within thirty miles of a tropical river. In more recent years, medical people discovered that just one pill a year breaks the life cycle of the insect, but earlier the people did not have that pill.[2]

Flies would sit on babies' eyes and keep them constantly infected with conjunctivitis or trachoma unless mothers are taught the importance of washing a child's eyes daily. Accidents also damaged eyes. Hand grenades left over from the Italian occupation 1935-41 became lethal weapons in the hands of innocent children who found them and played with them. When the grenade exploded, a child was killed, blinded, or maimed for life.

Clayton and Martha Keener, teachers at Lancaster Mennonite High School in Pennsylvania, were recruited to operate a school for the blind. During the summer of 1950, Martha attended the University of Wisconsin in Madison and took a crash course on teaching the blind. Fellow teachers in summer refresher courses took genuine interest in the Ethiopia project and gave her many helpful hints. The Keeners arrived in Ethiopia in November of that year and opened the Merha Ewourran (Guide for the Blind) School in 1952. The mission board asked for designated funds above budget to support the Keeners.

At the emperor's command, provincial government officials rounded up thirty-three young blind boys, aged six to twelve, a few from each region of the country. The government sent them to the new school for the blind in Addis Ababa, where the emperor and empress and many dignitaries welcomed them on opening day July 23, 1952.

Martha Keener, director of the Merha Ewourran School (for the Blind), Addis Ababa, encouraged each student to learn a craft. *1950s photo.*

Clayton and Martha were papa and mama of this boarding school for a decade. They helped a generation of young men, otherwise condemned to a beggar's life, to meaningful employment as teachers, craftsmen, lawyers, judges, attorneys general, and in other occupations.

Mama Keener, as she was called by the students, welcomed these frightened children, who had never been away from home. Mama Keener's love and acceptance were proverbial. She tried never to turn anyone away, even though all beds were full. The school, built for forty students, had sixty by the end of the 1950s. Creative teachers, both American and Ethiopian, helped the boys overcome their fears and taught them to engage in sports usually thought possible only for sighted people. Missionaries asked American Christians to pray for specific boys, especially those who also had other physical limitations caused by the accidents that took away their sight.

During those first days, some students were quite fearful in their strange surroundings. They lived with other blind children who spoke different tribal languages. Those who knew each other took turns sleeping while others "watched" so that no one would harm them.

Here the boys learned to read Braille, to make rugs and brooms and weave cloth, to sing and play musical instruments. From their teachers, they heard Bible stories from beginning to end. Lois Garber (Kauffman) from Mount Joy, Pennsylvania, wrote in early 1953 that the boys liked handwork so well that it was almost necessary to drive them out to play. Outside, they played ball by sound alone and ran races by sliding their fingers along a wire stretched across the playground. Beyene Chichaibelu and Haile Woldemichael, two of the early teachers, devised creative ways for blind boys to enjoy recreational activities. They took them on walks down by the nearby stream, where they were allowed to throw stones and hear them skip on the water.

Lois Garber asked the stateside church to pray for these boys "whom we claim for Christ." She noted that as the first school year ended, five of them said they were sure they were saved. The staff was not limited in teaching the Bible. Clayton said that after a year, there was hardly a Bible story new to them, even though few of them had any Bible knowledge when they first came. They memorized Scripture accurately and quickly, "far better than any American child I've ever tried to teach," Lois wrote. Twenty-four of them asked to have a special prayer meeting of their own on Friday evenings.[3]

His Majesty, Haile Selassie I, usually accompanied by Her Majesty, Itege Mennen, visited the school seventeen times during the first year. Once he brought a pair of shoes for each boy. He would quiz the boys on their studies and even their

Bible knowledge. Mama Keener usually escorted their Majesties through the building, attempting to converse in her broken Amharic. She talked about the school to anyone who would listen. Once, answering someone who asked her what she did, her Amharic got jumbled: "I work at the blind Haile Selassie school."

Eventually the blind students took their high school training along with sighted children in government schools. The staff at Merha Ewourran School, especially Alma Eby and Esther Becker, spent many hours reading their assignments to them when they came back in the evening. The school was their home until they were ready for employment or entering Addis Ababa University. A few went on to graduate school. Several became lawyers and teachers. Alemu Checole was a distinguished teacher at the Bible Academy. He has served as a church leader for many years, offering mature counsel. In 1962, the Mennonite Mission turned the school for the blind over to the Haile Selassie I Welfare Trust.

In August 1952 and at Nazareth, another educational

Emperor Haile Selassie I visited the Merha Euowerran School (for the Blind) 17 times during its first year of operation, 1952-53. Here he distributes shoes to the 42 students enrolled at the time.

institution opened, to teach hospital assistants called "dressers." This school was a continuation of the training given by the relief and service workers since they had opened the hospital in 1946. By the end of 1947, four classes had been trained. In the same year, J. R. Clemens reported that all of a class of seventeen passed the examination given them by the Ministry of Health, the only dresser school in the country to have such a record.[4]

When the administration of the hospital was transferred from the Relief Committee to the Mennonite Mission, the dresser school began a new chapter. In 1949 Chester and Sara Jane Wenger from Norfolk County (now city of Chesapeake), Virginia, were appointed to serve in Ethiopia as educational evangelists. They had trained for overseas service and chose Ethiopia after discerning carefully for several years where God would have them go. As proposed by Orie Miller, Chester's assignment was to help set up a school program as part of the Mennonite Mission in Ethiopia.

The Wengers left their home and church-school teaching position. With their three small daughters, they set sail in October 1949 on the *MS Garote* to become, in Miller's term, "teaching missionaries." Wengers were first assigned to Deder, where they lived in a small garage with a dirt floor. Two months later, during the first Mennonite Mission Conference in Ethiopia, Orie Miller recommended that they immediately transfer to the Nazareth Hospital. There Amharic was more commonly spoken, so they could study language as spoken by the Amharas. They spent a year in language study. Then they began developing education strategy for elementary, vocational, and secondary schools. All of the educational programs were designed to support church-planting efforts.

The government had designated Nazareth as a closed area for foreigners in mission. Therefore, it became a challenge for the missionaries to live within the law and still share their testimony of faith to those among whom they served. Many of those being trained in the hospital seemed to lack an essential ethical foundation for serving the sick with integrity. Hospital supplies and medicines were frequently stolen. At one point, the whole staff went on strike for higher wages and presented false claims of promises made by a previous administrator. The prospects for the hospital seemed bleak unless the missionaries were allowed to teach the gospel.

Therefore, in 1951 Chester Wenger with mission director Daniel Sensenig set about asking the government for permission to teach the Bible to fifty dresser (health-assistant) students at the hospital. Officials granted this permit in 1952, six years after the hospital was first opened by the Mennonite Relief Committee. The missionaries regarded this authorization as an answer to earnest prayer. Now students could learn the Christian faith and have it as a foundation for giving care to the sick. The school was named Nazareth Dresser Bible School.

Trained as an educational administrator, Chester expanded the school's curriculum, which was basically medical subjects, to include instruction in English, Bible, world religions, carpentry, and personal development.

Chester carefully thought through the purpose for such a school. He published the goals for the home church to read in the *Missionary Messenger:* (1) to be sure about the salvation of each student; (2) to help students know the love of Christ as expressed in Christian brotherhood; (3) to establish students in the Word of God; (4) to help Ethiopia in its need of dressers; (5) to provide students with means for an honest livelihood; (6) to supply dressers to assist in opening new areas to Christian witness; and (7) to awaken evangelistic conviction in the students.[5]

The government granted permission to open the Dresser Bible School (DBS) in 1952 with the stipulation that any Christian teaching must be restricted to the hospital compound. "Other mission societies have not been able to locate here, but God has opened a door to us. . . . The area is designated Orthodox Christian and closed to foreign mission work," Chester wrote in 1953. This permission from the government for the mission to function in a "closed area" was a definite answer to the prayers of many Mennonites in the United States.

Forty-five students enrolled in the preparatory course and the two-year program. The school issued a primary certificate at the end of the first year and an advanced certificate at the end of the second. Chester interpreted the government permission to allow students, who found new faith in Christ, to scatter over the country during holiday breaks to teach the gospel and sell Christian literature and Bible portions. Some students met severe opposition, and at least one was severely beaten by the people in a rural community who believed the students were teaching a doctrine strange to the Orthodox Church.

In an article in *Missionary Messenger* in 1952, Chester described the joy of teaching Bible truth to Ethiopian young people for the first time. Six weeks into the school year, he asked his students whether they believed what he was teaching. Twelve fellows said, "We like it, we believe it, we want more of it," and they made a personal confession of faith in Christ. A year later Chester wrote to the home church, "Many of the students are showing signs of real spiritual growth. . . . Pray for an abundant increase and harvest of souls. . . . May we never forget that more important than healing bodies is the saving of souls."

Three young men from the Hosanna area of Ethiopia were assisting in this work of bringing the message of Christ to Nazareth. In that area and before the Italian occupation, the gospel had found a response among the Kambatta people through the efforts of Sudan Interior Mission. Gemeda Baruda, Ephraim Okashe, and Watro Wachemo were committed Christians and assisted in leading morning prayers and Sunday worship for employees at the hospital. They also helped in teaching others who were seeking spiritual fellowship and baptism.

The hospital staff taught the medical subjects; Robert Garber of Mt. Joy, Pennsylvania, instructed in carpentry; and Chester Wenger taught Bible. Million Belete from Deder was one who made a faith commitment that first year, before he left the course to attend a government secondary school in Addis Ababa. Later he became chairman of the Meserete Kristos Church (MKC).

Seventeen students were graduated from DBS in June 1953. All of them "had made at least a confession of Christ, and many of them showed signs of real spiritual growth," Chester reported. The Nazareth DBS operated for twenty-five years, offering both primary (one-year) and advanced (two-year) training for dressers, later called health assistants.

During its operation by the Mennonite Mission and MKC from 1946 to 1978, Nazareth Hospital trained more than a thousand dressers, who served throughout the country in hospitals, clinics, and pharmacies. For many years the hospital had the distinction of giving solid medical and moral training to young people. Thus the Nazareth Hospital helped raise the quality of medical services throughout Ethiopia.

A dresser school offering just one year of training opened also at the Deder hospital in 1960. The Ministry of Health thought the hospital too small to operate a dresser school and found it inconvenient to send someone from Addis Ababa to give the final examination. The school was closed in 1968.

The largest educational institution started by the Mennonite Mission was the Bible Academy in Nazareth, opened in 1959. Chester Wenger, as founder and principal, began this secondary school with twenty-one students enrolled in ninth grade. During his first furlough (1955 and 1956) in USA, he had completed his master's degree in theology at Union Theological Seminary in Virginia. His goal was to pursue a curriculum with an educational philosophy based on the Bible. He wanted the school to give a good academic education while instilling Christian values.

Chester hoped some of the students would become church leaders. However, he wanted them to learn skills that would enable them to make a living without depending on a salary from the church. While working on the objectives for the Bible Academy in 1958, Chester in his annual report asked the stateside church to pray:

Sophomore class at the Bible Academy, Nazareth, 1961. From left: Marta Werkalemew, Shamsudin Abdo, Melkamwerk, Alemu Gebrewold, Tsegay Abreha, Mersha Tadesse, Desta Wedajow, Hailukiross Alemu, Seifu Haile, Negash Kebede, Semie Degefu, Abay Gebrewold, Samuel Bekele, Mena Tewahida, Abrehet.

> Brethren, pray for us that the forces of evil we encounter daily may be defeated, that the chains which are binding the hearts of many may be broken. Who can do this? "Now the Lord is that Spirit: and where the Spirit of the Lord is, there is liberty" (2 Cor. 3:17). We thank God for victories and trials, for his abundant provision throughout the year, and for your prayers and constant support. We pray that you may all be blessed with great joy when the Lord is revealed from heaven.[6]

His 1959 report indicates that Chester believed the development of youth was important:

> The preaching of the gospel challenges us as we see firsthand its saving power. Especially the young people thrill us with their fresh zeal and dedication to Christ. They make up the greatest part of the

congregations in our regular worship services, prayer meetings, singings, Sunday schools, and youth meetings. It is mostly youth who are studying in believers' instruction classes and taking Bible correspondence courses. Young people's Christian Life Conferences were held on three of our five stations with a total of 800 young people in attendance.[7]

The missionaries faced many obstacles while opening the Bible Academy. They had to purchase land for the campus. Missionaries feared the land price would be inflated beyond its real value if foreigners tried to purchase it. Furthermore, the law did not permit foreigners to own land. Neither could the church (MKC) hold the title because it was not organized and registered with the government. Finally three MKC members agreed to buy the land in behalf of the church.

The government was slow to give permission for the Nazareth Bible Academy to open. It feared that the academy might take students from government schools. So the Ministry of Education allowed the academy to admit students only from mission elementary schools. This was never enforced because government officials themselves wanted to enroll their children in the academy!

Church members had many questions. How would students be able to attend a school that charged fees for tuition and board? Would it become a school only the well-to-do could afford? Would the Bible Academy meet government standards for secondary education so graduates could be admitted to Addis Ababa University?

Missionaries also had their questions. Dr. Rohrer Eshleman was sure that the Dresser Bible School would suffer if its director, Chester Wenger, left it to be principal of the Bible Academy. Rohrer felt betrayed. He had devoted his life to medicine, to provide opportunities for other missionaries to do evangelism in the hospital. If the dressers in training to serve in hospitals were to be shortchanged in their biblical and spiritual development, Rohrer saw himself as merely the director of a secular institution. Chester, however, was sure that the founding of a quality secondary school would eventually prove its worth to the church. Paul Gingrich succeeded Chester as director of the Dresser School, maintaining its high level of biblical instruction.

Other missionaries wondered how much effort they should put into seeking government accreditation for a secondary school. Daniel Sensenig pointed out the country's great need for artisans of every kind—carpenters, mechanics, agriculturalists, clerical workers. Would it not be better to establish a vocational Bible school? he asked. At the end of a high-school academic program, some students might not pass the stringent University entrance exams. However, Chester persevered, and the Nazareth Bible Academy met the requirements to be an accredited secondary school, registered with the government.

Allen Byler from Belleville, Pennsylvania, directed the building of a new facility out of concrete block made on the site, two miles south of Nazareth along the road going to the Dutch sugar plantations of Wonji. There were classrooms, dormitory, dining hall, teacher dwellings. After using a rented building in Nazareth for the first year, the Bible Academy moved to the new location and added a grade each year until 1962, when a full four-year secondary school was in operation. That year the graduates took the standard government exam for entrance into the University; all passed! In addition to meeting government requirements, the academy included Bible courses in its curriculum. All students were required to study the Bible. Because subjects were taught in English, most students gained a good mastery of the English language.

Jan Bender Shetler, a staff member at the Bible Academy during 1980-1982, completed a research project on the 23-year history of the school. She found that 499 students had graduated and another 500 had attended. According to Jan, students are found in the higher levels of Ethiopian society today. Many of those filling out her questionnaire attested that they received quality training and developed moral standards to guide their lives and give them convictions to serve humanity. Many students made new commitments to Christian faith and to the church after they left the school.

The Nazareth Bible Academy helped the church to become known and gave the church a certain respectability in society. For students to pass the Ethiopian School Leaving Certificate (ESLC) examination became high priority for the church leaders and the academy staff. During the later years of the school, this may have led to a decline in the emphasis on Bible teaching and Christian nurture. However, the Christian faculty and a good percentage of evangelicals in the student body kept an active Christian witness alive.

Daily chapel, periodic spiritual life conferences, the emphasis on ethics, and the term *Bible* in the academy's name constantly reminded the community that this was a Christian institution. The Marxists, at least, were convinced that the academy did not support the atheism and the rigidity of their revolution.

Among the forty-some expatriate staff who served over twenty-three years at the Bible Academy, Calvin and Marie Shenk, Herb and Sharon Kraybill, and Esther Becker provided long-term continuity in teaching and directing. Calvin stretched students' thinking about theology and history. His close relationship to the church through the years brought him back to Ethiopia annually during the 1990s to conduct leadership training seminars. Calvin and Marie always encouraged excellence and challenged their students to do their best.

The Kraybills were true servants, ready for teaching, administration, maintenance, and counseling. They worked long hours and plugged in where they were needed. Esther Becker also worked several jobs at once, as instructor in English, librarian, matron of the girls, and in general management. These three, receiving their support from Mennonite Mission, were able to secure government employment after the Bible Academy was nationalized and continued to be present for the church during the underground years.

Pearl Gamber with students at Bedeno elementary school, 1962. *Arlene Hege photo.*

The Nazareth Bible Academy with its dining and lodging facilities was an ideal place to host board meetings, seminars, and conferences, and the church used it freely for these purposes. The loss of these buildings was a great disappointment to the church because it needed those facilities for its own Bible college. In 1997, the facility was still being used by the government for a teacher training institute.

Valley schools were another institutional outreach of Mennonite Mission. Nevin Horst from Hagerstown, Maryland, and Robert Garber from Mount Joy, Pennsylvania, had begun their missionary service in the early 1950s. In 1958, they began to contact communities in the towns and valleys around Bedeno and Deder, which were the market centers for about a hundred thousand people. Most of the rural people were Oromo Muslims, who were beginning to see the importance of schools for their children. The people eagerly erected school buildings in response to a promise by MKC to supply them with teachers. The plan was to open schools for only the lower grades in anticipation that those who wanted to pursue their education further would transfer to the full elementary church schools operating at Bedeno or Deder.

Shamsudin Abdo, who grew up at Deder, later supervised these schools as director of education for the church. Until imprisoned in 1982, Shamsudin served significant roles as a dresser, teacher, administrator of elementary schools, director of the Nazareth Bible Academy, and executive secretary of the church.

While still a Muslim, Shamsudin enrolled in the dresser school at Nazareth, insisting that the head of his bed be turned toward Mecca. For more than a year, he grappled with the Scriptures, constantly testing them against the Koran, from which he had memorized long passages as a child. One day he told his teacher, Negussie Ayele, that he could never accept the Bible because Hebrews 13:7 calls for Christians to imitate the faith of their leaders. Shamsudin had found no missionary good enough to follow. Negussie (now Dr. Negussie) replied, "Read the next verse."

Shamsudin found the words, "Jesus Christ is the same yesterday and today and for ever" (RSV). It was enough to remove his doubts. He declared his faith in Christ and never wavered from that commitment.

In 1962 as a student at the Nazareth Bible Academy, Shamsudin interrupted his education to become director of the elementary school at Bedeno, the first Ethiopian to replace a missionary. Later, as education director for the church, he was responsible for the twelve valley schools that opened from 1959 to 1966.

It soon became clear that supplying teachers for all of those schools would place too heavy a burden on the education budget. Therefore, Shamsudin had the thankless task of telling the communities that the mission and the church were not able to continue supporting the valley schools. Some communities had to close their schools because they were not able to pick up the cost of operation. Shamsudin then trained at the Evangelical (Lutheran) College at Debre Zeit and became director of the Nazareth Bible Academy, replacing

Chester Wenger, who left Ethiopia in 1966.[8]

The valley schools had the potential of being more effective than any of the church's programs in convincing Oromo-speaking people that the church had their interests at heart. The school closings must have appeared to them as one more sign that the good things of life come primarily to the town dwellers and to those who are fluent in the official language of the country. However, a few former Muslims in the church today trace their first introduction to Christian faith from hearing the gospel taught in the valley schools. The Deder congregation is beginning to reach Muslims through its twenty-two witness centers in the area.

An institution of a type different from those discussed so far was the Menno Bookstore, formed from a bookstore the mission took over from SIM, who had operated it for many years in Addis Ababa. As Ethiopia's only Christian bookstore of its size, it was essential for distributing Christian literature in the country. It supplied many small bookshops wherever missionaries served.

One day the SIM store manager spoke to Chester Wenger, interim Mennonite Mission director and director of the School for the Blind, about the difficulty of recruiting missionaries to staff the store. SIM missionaries thought they should be in a rural area, doing primary evangelism among tribal people, he said. Working in a bookstore did not fit their image of what a missionary does.

Chester thought a bookstore ministry would be an authentic witness and believed Mennonites would respond to such an opportunity. In 1959, Mennonite Publishing House, Scottdale, Pennsylvania, purchased the stock and furniture of the SIM Bookstore with the understanding that Eastern Mennonite Board of Missions would supply personnel. It was called Menno Bookstore. Through the efficient management of Alice Snyder, it became known as the place in the country where people could purchase or order books of all kinds in Amharic and English. By handling stationery and supplying textbooks for schools, the store and its branches in Nazareth and Dire Dawa were able to amortize the cap-

Alice Snyder shows a book to a customer in Menno Bookstore, Addis Ababa, 1960. Alice was manager of the store from 1963 to 1973.

ital investment and pay operating costs without church or mission subsidy. The store operated under Mennonite direction for twenty years until the Marxist government nationalized it in 1978.

During that period, the bookstore had six managers, and Alice Snyder had the longest tenure. Her efficiency was proverbial. She knew books and where to get them as well as the needs of the people and organizations served by the store. An employee tells of a customer coming to place an order for some books when Alice was on leave in the States. The customer asked to see the "Dutch Woman." When told that Alice was out of the country on leave and would not return for three months, the customer said, "I'll wait until she returns."

In addition to distributing Christian literature, the mission was also interested in producing it. Ever since Million Belete had translated a Mennonite Hour Bible correspondence course in the late 1950s, the Mennonite Mission was looking for a way to become involved in producing Christian education materials in Amharic. In 1958 six missions working under Light of Life Books Fellowship agreed to cooperate in the production of forty-eight titles, Pillar Books, designed as a pastor's basic library. The missions assigned the Mennonites to write or translate six of the titles.

In 1960, Mennonite Mission appointed Nathan and Arlene Hege from Lancaster, Pennsylvania, to work part-time on Amharic literature production. With Mulugeta Lule and Samuel Bekele serving as translators, the Heges produced *Christian Family Living, Abraham,* and *Jeremiah,* three of the Pillar Book series. In 1966, the Baptist General Conference Mission invited MKC to join their literature program in Addis Ababa. The two bodies formed Globe Publishing House and focused on producing Sunday school material for children. The partnership continued until 1974, when MKC experienced budget and staffing problems. The Baptist Church continued to operate Globe, preparing Sunday school materials in Amharic and also publishing books in the Oromo language. It published and sold to all the evangelical churches.

The final institution to be mentioned here—Good Shepherd School—opened in 1960 through the cooperation of four mission groups, including Mennonite Mission, to give their own children an American education. Later, two additional missions joined, making six partners. The school had grades 1-12 and grew to have an enrollment of over 300 students with 24 nationalities.[9] In the diplomatic community, many families from other countries sent their children to Good Shepherd. It operated for 17 years and had to close in 1977 because many missionaries were leaving the country. By that time, the number of children from sponsoring missions had dropped to less than 20.[10]

6

Medicine Opens Doors for Mission

If schools in Ethiopia were scarce in those days, clinics and hospitals were scarcer still. Medical needs were massive. Malaria, infections, complications in childbirth, dysenteries of various kinds—all had to be treated. People sometimes had to travel a hundred miles on foot or be carried by friends to receive treatment. The Nazareth hospital had been opened in 1946 by the Mennonite Relief Committee (see chap. 3). In addition, the missionaries decided to open a hospital at Deder and a clinic at Bedeno.

Dr. Walter and Mae Schlabach, originally of Greenwood, Delaware, were the first medical couple recruited by the Eastern Mission Board. They arrived at Nazareth in 1949 to take over responsibility from Dr. Meryl Grasse, of Souderton, Pennsylvania, who had served with the Mennonite Relief Committee. This began the transition from a short-term relief operation to a long-term medical ministry.

After language study and orientation at Nazareth, the Schlabachs transferred to Deder in 1951. Allen Byler, a builder from Belleville, Pennsylvania, arrived at Deder in the fall of 1950 and, with the help of many Ethiopian workers, started to construct a clinic. For several months Dr. Schlabach turned carpenter in the afternoons to help get the building fully operational more quickly. The clinic opened in the new building in April 1952, thus continuing a clinic which Mary Byer, a nurse, had run for a year previously in a room made of mud and sticks. A sixteen-bed hospital was opened in

February 1953. James Payne, a builder from Allensville, Pennsylvania, assisted Allen in construction.

Walter Schlabach was a graduate of the Hahnemann School of Medicine in Philadelphia. He brought the first modern medicine and surgery to this highland center for twenty thousand people, who carried their produce and coffee from the valleys to sell in Deder on market days. From here he traveled by four-wheel-drive Jeep to surrounding towns to treat patients. Ethiopian Christians were able to go along and distribute literature and share the gospel. Walter, along with two nurses, also started a small training program for dressers. They were encouraged to open outpost clinics under the supervision of the doctor. In addition, a leprosy clinic was opened in 1955 near the Deder Hospital to treat twenty-five people on an outpatient basis.

The Amharic word for doctor is *hakim*, which also included local medicine men without formal medical training. Walter insisted that staff and patients call him doctor, even though it was a foreign word to them.

Walter described the possibilities for witness as almost limitless: "Using the medical work as a direct approach to evangelism seems to be the best method for here. When folks are sick, be they Muslim or otherwise, they are in a mood to hear the gospel," he wrote after serving a year at Deder.[1]

The Schlabachs served only one five-year term in Ethiopia. Before they left, they had both a clinic and a thirty-bed hospital operational, and they had established a reputation for quality medical care. Walter was especially adept at surgical procedures.[2]

In 1942, Rohrer Eshleman enrolled in a premed course at Eastern Mennonite College in Harrisonburg, Virginia. He had left the farm to train to be a missionary. He chose medicine because he thought that would open the way for preaching the gospel in a foreign land.

Rohrer and his wife, Ellen Keener Eshleman, began at the Haile Mariam Mamo Memorial Hospital at Nazareth in 1951, after spending six months in frustrating study of the Amharic language. Rohrer could memorize the grammar, but he could not hear the sounds spoken. He resigned himself to using an interpreter for seventeen years.

Missionaries and Ethiopians joined Rohrer in grieving when Ellen passed away from a massive stroke in May 1953. Her ministry was brief but bright with the love of Jesus, which she shared with everyone. In 1955, Rohrer married Mabel Horst, a missionary nurse from Gap, Pennsylvania, who became bookkeeper for the hospital.

Keen about evangelism, Rohrer felt his medical efforts would provide opportunities for others to share the gospel. He spent long days at the hospital, seeing a hundred patients in the mornings and performing several surgeries in the afternoons. Often he was called out for emergencies at night and would have to carry his normal schedule the next day. When others seemed nonchalant about witness, Rohrer's morale would drop. However, Rohrer counseled evangelists not to take advantage of sick people by pressuring them into making a commitment to Christ.

Rohrer encouraged Ethiopian dressers to use their skills as soon as they received training. In 1952 he described the duties at the hospital: "One dresser diagnoses, one checks medicines, one does blood tests, one knows operating room technique." He was also concerned about evangelism. "With the many opportunities lying ahead of the students, you can readily understand how we covet these young people for the Lord. . . . Our efforts here will be in vain if these eager youths do not consecrate themselves to the Lord," Rohrer wrote in *Missionary Messenger.* He then appealed to the American church to pray: "With your prayers, there can be a tremendous testimony spread out over this country when the students graduate."[3]

Dr. Joseph Burkholder from Markham, Ontario, arrived in Ethiopia in 1954 to replace the Schlabachs, who had completed five years and were going on furlough. Joe remembered the challenges of adjusting to a totally new environment in a rural town. He had to learn to work with other missionaries, most of them culturally conservative recruits from Pennsylvania. As a single man, he had to board with a mis-

Nazareth Dresser Bible School students going out into the country to witness, 1955.

sionary family. With little experience in medicine after his training, he had to follow Walter, who by then was known in the community as a competent surgeon.[4]

A community grapevine message reached Joe's ears soon after his arrival at Deder: "If you need surgery done, schedule it quickly before Dr. Schlabach leaves, because the new doctor doesn't know how to do surgery." Without training in administration and without being given time to study the language, Joe was told to be the physician and administrator of the Deder hospital. "I had no training in anthropology or sociology, nothing in linguistics, and very little understanding of cross-cultural issues," Joe recalled later.

Another thing to make Joe's first year difficult was the appearance in 1954 of a popular Muslim prophet, Sayed Abeyo. He diverted the people from seeking medicine and promised them healing. Thousands of people of Deder and the surrounding communities followed the prophet, who told them not to plant their fields because God would provide. The hospital census dropped to almost nothing, and so did the income to pay the staff.

However, Joe's earlier call to missionary service was clear. He was raised in a Mennonite farm family, in a community where young people seldom finished high school. Joe, as the youngest child in his family, was given a special break. Once at a youth meeting where a film about a missionary doctor was shown, "something inside of me said, 'You are to be a missionary doctor.' " Characteristically reserved, Joe said nothing to his family. However, he knew this call would require a radical rethinking of his educational future. On completing high school, he knew he had to tell his parents that he wanted to continue his education. "I remember telling my dad, 'Look, I've got to go to the university.' "

His father consented, and Joe was amazed. "He thought people who went to University Medical School lose their faith, but he had the faith to believe that I wouldn't," Joe said. During his internship, a quirk of scheduling put Joe into surgery. That gave him more experience in this field than most of his colleagues received.

Before Joe shipped out to Ethiopia in 1954, he was introduced to Helen Witmer, a nurse who had just completed three years serving at the Nazareth Hospital. Later, when the Mission Board asked Joe to extend his first term from three years to five, he agreed on condition that Helen be sent out to marry him.

For thirteen years the Burkholders examined patients, many of them Muslims, visited outlying clinics, and made opportunities for a Christian witness. People came from near and far, often by foot, and from areas where no roads existed. A hospital in a rural community was a status symbol. So Muslims and Orthodox Christians tolerated the Christian teaching given by the staff and by the teachers at the mission school, even though they often did not care for an evangelical interpretation of the gospel. While patients waited to see the doctor, an evangelist would teach from the Scriptures in both the Amharic and Oromo languages.

Reflecting on those years, Joe says, "I had hoped that my medical efforts would have been followed through with evangelism, but we were not really integrating the two. We didn't have the skills to bridge our gaps. In 1966, the Burkholders transferred to Gondar to work in the government's program of training Ethiopians in public health and preventive medicine. Joe believed that teaching preventive care would be a better way to make a long-term impact on the nation's health.

Mary Byer, a registered nurse, served in Ethiopia from 1947-63. Here with health assistant Said Hasen, she opened and operated the Bedeno clinic. *Arlene Hege photo.*

At Bedeno, Mary Byer opened a clinic in 1954, treating thirty patients a day. She had grown up in a missionary family in Florida and previously worked both at Nazareth and Deder. Often she walked the mile to the town to make house calls, even at night.

The fourth doctor couple to be recruited was Paul T. and Daisy Yoder, in 1956.[5] P. T., as he was called, came from a family of ten children. He recalled that when he was five years old, the late Lloy Kniss, missionary on leave from India, visited in the Yoder home in Greenwood, Delaware. P. T. also remembered his great interest in the mimeographed letters sent to the churches from missionaries serving in Tanganyika. He chose medicine because he believed that would assure him the opportunity of becoming an overseas missionary.

Three months after P. T. started dating Daisy in 1948, he told her that if she was not interested in foreign missionary service, there was no point in their pursuing the relationship. From their first days, P. T. and Daisy became involved with Ethiopians and the emerging church. P. T. was the first doctor to eat a weekly meal in the hospital with student dresser trainees. The Yoders were the first to host Ethiopians in their home overnight, including low-income people.

The Yoders soon learned to swing with demands sprung upon them. Without orientation, P. T. picked up medical responsibilities at the Haile Mariam Mamo Memorial Hospital at Nazareth, a town of thirty thousand people. Dr. Eshleman was already in the States with his family, for their first furlough. He had told P. T. that a dresser trainee with four years of elementary schooling would show him how to do eyelid surgery!

P. T. combined medical practice with a spiritual ministry so completely that his colleagues often wondered whether he was a doctor or a preacher. He made it clear that he was a preacher first. P. T. learned Amharic and could diagnose patients without the need of an interpreter.

In 1963, the Yoders pioneered a medical ministry among the nomadic Afar people in the Awash Valley, fifty miles east

Dr. Paul T. Yoder and Getachow Woldetsadik outside the HMMM Hospital, Nazareth, ready to make a housecall, 1958.

of Nazareth. This story is told more fully in the chapter on development (chap. 7). The Yoders were active in famine relief during the drought of the 1970s. They continued serving until 1977, three years into the Marxist regime, working diligently for a smooth transfer of the Nazareth and Deder hospitals from church to government management.

The history of the Nazareth Hospital must include the story of Fissiha Wondemagenghu. One day in 1953, Fissiha was using a stick to help him walk on his one leg. He hobbled onto the hospital grounds and asked to be admitted to the dresser school. His leg had been amputated to save his life from a severe infection.

The school director did not see how a person with such a handicap could ever take care of sick people in the hospital. For four days Fissiha pressed his request and was finally admitted to a preparatory carpenters' course. Although disappointed, Fissiha applied himself diligently to any task given him and was soon assigned to manage the hospital patients' records. Fitted with a prosthesis, he threw away his crutches and eventually became hospital administrator, a position he held for ten years.

Later, Fissiha trained as a pharmacist and worked in the hospital pharmacy at Nazareth. In 1970, he opened Adam

Germa Gulti and Fissiha Wondemagenghu, owners of Adam Pharmacy, Addis Ababa, begun as MEDA project in 1970. *Jonathan Charles photo.*

Pharmacy in Addis Ababa with his colleague, Germa Gulti. During the underground years (1986-1991) Fissiha opened his home and hosted many cell groups who met there for Bible study. He spans the church's fifty-year history as a faithful lay businessman who faced every obstacle with prayer and unshakable trust in God. Fissiha's laugh is contagious.

In 1972, the Nazareth Hospital was upgraded with new buildings, financed by a grant from Bread for the World (Germany). With additional space available, P. T. Yoder and Carley Brubaker opened a Maternal and Child Health Clinic. This ministry encouraged mothers to bring their children for regular checkups. They hoped that the community would think of the hospital as a place where preventive rather than only curative medicine was practiced.

Peg Groff (Engle), Strasburg, Pennsylvania, rejoined the hospital staff after furlough in the States. She held monthly clinics at Abadar and Metahara, congregations of the Meserete Kristos Church (MKC) in the Awash Valley. Peg directed classes for women in the Neighborhood Associations at Nazareth as part of the Development Through Cooperation Campaign (*Zemecha*), run by the Marxist government. In the late 1970s, the Ministry of Health attempted to develop an overall plan for making health care readily available to the population.

In 1968, MKC's medical work was coordinated under the Mennonite Medical Board in Ethiopia. The board was composed of representatives from the church, the Mennonite Mission in Ethiopia, Eastern Mennonite Board of Missions, and the government's Ministry of Public Health. Two doctors from other organizations served as advisers. Paul Gingrich, director of the Mennonite Mission at the time, laid the groundwork for developing this board. It directed the church's medical programs until they were transferred to government administration—Deder Hospital in 1975, and Nazareth in 1977.[6]

It was a traumatic experience for the church to relinquish the Nazareth hospital to government control. Most of the leaders realized that management of such a large institution by a small denomination was problematic. Yet they found it hard to give up this ministry, which was a testimony to the Marxist government that the church was indeed concerned about social needs.

July 10, 1978, the date of the transfer, was a sad day. At this place, many MKC members had found training and employment, and many had found the Lord. During forty years they had witnessed a congregation come into being and had experienced the struggles of starting a new Christian denomination. They also enjoyed access to quality medical care for their families and had seen their children grow to adulthood.

However, God was calling the church to a new focus, away from curative medicine to community health, and to an era of church planting unparalleled in its history. God would use the past to help build a new future. The hospitals and clinics had provided a presence, a legitimate reason for missionaries and Ethiopians to be engaged in mission. As Nevin Horst wrote in 1997, "The institutions were not a mistake; God used them in a marvelous way. But God also calls us to new things."[7]

In 1970, the Nazareth congregation had erected a church building off the hospital compound and established itself as a viable entity apart from the hospital operation and employment. When MKC was closed in 1982, its members were prepared to move underground. The church proved that it could exist without institutions and even without church buildings. The Spirit of God kept bringing new life and power to the underground house-church groups that met in secret all over the city of Nazareth.

The doctors and nurses who served in Ethiopia from 1950 to 1978 were basically cut from the same cloth. All could have had lucrative jobs in the United States or Canada. Instead, they chose to enhance the mission of the church through their medical skills and to live on a missionary allowance.

During the 33 years the mission and the church operated medical services, 15 expatriate doctors served a total of 94

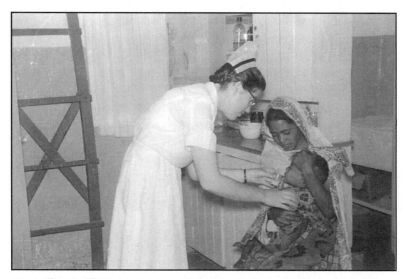

Mary Ellen Groff (Dula) giving medicine to a baby at the Deder Hospital, 1958.

years, and 40 nurses served a total of 200 years. The great numbers of Ethiopian dressers, nurses, and maintenance and administrative personnel far exceeded the number of expatriates. This is a subject yet to be researched and evaluated to make the MKC history complete. The Nazareth Hospital trained over 1,000 dressers; many of them still serve in hospitals and clinics across the country. Some took further training in medical and other fields. Some are among the Ethiopian diaspora living in dozens of countries across the world.

Were all these efforts through institutions necessary to plant a church in Ethiopia? Was this the way for missionaries to become established in a new land? The institutions made opportunities for them to contact Ethiopian students and employees. Small groups of Christians formed fellowships in the communities where schools and hospitals were located. But somehow the church became burdened with managing institutional programs that no longer stimulated church growth. Church leaders recognized that the evangelism of earlier years no longer seemed to be happening. The hospital at Nazareth was expanding so rapidly that the church could not supply enough dedicated staff to meet the demands.

Nevertheless, MKC was determined to carry on the ministries started by the mission. The church set about applying for funds from donor agencies for capital expansion at the Bible Academy and the Nazareth Hospital. A grant from the Netherlands enabled the building of a chapel, a science building, and library. Student enrollment doubled to 250 students. A grant from Bread for the World (Germany) was used to improve the services of Nazareth Hospital, with a new outpatient clinic, a new operating room, and additional wards.

Operating these enlarged institutions required a great deal of energy. Yet the church never blamed the mission for having started them. There were constant discussions, however, about how much a young church should be expected to manage. The bookstore and the hospitals were self-supporting (with the contributions of staff from North America), but other projects had to be subsidized: elementary education, the Bible Academy, Amharic literature production, and the Awash Valley medical outreach. The annual amount coming from the Mission Board was only $40,000 U.S. Church membership had increased from 150 in 1958, when the General Church Council first met, to 400 in seven congregations eight years later. However, this was still a small body to be responsible for so many programs.

"What did we do wrong?" Nathan Hege asked in an article in *Missionary Messenger* in 1966. "Perhaps we did not recognize the point at which institutions ceased to be productive in terms of church building. Without a well-developed church, institutions have become our masters, too large and too unwieldy to turn over to a young church. There seems to be two vacancies for each qualified person. To pull a man out of one post to fill another often seems to threaten the entire organizational structure." Thus Nathan described his frustration with the large amount of administrative detail the church had to handle.[8]

To better coordinate the church's programs, MKC

appointed Nevin Horst in 1966 as the first full-time executive secretary. New emphasis was placed on evangelism, and the church started gradually to grow again. However, it would take another twelve years to complete the transfer of the hospitals to government management.

In retrospect, MKC sees the institutions as quite important to create momentum for getting a church started. The schools and hospitals provided opportunities to carry on evangelistic work. Mennonites worked in Orthodox and Muslim areas, so early growth was slow. A 10 percent annual growth in those early years did not seem to be dramatic. However, it is not appropriate to compare that rate with the thousands coming to faith which SIM was reporting among peoples of traditional religions. Nor should those early efforts be compared to growth happening today when people are more open to new ideas and surrounded with many evangelical influences.

Institutions were important, because of the great needs for schools, clinics, hospitals, and bookstores, commented Nevin Horst in a letter to the author in 1997. He went on to explain:

> As we started them in the early days, it was with a sure sense of direction and guidance, of God opening doors. Of course, there were hassles in running them, but that does not make them invalid. As I reflect on my involvement in the institutions that we had, I see them mostly as positive. On one hand, the [Marxist] Revolution was a blessing in that it took some of the institutions which were becoming difficult to operate. On the other hand, we lost some valuable ones.[9]

Negash Kebede, who as a child witnessed the opening of schools and hospitals operated by Mennonite missionaries, in 1997 reflected on more than a quarter century of that experience and gave an Ethiopian perspective to those years:

People understood that the hospitals and schools run by the mission were not motivated by profit. They understood the goal of the mission to be compassionate and humanitarian in healing the sick, in response to the gospel of Christ. Although the schools charged a nominal fee, the general understanding was that the schools were there to help people see the light of education. Schools, hospitals, and clinics were a place of test in Christian commitment and character for those who worked there. Indeed, this has resulted in the belief by the general public that churches and missions provide the best service in their hospitals and clinics, and education of the highest quality.

While the positive testimony through the institutions continued to be true, administering them became a difficult task for the church. Today, as we look back, we believe the institutions were a legitimate strategy in church planting, but it was not easy to run them. One of the negative effects of the institutions was the assumption that all employees would be church members. Perhaps this is one correction that can be made if the church ever runs institutions again. Today, many people would like to see schools, clinics, and hospitals opened and run by the church or by church members. It seems the problem is not whether running institutions is the proper thing to do. Rather, it is a matter of counting the cost and identifying priorities before undertaking the responsibility.[10]

Regardless of how we may look at them today, institutions were a major part of the witness and work of the Mennonite Mission in Ethiopia and Meserete Kristos Church for thirty years.

7

Development— An Urgent Need

It was 1953. The first-term missionary directing the elementary school at Bedeno needed firewood for the cookstove in the mission's house where he lived on the hill. Wood was cheap. For 15 *birr* ($7.00 U.S.) he negotiated with a neighbor to purchase a large *zigba* (pine) tree for workmen to cut into stove-length pieces and stack on a huge pile behind the house.

The wood cutting provided a meager income, one *birr* per day, for several day laborers. They were happy to get some money to buy salt and oil at the weekly market so they would not have to sell grain needed to feed their families.

The next year the missionary needed another tree.

Those were the days when Ethiopia was well forested. Over 60 percent of the land surface had trees covering the steep hillsides—pine, cedar, as well as fig, acacia, and a number of hardwoods. Streams flowed out of those hills even during the long dry season and supplied water to irrigate the coffee, orange, and banana trees in the valleys below.

The fertility of the land was proverbial. Black volcanic topsoil more than a foot deep produced crops year after year without the need of fertilizer. People often claimed that Ethiopia could be a natural breadbasket for Europe if a marketing system were set up to airlift fruits and vegetables for Europeans during their long winters. No one thought much about ecology, and missionaries had little concern for development.

Then within twenty-five years, the population of Ethiopia doubled to fifty million. People cut trees for firewood and while clearing land to expand their farming areas. To satisfy a constantly growing demand for cooking fuel in the cities, they cut more trees for making charcoal. Soon the annual torrential rains of July to September washed topsoil off the hillsides, cut gullies deeper, and created floods during the rainy season and waterless streambeds during the dry season.

From 1960 to 1980, the tree coverage of the nation was reduced from 60 percent of the land area to 10 percent. People wondered why the hillsides were not producing crops and why the streams dried up as soon as the rainy season was over. Missionary Carl Hansen, who started a development program in the early 1970s at Bedeno, was en route home from Dire Dawa one day. He noticed that a group of farmers had built a fire and were obviously getting ready to sacrifice a goat. He stopped and asked what they were doing.

"We are offering a sacrifice in the hope of getting the streams to flow again," they answered. Carl asked for how many years the streams had stopped. He also asked whether they could remember whether the hillsides were forested during the days when the streams flowed even during the dry season.

"Oh, yes," they said. "There were trees all over this area as far as one could see."[1]

In the late 1800s, Emperor Menelik II had introduced fast-growing eucalyptus trees from Australia to provide firewood and building materials for the fast-growing capital, Addis Ababa. At that time, the forests of the countryside seemed limitless, and few people imagined that they could be depleted. Some people put forth notable efforts to avert the coming plight, and so did the government. However, those efforts were not enough to preserve the forests. Today, Ethiopia is attempting to replant her forests, a project that may take fifty years.

Robert Garber, assigned as teacher-evangelist for church planting, was the first Mennonite missionary to emphasize that Ethiopian farmers would need to learn about nutrition

Henry Gamber directs student gardening, Bedeno, 1958.

and the care of the soil if they were to feed their families adequately. Orie Miller, the Mission Board secretary who recruited Robert, had once encouraged him to be an agricultural missionary. Robert was raised on a farm in eastern Pennsylvania and was himself a farmer for eight years before going to Ethiopia. In addition to his teaching and church responsibilities, he prepared experimental seed plots at Deder as early as 1954 and involved the students at the mission elementary school in caring for gardens.[2]

Nevin Horst and Henry Gamber did the same during their terms directing the elementary school at Bedeno. The results of these efforts were discouraging. Seeds brought from America were not acclimated to the constant coolness at elevations of seven thousand feet.

The Meserete Kristos Church (MKC) Executive Committee frequently talked about development. Dr. Beyene Chichiabelu, trained in agriculture, many times urged the committee to use church funds, including subsidies from the mission board, to establish income-producing projects. He thought that would be better than simply funding service projects that needed to be supported each year from the budget. His aim was to enable the church to be self-supporting and her members self-reliant rather than depending on foreign subsidies. Years went by before the church began to act on these ideas.

More serious development got underway in the early 1970s when the church invited Carl Hansen of Alberta to return to Ethiopia and direct a development program. Earlier, while teaching at the Bible Academy, Carl had noticed that only a small percentage of high school graduates were admitted to the Addis Ababa University. He saw that students from the academy could not always find employment upon graduation. "I felt that our schools should be more than just traditional schools, that they should give training in agricultural development or other kinds of skills so people could support themselves," he reasoned. "Why are we educating people for joblessness?" he wondered. He also noted that the elementary schools operated by the church were not meeting the needs of farmers.

Since Carl had grown up on a farm in Alberta, he pondered what could be done to help Ethiopian farmers. He used all his spare time while teaching at the academy to farm one of the school's plots, showing interested students how to raise vegetables and *tef* (a grain) for sale at the local market. Noticing his interest in agriculture, MKC assigned Carl and Vera Hansen to work at Bedeno in agricultural development. About the same time, the church assigned Henry and Pearl Gamber from Scottdale, Pennsylvania, to do development at Deder. They were previously involved in education.

As one of the first projects, Carl and Henry arranged for a shipment of 47 dairy goats from Switzerland to improve the milk and cheese production of local herds at Deder and Bedeno. A farmer receiving a goat was to return the first female offspring, which in turn would be given to another farmer. "About 20 of the 47 Swiss goats are now out to local farmers or in villages at breeding stations," Henry wrote in 1975. "These add contacts and open doors where we can also share the Good News."[3]

At Bedeno, Carl set up a small demonstration farm with a five-cow dairy herd, 75 leghorn hens to produce hatching eggs, a wool-sheep breeding program, and a beekeeping project. A farm supply center made new tools, seeds, fertilizers, and chemicals available to farmers. These projects were funded by grants from MCC, Swiss Mennonites, Bread for the World (Germany), and the Swedish International Development Association (SIDA).

"The MKC sees agricultural development as a means to make the gospel message practical and understandable," Nathan Hege wrote in *Missionary Messenger* in 1973. Nathan noted that the elementary school program with its academic emphasis, although necessary, did not give much help to farmers. For twenty years many of the students had migrated to the cities for jobs or additional education. Few took up farming as an occupation.

MKC's goal was to teach farmers along with their sons in their villages without removing them to a formal school situation. This included literacy and Bible teaching as part of the development program.[4]

In 1963, Dr. Paul T. Yoder (P. T.) with his wife, Daisy, and their four children moved to Awash. This town is a market center for the nomadic Afar people, eighty miles east of Nazareth. The move was in response to P. T.'s vision to take the gospel to the Awash desert. He wanted to do this ever since he had admitted an Afar patient to Nazareth Hospital in 1957. At that time, the staff had tended to avoid the patient because of stories circulating about the Afar being fearful warriors.

P. T. prayed that God would open a way for this unreached people group to hear the gospel. He frequently remarked that he looked forward to the day when he would have communion with an Afar Christian.

The Yoders lived in a rented house in Awash, a town on the railroad line between Addis and Dire Dawa. They worked with Christian health assistants, operated a clinic, and made trips into the desert to provide medical care for the nomads. An evangelist accompanied the team and taught the Scriptures to the people as they waited for their examinations and treatment. They also organized summer Bible schools taught by volunteer students from Nazareth. Three years later, the Yoders transferred back to Nazareth, to assist in operating the expanding hospital.

In 1972, with grants from Oxfam (England) and Bread for the World (Germany), the Yoders started the Awash Community Health Services. This included a mobile health unit, based in Nazareth and composed of Yoders and medical assistants. The team would pack their supplies every Monday morning and drive to locations in Awash Valley. They visited villages, providing vaccinations and medical treatment. In the evening they pitched tents for the night, then moved to a new location each day until Friday.

When drought struck in 1973, the MKC team turned to relief work and directed the distribution of 800 tons of corn donated by the Red Cross. In Awash Valley, they distributed 145 tons of grain from March to May 1974, to help the Afar people recover from the famine.[5]

P. T. also wrote proposals to Bread for the World for funds to install a new and improved water supply for residents in Awash town. Prior to this, the people were limited to two barrels of muddy water each week, brought directly from the Awash River. Sometimes fights broke out if someone's barrel was moved out of the line at the one faucet in the town.

The new system provided for the water to be filtered and treated for safe drinking. The system became operational sometime after the Yoders left Ethiopia in 1977.

MKC development workers also showed the people how to dig wells in the desert floor of the Awash Valley. First workers made concrete rings, using iron molds supplied to them. As they dug under the rings, the rings would sink into the opening, thus reinforcing the wall of the well. As the rings sank, they added new ones from the top. The workers usually struck water at a depth of about twelve feet. People drew water by using a bucket on a rope.

In still another program, P. T., in cooperation with local officials and with the support of the Orthodox priest, was able to negotiate with the Ethiopian Electric Light and Power Authority to extend the electric lines from Metahara to Awash.

Mennonites in North America engaged in an ongoing

Yechalu Kebede weighing a child at the Well-Baby Clinic at HMMM Hospital, Nazareth, 1972.

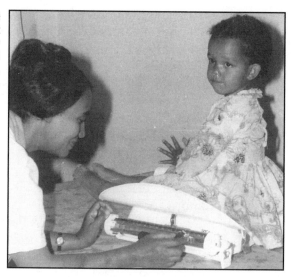

debate in the 1960s and 1970s over the purpose of evangelizing. They asked whether a church opens hospitals and schools to evangelize, or whether such ministries are valid in their own right as expressions of faith. MKC believes that all ministry is evangelism. The church honors the variety of gifts that meet needs in the community (1 Cor. 12). Whether a missionary bandages wounds, feeds the hungry, digs wells, teaches school, or preaches the gospel—all give witness to God's love.

However, affluent North Americans have the luxury of debating the relative importance of evangelism and social service. They needed to learn that the two are inseparable.

David Thomas, then moderator of Lancaster Mennonite Conference, made this point after visiting Ethiopia in 1977. Starting from Dire Dawa in the east, he traveled overland through the Awash desert. By the time he arrived in Awash town that evening, he was completely covered with dust. At the time MKC was working on a project to pipe water from the Awash River into the town. When David reported to the Lancaster Conference Annual Meeting that year, he described his dusty ride and his anticipation of a bath at the hotel stopover. "We even felt dust in our teeth," he said.

However, David learned that the hotel had no running water. He was given a pail of muddy water for his ablutions.

Raising his voice a few decibels as he concluded his story, David said, "No one should condemn the social services of our missionaries. When I hear people talking about Dr. Yoder trying to get water into Awash town as a social gospel, I tell them they are wrong."[6]

From the beginning of their ministry, Mennonite missionaries working in Ethiopia were committed to a gospel that included improving living conditions. They and the Ethiopian church leaders that came after them never considered separating preaching from social service. Whatever concerns North American Christians had about missions overemphasizing social service, one trip to Africa usually convinced them that their fears about a "social gospel" did not fit the situation.

When the Marxists took over the country in 1974, MKC wanted to convince the new government of the church's interest in helping meet social needs. They wanted to show that the kingdom of God is *now* and not "pie in the sky," as Marxists think Christians believe. In 1975 the church made an agreement with MCC for increasing its development activities. MKC's development board assigned Eric Rempel to lead the church in its development program, for expansion and increased effectiveness. MCC and MKC determined to base the program in Ethiopia on the development priorities of the national church. This cooperation with the MKC represented a new model for MCC programs in Africa.[7] The program included simplifying electric cookers for making *injera* (Ethiopian bread), developing several types of solar ovens, and designing a simple incubator for hatching chicks.[8]

In a picture caption in 1975, *Missionary Messenger* noted, "MKC is planning to give evangelists and local church leaders basic training in gardening, crop rotation, and general community development as an important arm of its spiritual ministry among Muslim farmers of eastern Ethiopia and also among the nomadic Afar people of the Awash Valley, who are being urged to settle on the land." At that time the over-

Peg Groff (Engle) with one of her friends in the development project at Bale, 1981

seas office was looking for another agricultural development worker to strengthen the team in Ethiopia.[9]

Development and relief activities, however, did not endear the church to the Marxist government. Once when an MKC delegation to Hararge Region offered grain to a famine-stricken area, an official said, "We are not sure we can accept aid from you. Although you bring grain in your right hand, you have the Bible hidden in your left hand."

In 1978, the partners MKC and MCC began another relief and development project in Bale Region, in southeastern Ethiopia. The MKC needed people to monitor relief goods being shipped to Bale. Peg Groff (Engle), a public health nurse, and Arlene Kreider, a teacher, had served with MKC for ten years. They were sent to work among people displaced by famine conditions and war between Ethiopia and Somalia. Here they could observe the distribution of food and clothing shipments sent by MCC.

For two years, Peg and Arlene operated a mobile clinic, helped the refugees plant gardens, and held cooking classes with mothers. They learned to do the necessary maintenance on a Toyota Landcruiser, lived in the cramped hotels of small towns, and ate simple country fare. Eventually a mud-block house was built for them at Ghinir as a demonstration project to see whether such a house would be satisfactory for local people and thus conserve trees.

At one point local authorities thought it unsafe for Peg and Arlene to move about the countryside without an armed guard. A rumor had spread that someone was planning to kidnap the foreigners. The women declined this assistance and told their supervisor, Eric Rempel, that God had called them to this assignment. If anything did happen to them, Eric could tell their families that the decision to stay was their own. The small group of Christians, a Kale Heywet Church at Ghinir, encouraged them and prayed daily for God's protection over them.

Later, four other nurses participated in the Bale project: Judy Buckwalter, Andover, New York; Alice Russell, Los Angeles, California; Linda Wiens, Yarrow, British Columbia; and Charlene Neer, Michigan. The nurses with an Ethiopian staff formed two groups and circulated among ten villages, examining up to 150 patients daily. This project continued for several years after the church was closed because it operated under the name the Mennonite Mission in Ethiopia.

The work of the Bale project came to the attention of the Regional Health Department at Goba. Officials there invited Peg Groff to train Ethiopian health assistants to operate clinics in remote areas. She helped train forty-five health assistants, who graduated in 1984. The Ministry of Public Health of the central government then invited Peg to join a team in Addis Ababa that was preparing new curriculum materials for government training programs.

In 1980, Million Belihu of Ethiopia and Eric Rempel of Manitoba directed afforestation projects near Nazareth. They showed that trees would grow and erosion could be checked if farmers would follow simple directives about planting trees and terracing the land. The program was not unique, but MKC employees demonstrated integrity and honesty while working with local farmers. Together they created several forested hillsides around Nazareth. This was a semiarid area at an elevation of 5,000 feet. MCC provided food for work to the families who toiled on the hillsides, digging holes to plant trees and forming ridges around the trees to trap water during the rainy season.

The plan was to plant 1,200 acres of fast-growing trees each year for five years, using funds from MCC and the Canadian International Development Agency (CIDA). The Ethiopian government supplied 182,000 seedlings during the first year of the project. Located only 50 miles from Addis, the site could easily be visited by representatives of international donor agencies looking for ways to assist in development.

To help the people conserve wood, the MKC team worked on developing a more efficient woodstove and introducing solar and biogas power. They also showed the people how to build their houses from compressed soil blocks, without the wood frame needed for traditional mud houses. Sadly, this project could not be continued after the church was outlawed in 1982.[10]

During this time, MKC was also distributing grain sent to Ethiopia from North America to famine areas. Three thousand tons of wheat were distributed in Awash and Hararge regions during 1981. About thirteen thousand tons of corn were at the port of Assab on the Red Sea when the church was closed. MKC then had to carry on development work through MCC, its partner.

MCC employed members of the church and operated under the name Mennonite Mission in Ethiopia (MME), the only Mennonite agency at the time having government registration. Underground church leaders told expatriate and Ethiopian workers that they must now refer to the Mennonite Mission only and not to MKC when discussing their assignments. "It was hard for us to change our speech," Arlene Kreider remembered, "but we had to do it if we wanted to stay, and the church wanted us to stay."

When the shortage of rainfall caused famine in the mid 1980s, most development agencies had to bend their energies toward meeting the emergency by distributing food. Canadian Mennonites, whose grandparents were on the edge of starvation during World War I, remembered stories of food shipments sent to their families in Russia. They urged their government to make food from the Canadian Food Bank available for hungry people in Ethiopia.

Ray Brubacher from Ontario was on a special investigative assignment with MCC in 1984. He reported that the "seriousness of the tragedy had not been exaggerated." As a result of these findings, MKC decided that it must start long-term development plans.[11] MCC asked the government for a development project.

In 1985, MCC gave $40,000 to help build a much-needed warehouse to store donated grain from the countries helping Ethiopia. John Hostetler, MCC Material Aid director, visited Wukro, 35 miles northeast of Mekele, and reported, "The people, unable to give cash, collected stones, chipped them to a uniform size, carried them to the main road, and stacked them in neat piles. We walked away from the new warehouse in Wukro with a feeling that God is as pleased with the construction of this building as he was when the Israelites had completed the tabernacle."[12]

In 1986, Bob Hovde, MCC representative, reported that the Ethiopian government and the Mennonite Mission in Ethiopia signed an agreement for the first three-year phase of a nine-year development project in the Gerado River Valley near Dessie, 250 miles north of Addis Ababa. In that area, 63,000 people were affected by drought made worse because of erosion and deforestation. The project called for reforesting, terracing of hillsides, and the construction of 40 miles of rural roads. MCC was to provide $1.2 million U.S., along with 7,000 tons of grain and 285 tons of oil to be used in a food-for-work project. Most of the oxen had been lost in the drought. The Relief and Rehabilitation Commission of the government coordinated and supervised the project. MCC implemented it and provided oxen, seeds, fertilizers, pesticides, and other agricultural assistance.[13]

This Gerado project gave Mennonites the opportunity to maintain a presence in the country. This assured the underground church that their North American brothers and sisters had not forgotten them. In 1996, MCC began reducing the size of the Gerado project to free MCC for working more closely with MKC's own programs.

MKC, the so-called "outlawed" church, was never outlawed by the society, by its partners, or in its own mind. It simply had to take a different form in order to carry on its ministry.

Ethiopia gained worldwide attention for its 1984-1985 famine. Millions of people were emaciated, and many thousands died. Cholera swept across the land, bringing untold misery and death to many more. About six million people suffered through several years of severe drought. Millions of domestic and wild animals perished. Even perennial plants died.[14]

In response to this great need, Jerry and Ann King Grosh were sent by MKC to work with Southern Baptists who were operating a feeding center and clinic at Rabel, in northern Shoa Region. They began in April 1985. "How do you take care of 100,000 people, many of whom are sick, who come from across the canyon looking for food, and at the same time keep the town people happy?" This was the staggering question facing the relief team.

The task was so overwhelming that the team had to learn to do what they could and not feel guilty about what they could not do. "God wants to teach us that sometimes we need to just bear the burden of our helplessness, for if we try to fix all the problems, we will become burned out and have to leave the area," Jerry Grosh said.[15] The television coverage was so widespread that even today, when Ethiopia is mentioned, many in the Western world think only of children with emaciated bodies.

The rains returned to Ethiopia in the late 1980s and early 1990s. However, Ethiopia's task of reforestation will be a

Beyene Mulatu, administrator of HMMM Hospital, Nazareth, 1962-65, and 1969-77; Deder Station Superintendent 1965-69; MKC Secretary, 1962-66; MKC Chairman 1966-68; MKC/MCC development, 1977-97. *Jonathan Charles photo.*

major concern for years to come. Many rural dwellers hope to find better opportunities for education and advancement in the cities. Only a few are able to advance this way. Many who migrated to the city are living in shacks and constant poverty. The unemployment rate in the cities is high.

Tilling the soil, planting trees, terracing the hillsides, building dams, and constructing catchment tanks—these will have to become fully as honorable as teaching school, driving a car, operating a computer, or being a governor. When farmers can care for the land so that they are able to raise two crops a year, they must have respect equal to that given to doctors and lawyers.

In 1997, MKC's development board was trying to give status to farmers. It was interested in grassroots projects. The board's administrator, Zemedkun Bikeda, was helping congregations develop projects, using their own resources. MKC and most development agencies have learned the need for local ownership. Programs that remain the vision of foreigners and are administered by a central office do not bring long-term benefits like projects owned by the local people.

According to Western thinking, development would flourish if new laws made it easier for private ownership of land. Occasionally one hears a farmer say, "Give me that eroded hillside as my own, and I'll plant trees. I'll guard them with my very life and pass them on to my children." It sounds right. However, the equitable distribution of land is far more complicated than the typical armchair theorist realizes.

MKC wants to guard against projects using outside funds, which may create dependency or overshadow the church's evangelism and nurture programs. Often development programs seem to be more important and have better funding than the church's other programs, so the church tends to be wary of development. Jerry Grosh pointed out that MKC is helping people to think of development in terms of ministry and service and in starting with what they have—not projects conceived and funded by an outside agency.

The MKC development department tries to show congregations that development is part of a holistic gospel, and that Christians should be the first to promote sound ecological practices. Development should not be equated with an outside agency doing a project with large amounts of capital.[16]

Because of the negative image that development sometimes causes in the church, MKC needs to create a new word for grassroots development, where local people take initiative and ownership. Ready at hand is the word *limat*, the Amharic word used to translate the English word *development*. It actually means verdant and lush, a concept the church can promote. The word *development* comes from the French and has to do with opening an envelope. It would be much closer to the culture to talk about God leading his people into green pastures, as in Psalm 23, which in translation uses a form of the Amharic word *limat*. People need to think in terms of making the earth green, of setting out vegetable gardens to supplement their diets of grain, of planting trees and keeping the goats from stripping their bark during the first years. It will take a reeducation, so that when people hear the word *development*, they will think of *limat* and something they can do—not something somebody else will do.

Ponds need to be built and dams constructed to conserve the water of the rainy season. Farmers can terrace their fields to keep the runoff from making deeper gullies. Crop stubble needs to decay in the fields to enrich the soil and not be burned off, as the custom often is. Mekonnen Desalyn, who has worked in MKC and MCC development for many years, said that we cannot continue development as we did twenty years ago. He believes the church's development committee needs to work with each congregation. The congregation must identify its own needs and supply the resources—the mind, the energy, and the strength—for meeting those needs. People must be trained to see things they themselves can do.[17]

Governments, as well as many Non-Government Organizations (NGOs), think in terms of large projects and a major input of capital. However, when the agencies that start these programs leave, the programs stop because the people have not perceived them as their own. Mekonnen noted that the technology introduced by an outside agency is often not the type that a local rural community can maintain or repair. Development techniques introduced must be the kind that are sustainable by the congregation and not by a central office. If the community participates in designing the project and if sustainability structures are put in place, development can be positive.

"As a Christian," Mekonnen said, "when I think about development, I think about service, service just like evangelism, just like Bible study, or prayer, or the great commission. The church has to see development as part of its service. We must teach development as service. I believe churches are ready to do service."

Training courses are needed. At least a few people in each congregation need to understand the right meaning for development, Mekonnen said.

Carl Hansen, a former development worker for MKC who became acting director of the MKC Bible College in Addis Ababa in 1997, emphasized the biblical basis for development. Carl taught that people are codevelopers with God, custodians of his garden, so that Eden can be extended to all people. God insists that the poor be protected and that land accumulation be limited. God's interest in *shalom* for all creatures is forcefully set forth in Jesus' prayer to our Father in heaven: "Thy kingdom come. Thy will be done on earth, as it is in heaven" (Matt. 6:10).[18]

Carl has observed that when the churches try to manage a large project, sooner or later someone will act irresponsibly and earn a bad name for the church. He believes that such projects need to be privately owned and operated by an individual or by a group of families who have caught the spirit of community. They must be willing to commit themselves to the hardships of keeping a project going.[19]

Development will find its proper niche in the life of MKC. It is still a young church. Although its administrative structure dates from 1960, fully 85 percent of its people became members since 1982, and more than half of them became members since 1992. In 1997, the emphasis is on growth and the nurture of new believers. As these believers mature, they will be searching for ways to develop the resources of Ethiopia for the good of their posterity.

God is leading MKC in setting priorities. The church has zeal and fervor in putting people in touch with Christ. In evangelism, church growth, and nurture, the Meserete Kristos Church is a model for Mennonites everywhere. The church wants its development efforts also to help in demonstrating how the gospel can transform life on God's good earth.

8

Opening the Holy Book

Bati Insermo, a nominal Orthodox Christian whose grandfather had converted from Islam, worked as a day watchman at the Nazareth Hospital in 1946. Living with his seventh wife, he was addicted to cigarettes and was deep into occult practices. Because he had free time between his rounds, he tried to teach himself to read. Loretta Mayer, one of the first nurses to work at Nazareth, saw his interest and introduced him to the Amharic Bible.

With the help of an Ethiopian tutor, she memorized John 3:16 in Amharic, writing out the sounds in Latin script. She did not understand the words she was saying. However, she recited this verse to Bati, directing him to run his finger along the line in the Amharic Gospel of John as he repeated the

Bati Insermo, evangelist at HMMM Hospital, Nazareth, witnesses to an outpatient. Bati was in the first group to be baptized in 1951. *Paul Kauffman photo.*

words after her. Bati was the first person at Nazareth to become a new believer in Christ, through the witness of Mennonite missionaries, and his life began to change dramatically.[1]

Dr. Paul Conrad, physician at the Nazareth Hospital, helped Bati understand the first chapter of John's Gospel. "How does one become a son of God? Is it as easy as this word says?" Bati asked. "If so, I want to be a son of God."

Bati, who never completed elementary school, became one of the founding fathers of Meserete Kristos Church (MKC). He took his faith seriously and began witnessing to patients who came to the hospital for treatment. Each morning he gave a Bible lesson to patients in the waiting room of the hospital clinic. Anna Mae Graybill (Schaffer) described his ministry: "Bati is seen with his well-used Bible. . . . With a face radiating the love of Christ, he tells others of the peace of the Holy Spirit's abiding in his heart."[2] After Bati was baptized, the church elders selected him to baptize others. This he did secretly at night, in his home. He also traveled to Dire Dawa and Deder to baptize believers at those places.

Bati carried his Amharic Bible wherever he went. He walked to villages in the Nazareth area and taught the people. Often he used his own language, Oromo, when teaching country folk, who had a limited understanding of Amharic, the official language. He did not accept the government's edict that Nazareth was a closed area just because the population was considered members of the Orthodox Church. Such a regulation might apply to foreign missionaries, but he did not believe it could apply to him, a citizen of his own nation, a country that professed complete freedom of religion. However, in those days freedom of religion was often interpreted to mean freedom to remain what you already were—not freedom to change your religion.

"Little by little, God has given fruit," Bati said when telling his story in 1961. "This has encouraged me, and I am bold to speak to small and great about the One whom few seem to really know. . . . I have my greatest joy when I'm telling others what Christ has done for me."

The Scriptures have been revered in Ethiopia for 1,500 years. Monks in the Orthodox monasteries carefully copied the holy words in the Ge'ez language from parchment to parchment. They passed along stories to their successors, telling how God miraculously saved these Scriptures from the flames when infidels invaded their country centuries ago. The Amharic name for the Bible is Holy Book.

So when a missionary opened the Bible, Ethiopians listened. If he was wise enough not to criticize the Apocrypha of the Orthodox Bible and not to make a big deal over the fact that his Bible had 66 books while the priests' Bible had 81 books, people were ready to hear the teaching and to discuss what the holy Word meant for their destiny.

The mission opened social service institutions and assigned teachers, doctors, and nurses. To provide balance in ministry, the Mission also recruited workers to teach the Bible and establish churches. These were called teacher-evangelist couples. Eventually seven couples were appointed: Henry and Pearl Gamber, Robert and Alta Garber, Chester and Sara Jane Wenger, Calvin and Marie Shenk, Nathan and Arlene Hege, Paul and Ann Gingrich, Nevin and Blanche Horst. They were commissioned to instruct Ethiopians for the purpose of leading them to saving faith in Christ, and to urge those who carried the name *Christian* to make new commitments.

These missionaries called all people to salvation, including members of the Orthodox Church. They did not think in terms of working for a reformation within the Orthodox Church, as did the Bible Churchman's Missionary Society (BCMS) from England. The missionaries believed that an Orthodox person who made a serious faith commitment to Christ would want to receive adult baptism. They would receive rebaptism such as the Anabaptists received when breaking from European state churches in Reformation times. The missionaries did not see this as proselytizing, but as giving options to people who experienced new life in Christ.

The missionaries were serious about evangelism. They

looked for responses from their teaching. Students who made a profession of faith were sent out on weekends and during vacation times to evangelize in the marketplaces of small towns and distribute Christian literature.

Missionaries taught Ethiopians to go to the Bible for their answers. If they had questions about any teaching, they could test it by the Bible. In the Orthodox Church, Ethiopians were reciting traditions and practicing rituals they little understood. Now young people appreciated their own opportunity to study the Scriptures.

Students at the Bible academy took their Bible courses seriously and showed genuine enthusiasm about discussing the Scriptures with their teachers. In addition, the Bible was opened and expounded each morning in a daily chapel service and in worship on Sundays. Students interested in witness joined the Young People's Christian Association (YPCA) and went into nearby villages to teach the people. Some spent weekends teaching at the fledgling churches in Wonji and relating to youth of the Semay Birhan (Heavenly Sunshine) group in Nazareth.

Paul Gingrich witnesses to Ethiopians who gather to hear the gospel message in the Oromo language played on a phonograph, Nazareth, 1958.

During its second year of operation, Emperor Haile Selassie I visited the Bible academy and asked the director the nature of the school's curriculum. The director replied, "We meet the requirements for secondary schools in the country, and we also teach the Bible." His Majesty said, "Why do you say *also*? Isn't the Bible the basis for all learning?"

The emperor asked for the privilege of testing the students on their Bible knowledge. He first asked, "What is found in Isaiah, chapter 7?" A student put up his hand and quickly replied, "Behold, a virgin shall conceive, and bear a son, and call his name Immanuel." The emperor's next question was about Daniel, chapter 2. There was a moment of hesitation, and then a student replied, "It tells of an image made of gold, silver, brass, iron, and clay."

Clearly impressed, the emperor said, "I need test you no further."

When Orthodox Christians discovered the meaning of personal faith, they usually were ready to tell others about it. In the 1950s, students at the Dresser Bible School at Nazareth spent vacation times during Christmas and Easter traveling, selling Christian literature, and witnessing in marketplaces. Lois Marks (Hahn), a teacher from Indiana, wrote in 1953 that "eleven students spent an entire month traveling to various parts of the country, preaching the word and selling literature. Upon returning, they told of many contacts made and of the eagerness with which the people received the message."[3] On the other hand, sometimes students were ridiculed, and in one incident a student was severely beaten and put in jail.

During Easter vacation of 1954, two young men, staff persons at the Addis Ababa School for the Blind, went into the interior on a preaching tour. The following year, they added a third person and returned to the same area. The people were eager to hear the Word and had begged them to come back. Lois Garber (Kauffman) wrote, "These Christian young men, filled and impelled by the Spirit of God, are the hope for the evangelization of Ethiopia. We can't go out as they do, but we can and need to uphold them in prayer."[4]

During the late 1950s, spiritual life conferences began first at Nazareth, then at Deder, Bedeno, and Dire Dawa. These meetings were an evangelistic tool, leading youth to make commitments. Community people noticed the preparations and wanted to see what it was all about. Using power from diesel generators on the mission grounds, the conferences showed gospel films at Deder and Bedeno, a first-time event for these rural communities.

The story of Million Belete's faith pilgrimage is typical of others. In the confusion of Orthodox, Catholic, and Protestant teachings, Million determined that he would find his answers in the Bible alone. "I love the Bible, and I want to do what this book says," he told Chester Wenger at the Nazareth Dresser School, where Million was enrolled for only six weeks. Chester gave him Proverbs 3:6, "In all thy ways acknowledge him, and he shall direct thy paths" as a motto for his life.

Million continued his search, reading his Amharic Bible faithfully every day while studying at the Technical Institute in Addis Ababa. Once a fellow employee at his first job commented that Million was not Orthodox and so must be a Protestant. Million was surprised by the comment but kept searching the Scriptures while arguing about them with anyone. Finally he told his friend, "The Bible tells me I am a sinner. Because of my sin, I'm going to hell. But Jesus Christ died for me so that I don't go to hell. My religion is to accept Jesus Christ and follow him by reading this book."

It seemed to Million that he had three sets of teachers: the Orthodox priests, the morals teachers in the public schools, and the missionaries. He concluded that he did not care what people said; he would follow only the Bible. After a lot of turmoil, he was convinced that the Bible taught baptism, which he accepted at the hands of Asfaw Bachore, an MKC layperson, in July 1955. The next year Million left for the United States, using a government scholarship for further training. Eventually Million became the first Ethiopian chairman of MKC.

Slowly groups of believers emerged at the five locations where the Mennonite Mission in Ethiopia had begun school and hospital ministries. They identified themselves as members of a new church, but the community basically saw them as groups of Ethiopians who had taken on the ways of the foreigners. Members in the 1950s and 1960s were mostly under thirty years of age, and many of them were not yet married. Older people could not risk the ostracism they would face if they would declare their adherence to evangelical teaching.

There was one notable exception. Menbere Woubi, wife of a Nazareth businessman and mother of eight, declared herself a believer in Christ at a spiritual life conference in 1959. Nurtured by missionary women, she began to teach the Bible to other women. For many years she bore the stigma among her middle-class friends of being an evangelical. Yet she attended the Bible studies and sewing clubs sponsored by the missionary women at Nazareth. She encouraged Christian women working at the hospital to gather and pray for the growth of the church, even though she could not risk accepting rebaptism by MKC leaders.

Daisy Yoder remembers that the prayer meetings were serious and intense. The women would kneel, putting their faces down against the floor as they prayed for God's blessing on their city. Many of them received the gift of tongues during those meetings. Often the women all prayed at the same time, using the language they knew or sounds that came to them. Timid women could thus participate in prayer without feeling embarrassed.[5]

Daisy and Menbere would go to a village on the edge of Nazareth and have Bible study with the women. Menbere did the teaching. The country women were greatly impressed that Menbere would leave her nice house in the city and come to sit on one of their stools or on the floor, teaching them about the Lord.

Prayer meetings among the women began before the renewal happened among the youth of the Semay Birhan (Heavenly Sunshine) group (see chap. 10). "The women's

Ethiopian women and Daisy Yoder discuss God's Word while they fellowship around the coffee cups.

prayer meeting was a powerful force in the revival movement that started," Daisy says.

Out of such prayer meetings came the urge to be more diligent in evangelism. Ann Gingrich wrote in 1956, "The believers [at Nazareth] have seen the need for greater evangelism. . . . As a result, the believers have begun a weekly youth meeting geared especially for the school students."[6]

Ethiopians were frequently positive about an opportunity to study the Bible. In 1957, just after the chapel had been built in Dire Dawa, a hundred students registered for English classes. When Daniel Sensenig announced a Bible study on Wednesday evenings, almost all the students came. Dan reported, "Over and over we hear students saying they want to study not only English but the Bible, too. Many are hungry for the Word of the Lord; the husks of the world do not satisfy their hungry hearts."[7]

Paul Gingrich, writing from Nazareth in 1957, said, "We have been making a very definite effort to get into many of the homes of our community. This has been a most fruitful ministry, and we have found doors which are wide open, and many people are very eager to be taught the Word of God."[8] Later in the year, he reported, "All around us we have many friends who are very hungry for the Word of God. They are starving for true friendship and thirsting to know 'The Way.' "[9]

In 1955, Lois Marks (Hahn) wrote, "There are yet many who have not accepted the great invitation, but we rest assured that the Word of God will not return without accomplishing its purpose [Isa. 55:11]. We know that the rock we are striking against is a difficult one, but it must surely break under the hammer of God's Word."[10]

9

Believers Form a New Church

All nine of them packed onto the back of the half-ton Chevy pickup, the multipurpose vehicle used for hospital business and staff transportation at the Haile Mariam Mamo Memorial Hospital, Nazareth. It was Saturday, June 16, 1951. The group was headed for Addis Ababa, the capital city sixty miles west, to become the first national believers on Ethiopian soil to be baptized by Mennonites.

In the group were Bati Insermo and his wife, Fayetu; Amde Woldegebriel and Lazib; Badi Tasew and Felekech; Zewdie Daba, Assefa Damena, and Kebede Teklemariam. Most of them were employed by the Haile Mariam Mamo Memorial Hospital—Bati as a day guard, Badi and Zewdie as dressers, and Kebede in the kitchen. Amde was a merchant who sold fresh vegetables to missionaries and the hospital kitchen. A tenth person, Asmare, joined them in Addis. Ephraim Okashe and Watro Wachemo, mature Christians from southern Ethiopia who worked at the hospital, also accompanied the group.

Addis Ababa was the venue for the baptism, an "open" area where missions could teach without restrictions. Nazareth was "closed," which meant missionaries were not free to disseminate evangelical ideas beyond the hospital compound. Daniel Sensenig and Chester Wenger reasoned that baptisms in Addis Ababa would not be illegal. So they scheduled it there for a Saturday night, in the rented home of Clayton and Martha Keener, who had come to Ethiopia to open a school for the blind. The missionaries did not even discuss whether Orthodox infant baptism would be acceptable for church membership. They saw themselves re-enacting the first baptisms of the Anabaptists in Zurich, Switzerland, in 1525.

When Dan asked the group to kneel to receive the baptism, they showed their complete commitment by going the whole way down, their faces on the floor. Dan didn't know how to perform a baptism that way, so he instructed them to raise up a bit for the application of the water. Arlene Hege, who was present at the occasion, wrote, "It was as thrilling a baptism service as I've ever attended—to hear these Ethiopians give their promises. About all of them are in their twenties or late teens; it was very impressive to me."[1] The Meserete Kristos Church (MKC) today marks this event as the beginning of their church and the date from which they will count for celebrating the fifty-year jubilee in 2001.

The next morning, the group had a worship service together. They shared in communion, were introduced to the strange custom of foot washing as a religious rite, and returned to Nazareth in the afternoon.[2]

However, the Mennonite church being established in Ethiopia had to face opposition from the beginning. Within three days of the baptisms, word of the event had reached the Nazareth governor's ears. He summoned the doctor at the hospital, Rohrer Eshleman, to explain this

Amdi Woldegebriel and Lazib were two of the first MKC believers to be baptized.

breach of government policy. At the time, Chester Wenger was away from Nazareth on vacation.

"Yes, there was a baptism. Yes, it was held in Addis Ababa. No, we did not understand it to be a violation of government law." Eshleman was forthright in his answers. When the governor learned that the rumor was indeed true, he reminded Eshleman that it was not the business of missionaries to baptize Ethiopians, especially anyone of the Orthodox faith. The change of venue to Addis Ababa, which had been designated as an open area for missionaries, was not a sufficient alibi.

Doctor Eshleman promised that the missionaries would not baptize any more Ethiopians. When he reported the incident to other missionaries, he asked, "What can you say when you, a guest in the country where you profess to be a law-abiding resident, are caught in violation?"

His Imperial Majesty, Haile Selassie I, apparently also heard the report about Mennonites rebaptizing. Once during a contact with Daniel Sensenig about other mission business, he expressed his disappointment to learn that Mennonites also baptize Orthodox Christians. Dan learned that another group had done the same, and the missionaries were immediately expelled from the country. He tried to explain that most of the persons in question were not strictly of Orthodox background and probably had not received a previous Orthodox baptism. He also pledged that it would never happen again.

The event was not published in any written form. Chester Wenger wrote in code to the home mission office that "ten trees had been planted." No membership statistics were reported during those early years so that no officials of the Orthodox Church or the government would ever be able to get their hands on a written record. However, when Chester went to the United States for furlough in 1954, he carried with him the names of fifty-two members, a third of whom had transferred from the Kale Heywet Church in Kambatta. Seven were listed as "backslidden" or "address unknown."

After that first baptism, no Mennonite missionary baptized an Ethiopian. Instead, national lay leaders, persons who had already joined the fellowship, secretly baptized new believers in the presence of a few trusted witnesses, as they met in someone's home at night. Missionaries did not even attend these events.

From Nazareth, Bati Insermo and Gemeda Baruda, although never ordained, traveled about and performed most of the baptisms in the early years. For fifteen years, baptisms were referred to as tree plantings.

In 1973, seventeen years after arriving in Ethiopia, P. T. and Daisy Yoder told about attending a baptismal service in Nazareth. About twenty persons met in the home of Gemeda Baruda. The two candidates and those who administered the baptism went into a bedroom; the rest of the people remained in the living room. They had agreed that if anyone came to investigate, they would say they were visiting the Gemeda home.

In contrast to this secrecy, by 1976 MKC leaders, under a fresh anointing of the Holy Spirit, bused baptismal candidates to the Awash River near the Wonji sugar estate. There they chased away crocodiles and immersed scores of people.

Throughout the 1950s, Sunday school and worship was held at the five locations where missionaries worked: at Addis Ababa in the School for the Blind, on the Nazareth Hospital compound, in a rented dwelling in Dire Dawa, and in the elementary school buildings at Deder and Bedeno.

Evangelism was a constant theme of missionary teaching. The missionaries knew that if Ethiopia was to be evangelized, Ethiopians themselves would need to do it. They did not want their influence limited to those employed in the hospitals and students attending the schools. So the missionaries encouraged Nazareth Dresser Bible School students to spend weekends and vacations witnessing in nearby communities.

Near Nazareth were the hundreds of families moving into Wonji to work on the sugar plantation established by the Dutch in the early 1950s. Bible classes were held in the homes of dressers who moved to Wonji to work in clinics the Dutch company opened for field and factory workers. Bati Insermo, day guard and evangelist at the Nazareth Hospital, regularly trekked five miles to Koka, near Wonji. There he taught the village people to trust Christ, who would rid them of their fears of evil forces.

The early believers were anxious about the uncertainty of a burial place. The Orthodox refused to allow evangelical Christians to be buried in their cemeteries. Missionaries had difficulty appreciating how deeply Ethiopians felt about this matter, although there was not much they could do about it. In 1954, MKC experienced the death of its first member, Lazib, wife of Amde, the "vegetable man." Because Addis Ababa was only sixty miles away, her body was taken there for burial in a public cemetery, open to all religions. It was about the only such place in the country.

The event was significant for the new church. It assured believers that missionaries would not allow the deceased to be thrown to the hyenas. However, until Nazareth had its own burial ground for evangelicals, believers could hardly make a complete break from the Orthodox Church.

On the Wonji Sugar Estate, seven miles south of Nazareth, a house fellowship began in 1958, in the home of Badi Tasew, one of those in the first group to be baptized. His wife, Workinesh Bantiwalu, was a loyal Orthodox who later said that at that time, she knew nothing about the Lord. Her friends had warned her to keep away from evangelicals. She stayed in the kitchen and watched the service through a crack in the door. "It was the singing that attracted me," she said, "especially the song which says 'the door to life is narrow; strive hard to enter it' " (see Luke 13:24). Soon Workinesh pushed the door open a bit to get a better view of what took place. "I listened to the messages, and my heart was very touched," she recalled. She opened the door and began to listen to the teaching. Finally she was brave enough to join the rest as they studied the Bible and prayed. In 1960 at her house, she received the Lord.[3]

In 1959, Bible academy students began to make weekly trips to the sugar plantation at Wonji to teach in the camps

Shamsudin Abdo gives the charge to the Nazareth Church counselors at their appointment, December 5, 1965. From left: Gemeda Baruda, Fissiha Wondemagenghu, Rohrer Eshleman, Gebreselassie Habtamu, Million Belete, Nathan Hege.

and encourage the Christians. Badi Tasew and Asfaw Bachore, who had been helping to organize house fellowships in the worker camps, appealed to the Mennonite Mission in Ethiopia for assistance in purchasing land and building a meetinghouse for the believers. In 1961, believers acquired land and built a small church at Wonji-Gefersa, just outside the Dutch sugarcane concession. Badi Tasew and Million Belete, who had bought investment plots side by side near the sugar factory, gave their plots to the congregation to build on.

This first MKC church building, large enough to seat 150 people, opened its doors in 1961. Elders were chosen to give leadership: Asfaw Bachore, Badi Tasew, Tegesse Dutebo, Yohannes Germamo, and Desalegn Hereno. Academy students did much of the Bible teaching. Students involved in this outreach were Tesfatsion Dalellew, Lapiso (Getahun) Dilebo, Negash Kebede, Tilahun Beyene, and others. Wonji-

Gefersa was the first congregation to be established apart from a mission station.

In 1964, a second congregation was formed at Wonji-Shoa, about five miles from Wonji-Gefersa. Both congregations were composed mostly of evangelical Christians from southern Ethiopia, believers who had moved to Wonji to work at the sugar plantation and factory. They had been members of the Kale Heywet churches resulting from the mission work of SIM, begun there in 1927, before the Italian Occupation. After graduation from the Bible academy, Getahun became full-time evangelist and supervised the construction of the church building at Wonji-Shoa.

There was an intense struggle for burial rights. Once the Orthodox refused to bury the child of evangelist Fetamo Achiso. After the church elders negotiated with the local police for a week, the police finally released the body and allowed it to be buried beside the Wonji-Shoa church building. After a long hassle with authorities, Wonji-Gefersa was able to buy land and have it designated as a burial site. Even so, their right to bury was challenged again when the church was closed in 1982.

In 1958, counselors were chosen at six locations, one for every twenty members, to represent the believers at a General Church Council which would meet twice each year. Chester Wenger had just returned from studies at Union Theological Seminary in Virginia in 1957. He suggested a structure that he believed would suit the needs of the emerging congregations.

At Nazareth on January 17-19, 1959, Ethiopian and North American believers related to the Mennonite Mission held their first organizing meeting. They wanted to arrange for implementing the new church structure and to choose a name for it. Chester served as chair. Also present were Haile Woldemichael, Kiros Bihon, Million Belete, and Negussie Ayele, who served as secretary. These persons represented their congregations. Clayton Keener participated as business manager for the mission. Eight observers also attended.[4] At this first meeting, the name *Meserete Kristos Church* (The church of which Christ is the foundation) was among the proposals, the one eventually adopted as the permanent name (MKC).

Daniel Sensenig, on furlough at the time, called the meeting a "milestone." He wrote in his annual report that "the spirit and vision of our Ethiopian brethren was most heartening, and their helpful suggestions appreciated."[5]

Gemeda Baruda, at the time active in evangelism at Wonji and Shoa, had a vision that reached beyond Ethiopia. He asked EMM treasurer Ira Buckwalter, who visited Ethiopia in 1959, how many congregations the Mennonite Church had in North America and how the membership increased during the previous year. In his report to the mission board, Ira called Brother Gemeda's query a pointed question. However, Ira did not say how he answered Gemeda or how he explained the almost static membership level of North American Mennonites.

At a second meeting, in September of the same year, the committee carefully studied the Mennonite Confession of Faith. The ten Ethiopians present affirmed it as their personal faith. The group also reviewed the church's evangelistic methods and agreed to begin additional small places of wor-

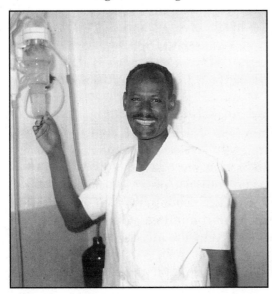

Gemeda Baruda, chairman of the Nazareth congregation in the 1960s. He worked as laboratory technician in the HMMM Hospital, Nazareth. Gemeda served a vital role in the spiritual nurture and development of the church for over 30 years.

ship away from the mission compounds, in the homes of the people.

In his annual report for 1961, Daniel Sensenig wrote, "Now that the General Church Council will assume a more direct administrative role—if all the bodies involved accept the recommendation—the [Ethiopian] brethren will be able to take a larger responsibility in building the church."

For several years believers debated whether the word *Mennonite* should be included in the church's name. Some suggested that it be called *Meserete Kristos (Mennonite) Church.* Ethiopian leaders who had traveled to America and had firsthand contact with stateside Mennonites opted for *Mennonite* to be included, to help relate the emerging Ethiopian body to the worldwide denomination. Others, who did not have these opportunities, felt the name *Mennonite* had no meaning at all for Ethiopians and could even refer to some false religion. Furthermore, since *Mennonite* is based on a man's name, it might suggest that members were following a cult. Today, most Ethiopians agree that a strictly Ethiopian name gives an authenticity to this evangelical church which could not be achieved with a foreign name. However, Ethiopians are quick to point out that they are members of Mennonite World Conference and send delegates to meetings held every six years. They are also members of the All Africa Mennonite and Brethren in Christ Fellowship.

In 1962, the mission board's overseas secretary, Paul Kraybill, prepared a Memo of Understanding that provided for three missionaries to serve with five Ethiopians on an MKC executive committee. The mission board chose the chairman and treasurer; MKC chose Beyene Mulatu as secretary and Desta Alemu as assistant treasurer.

The next step, taken in 1964, provided that the MKC General Church Council (GCC) choose its own officers from the eight-member executive committee, which still included three missionaries appointed by the mission board. The GCC chose Chester Wenger as chairman. At that point, MKC assumed "responsibility for allocation and administration of church budget, administration of medical, educational, literature, and evangelistic programs, and assignment of missionary personnel."[6]

In a third step in 1965, Ethiopians who had been serving as assistants became officers of the executive committee, and missionaries became their assistants.[7] This helped facilitate the church's application for registration by the government, which required the officers of an organization to be Ethiopian. The government also required that a detailed constitution be submitted. Preparation for writing this constitution required weeks of discussion. The executive committee had to develop detailed procedures for accepting members and administering local congregations. They had to work out the purpose and goals of the church, and agree on a doctrinal statement.

What would they do, for example, about the Mennonite belief that Christians should not join the armed forces? No Ethiopian citizen dared think in terms of not defending the motherland—with the Italian occupation still fresh in memories and the constant threat of Somalis to Ethiopia's eastern border.

The executive committee eventually drafted a statement that adapted the article on nonresistance from the *Mennonite Confession of Faith* to read that the church believes in the principle of love for all peoples.

The government refused to grant legal registration of Meserete Kristos Church. Apparently officials were not happy to have still another evangelical church recognized. The Mekane Yesus Church (Lutheran) and the Kale Heywet Churches (SIM) had registration. However, sometimes even that recognition was challenged in rural areas far from the capital city.

So MKC printed letterheads, opened its own bank accounts, and started to function as though it were registered. However, the Mennonite Mission in Ethiopia was the legal entity and thus held titles to vehicles. This was a helpful fringe benefit when the government confiscated church properties in 1982. After 1965, Ethiopians were fully in

Meserete Kristos Church Executive Committee, 1965. From left: Desta Alemu, treasurer; Nevin Horst; Shamsudin Abdo, educational director; Chester Wenger, assistant chairman; Beyene Mulatu, secretary; Daniel Sensenig; Million Belete, chairman, Gemeda Baruda, assistant treasurer, not pictured.

charge of decision making for the church, and missionaries served at the invitation of the church and in institutions under the church's administration.

Ethiopians have emphasized that Mennonites used an approach distinctly different from other missions as they were transferring leadership responsibilities to nationals. They remember that Mennonite missionaries did not ask to be called *Geta* (Master), the customary address for persons in authority. Missionaries invited Ethiopians into their homes to eat at their tables and respected their cooks and child-care helpers as employees having rights to reasonable hours. They encouraged Ethiopians to continue their schooling beyond the elementary level and helped them find such opportunities.

Sometimes Ethiopians described Mennonites as using the John the Baptist principle: "He must increase, but I must decrease" (John 3:30). Missionaries also respected Ethiopian culture and freely participated in funeral and wedding ceremonies.

During the interviews conducted in 1996 for this book, someone recalled the stand that Mennonite missionaries once took when they met at the guesthouse of another mission for their annual retreat. Several Ethiopians were invited as observers, a practice begun in 1960. The guesthouse host reported that he could not accommodate the Ethiopian nationals because the facility had been built for missionaries needing a place for their annual vacations. The Mennonite Mission director said, "Either you will give the Ethiopians beds, or we will all have to leave." The retreat did not need to be canceled.

In the mid-1950s, the church began to hold annual revival conferences on the hospital compound at Nazareth. Beyene Chichaibelu (now Dr. Beyene), serving at the time as instructor at the School for the Blind, remarked to Daniel Sensenig that if it was necessary for missionaries to meet in an annual conference for spiritual refreshment, Ethiopians should have the same opportunity.

Ethiopians planned these significant conferences and invited interested people from all areas of the country to come to Nazareth for a three-day weekend to sing, study the Bible, and hear sermons on salvation and revival. It was an ecumenical experience. Both nationals and missionaries from various evangelical communions participated as speakers. People came, several hundred of them, some from far away. They slept on the floor of the large storage shed which housed the dresser school, the same room where the meetings were held. They ate meals prepared in the hospital kitchen and developed friendships to last a lifetime. Participants gave testimonies of God's leading in their lives, and many accepted Christ as their personal Savior and Lord.

The long sessions, wearying to the missionaries because of their limited grasp of the language, exhilarated the Ethiopians. This was a conference they arranged and executed. People of all ages attended, to experience and share God's love through the teaching of the Word. The annual conference at Nazareth became a highlight for people as far away as Asmara. They flocked together to make new friends and meet old ones. Today, Ethiopians still talk about those conferences as a definite milestone for them in their Christian walk.

Young people talked of ways to evangelize Ethiopia. Beyene Chichaibelu, Negussie Ayele, Haile Woldemichael, Ingida Asfaw, and Million Belete discussed plans to establish an Ethiopian mission, much as the missionaries had done, to provide a wholistic ministry to society. One would train in agriculture, one in medicine, several as teachers, and one would be a builder. Million Belete recalled those conversations: "We wanted to run an organization like the missionaries were doing; we didn't know enough to talk about church in those days."

One of the highlights of annual conference at Nazareth was the choir of students from the School for the Blind in Addis Ababa. Alice Snyder, secretary and bookkeeper for the mission, spent her spare time instructing blind students in instrumental and vocal music. She organized them into a choir that was often asked to sing in churches. Alice encouraged the students to translate English hymns that she compiled and published in 1964, the first Amharic hymnbook to have the words set to music. Although culturally not grounded in Ethiopia, the book, *Mahilete Egziabiher* (Praise God), was a bridge to a new day. The choir of blind students was an early model for the hundreds of choirs in MKC today.

Since the mid-1970s, evangelicals have created songs and lyrics, many for special occasions, giving rise to a new generation of hymnody. The charismatic renewal sparked new melodies that are unlike either the translated hymns from Europe and America or the Orthodox hymns. The new melodies have grown out of the culture, and they give Ethiopian evangelicals a sense that "this is our music."

The first formalized General Church Council met at Nazareth September 22, 1962, with sixteen Ethiopians and six missionaries present. It was the first opportunity for Ethiopians to speak to budget planning for the church and mission.

Million Belete recalled that Daniel Sensenig had tears in his eyes as he said, "This is the day I have wanted to see; I thank God." Daniel reported a thousand people attending congregations at seven locations and a 10 percent increase in membership during the year. About half the churchgoers were in the Wonji and Shoa congregations. "Never was the harvest so great, and so many opportunities are all about us that we are utterly amazed. You will want to share in this great harvest by praying, giving, and coming," Dan wrote in his 1962 annual report.[8]

In the 1963 report, Dan told of an Orthodox monk who happened to see a sign in the Menno Bookstore window in Addis Ababa. The sign offered a free Bible correspondence course. Inside, he was introduced to the twelve-lesson Mennonite Hour Bible study course, *God's Great Salvation*, which Million Belete had translated into Amharic. The monk was not willing to take the course without paying, so he insisted on paying twenty-five cents. About a month later, after completing two other twelve-lesson courses, he came to the mission office where the lessons were corrected and announced, "I've just been born. I'm going home to tell my

The first believers to be baptized in MKC, June 16, 1951. From left: Lazib, Amde, Kebede, Ephraim, Zewdie, Watro, Bati with son Yohannes, and Fayetu. Ephraim, and Watro, evangelical Christians from southern Ethiopia, had assisted in their instruction. *Arlene Hege photo.*

people what I've found."[9] At that time it never occurred to either missionary or national that such small happenings could be the beginnings of a wide-sweeping renewal which would take place in the 1990s.

In 1964 Chester Wenger, as chairman of Meserete Kristos Church, wrote his first annual report to the stateside church. "The most outstanding development of the Meserete Kristos Brotherhood during 1964 was perhaps the dissolution of the former mission-directed organization and the preparation and approval of the first church constitution. The constitution provides for a Church Council, which elects the Executive Committee of eight members, including chairman, secretary, treasurer, and assistants. Meeting approximately every two months, the Executive has shouldered its new responsibilities."[10]

The new structure put all the Mennonite Mission programs under the MKC General Council, except for Menno Bookstore and the Good Shepherd School for missionary children. The move did not yet make MKC a new conference, but it did mark a new stage of partnership. Chester wrote that the rapid changeover was done with "a minimum of stress and frustration of personnel and institutions because of three things: Ethiopian brethren have been most understanding and cooperative; the Mission and the Mission Board have always been encouraging and helpful; and all of us have a genuine desire to see the work grow and to gain government recognition for MKC."

The Mennonite Mission and MKC used a system of apprenticeship for nationals to take over managerial posts and leadership responsibility. MKC leaders who remember those days affirm that process as a perceptive strategy: "You did not just turn over leadership and leave us to struggle. First you showed the way; then you stood alongside."[11]

The new officers of the Church Council were Million Belete, chairman; Beyene Mulatu, secretary; and Desta Alemu, purchaser for the mission, treasurer. Missionaries held the assistant positions. Shamsudin Abdo was chosen as director of the church's educational program. A mission committee of three members was appointed to handle a few purely mission items and to serve with five Ethiopians on the church Executive Committee.[12]

Paul Gingrich was one of the missionaries who helped to keep clarifying the goal of giving responsibilities to Ethiopians. Reflecting on the early days, Paul said, "We had a strong feeling that we had to indigenize, to put Ethiopians in charge." At Nazareth, Paul was always training someone to take over his responsibilities—Manoro Abiyo for maintenance work, Beyene Mulatu for hospital administration, and Fikere Yesus Bekele for directing the Dresser Bible School.

This freed the Gingrichs to transfer to Addis Ababa in 1964, where Paul served as director of the Mennonite Mission and general director of Menno Bookstore. He and his wife, Ann, managed a hostel for Addis Ababa university students, relating closely to young people destined to be leaders in the church and nation. The Gingrichs were happy to see the shift from missionary control to Ethiopian management.

Paul and Ann took initiative in building friendships with Ethiopians. Paul had a gift for making friends and carried the aura that something significant was about to happen. The Gingrichs encouraged missionaries and Ethiopians alike to live life with anticipation.

The Gingrichs were the first of the missionary team to urge Ethiopians to write their own songs instead of translating songs from the churches of Europe and North America. This new movement in hymnody began to take shape in the 1970s, along with the charismatic influences affecting evangelical churches.

Today MKC is blessed with trained leaders—not so much because missionaries did things right, but because the Holy Spirit called people with training to dedicate themselves to serve the church. Frequently Ethiopian leaders postponed higher education or left lucrative jobs in obedience to God's call on their lives.

Lay people did much of the work in developing the church. Missionaries, as well as Ethiopian believers, had reservations about ordaining nationals because they did not want to perpetuate the image of the typical Orthodox priest. The Orthodox priest spent much of his time performing the mass and celebrating the many holiday feasts in honor of saints, angels, and Mary. Also, MKC emphasized the priesthood of all believers and feared that a clerical hierarchy would give a wrong message to the people.

Bishop J. Paul Graybill, during a deputation visit from Lancaster in 1952, was determined to ordain the Ethiopian men who were baptizing believers in secret. Daniel Sensenig firmly stated that if there was any greater offense to the government than baptizing an Orthodox person, it would be to ordain someone to do such work. Furthermore, the missionaries reported that they could not find Scripture to say one had to be ordained in order to baptize. Graybill went home without achieving his mission. When he reported on his trip to the bishop board, one of the Lancaster bishops was quite disturbed about lay leaders baptizing. He predicted that with such a breach of Mennonite polity, the Ethiopian church would never get on track.

Nevertheless, by 1965, fifteen years after the mission was established, Chester Wenger believed that ordination would help the fledgling church to see itself as an authentic body with a mandate from God to evangelize and grow. He explained the procedures to the Nazareth congregation and asked them to set apart two people from among the previously chosen counselors, who would be ordained as pastors. Million Belete was chosen and ordained. Nathan Hege was also chosen to serve as a pastor, having been ordained by Lancaster Conference in 1952. From that time until the Marxist Revolution in 1974, only five other persons had taken ordination vows—Daniel Lemma in Dire Dawa, Kiros Bihon and Abebe Gorfe in Addis Ababa, Gebreselassie Habtamu in Nazareth, and Beyene Mulatu at Deder. Through the years, many lay people have served as evangelists, deacons, elders, and pastors, and little mention has been made of ordination. Designated lay people have performed baptisms for many years.

During the 1960s, MKC grew slowly. Much energy was

put into developing an efficient managing system. The Executive Committee met often, revising the constitution, setting up boards and committees, such as those on education, evangelism, and medical service. The executive had to develop and update policies for the growing institutions. In the 1950s, Eastern Mennonite Missions appointed missionaries. By the 1960s, the executive acted with Eastern Mennonite Missions in approving missionary replacements. Meetings sometimes lasted late into the night.

Reflecting on those times, Negash Kebede wrote,

> There were many clashes and stormy meetings. I remember once when we were having an Executive Committee meeting, a misunderstanding arose between two brothers. One of them stood up, took his briefcase, and said, It is a waste of time to attend the meeting since "we are going nowhere." A missionary in the committee felt frustrated, thinking that the church will never grow if we continue with such squabbles. As a result of his deep concern and sadness, he began weeping. Unable to control his tears, he tried to walk out, only to be seen by a house guard who wondered what was the matter with a missionary crying like a child.
>
> I believe that period of struggle as we tried to set up organizational structures was important. Church leaders today talk of how they have benefited from having a firm foundation of church organization. Now they do not have to spend their time and energy on procedures and management philosophies.[13]

In 1997, the MKC had a worshiping community of more than 100,00 but no more than ten ordained pastors (*megabi*). Most of these ordinations were a recognition of work the men were already doing and have not changed their responsibility. Lay leadership continued as much the norm for MKC.

Administrators or overseers coordinate the work of the districts and are appointed for a specific term. Elders and deacons are also commissioned for a specific term. Evangelists are "set apart" for life after they have proven themselves by serving in the One-Year-for-Christ program.

Although the church has few pastors, it has many evangelists. These are commissioned to win others and disciple them in the faith. The church tries to keep clear the distinction between the responsibilities of pastors, who focus on training leaders and administration, and evangelists, who call people to commit their lives to Christ.

10

A Fresh Move of the Spirit

In 1962, six students stood together outside the doctor's house, shifting their weight from one leg to the other as they awaited an answer to their knock. They could not predict the doctor's answer. They knew he was busy administering the town's only hospital, examining a hundred patients in a morning, and doing surgeries each afternoon.

However, they wanted to improve their English, and they knew the doctor could help them. They also knew that the doctor's limited ability with Amharic ensured that he would stick to English and not switch into Amharic to give explanations. He would be an ideal teacher.

Dr. Rohrer Eshleman, from Paradise, Pennsylvania, was the medical director of the Haile Mariam Mamo Memorial Hospital in Nazareth. He never took long to make a decision. "Yes," he said. "I'll teach you English, and we'll use the Gospel of John as our textbook."

Every Saturday evening the doctor met the youth in his living room. They read part of a chapter and then discussed its meaning. Before long, the students were discussing among themselves what the text meant in their own language. The message of this Word became more important to them than learning English.

Some of the students were attending public worship services held on the hospital grounds. Youth for Christ met there on Saturdays, attracting hospital employees as well as students from the public high school in Nazareth. They all liked the singing. However, the students in particular were wary of relating too closely to the mission because the public referred to the Christianity taught there as "the religion that came to Ethiopia loaded on a ship."

Everyone "knew" that the Orthodox Church was the true expression of Christian faith for Ethiopians. The students did not consider becoming evangelicals because that would identify them with the foreign missionaries. Those missionaries were perceived as the enemies of Mary because they would not accept her as an intercessor between them and Christ.

However, missionaries tried to point out to the students that their own Bibles would show them the Christian way. They explained that becoming a born-again Christian did not necessarily mean they had to leave the Orthodox Church. It meant that for their salvation, they were trusting Christ rather than the practice of rituals. A number of them, including several who were attending Rohrer's English class, made this faith commitment and immediately wondered how they could best witness to their fellow students at the local secondary school.

"If we could have a meeting place away from this compound of foreigners, we could invite our friends to study the Bible with us," they reasoned. Rohrer encouraged them in this proposal and even promised to pay the rent for a building off the compound, if they wanted to use this approach to reach their friends.

Accordingly, a handful of students from the Atse Gelawdeos High School who had experienced salvation announced regular prayer meetings and Bible studies at the rented house, now used as a chapel. They named themselves Semay Birhan (Heavenly Sunshine), from the title of a song they often sang.

The annual Christian Life Conference of Meserete Kristos Church (MKC) met at the Nazareth Bible Academy in 1964. At the meeting, Solomon Kebede (by 1997, chairman of the church) met his friend Zeleke Alemu, who already had come to a saving knowledge of Christ.[1] While discussing about life and growth in Jesus, Zeleke, who had some contact with Getachew Mikere in the Finnish Pentecostal Mission in Addis Ababa, told Solomon that God still baptizes believers with the Holy Spirit just as on the Day of Pentecost (Acts 2).

Both resolved to earnestly pray that they would receive this baptism and become servants of the Lord. Zeleke left for Harar, a city 250 miles to the east, where he was a student at the Teachers' Training Institute (TTI). Later, at about the same time, both received the baptism, Solomon in Nazareth and Zeleke in Harar.

Eventually, all the students who had met at the chapel outside the compound, finished high school and went to Addis for further studies or to seek employment. They gave Solomon the key and put him in charge of the chapel. Solomon and four others, who came to the Lord through personal witnessing, started to fast and pray for the baptism of the Spirit, for the gifts of the Spirit, and for people to be saved. The spirit of fervent prayer came upon them, and they prayed three times daily: early morning, at lunchtime, and after school until dusk. As the group grew, they began to pray simultaneously.

"No one taught us about mass prayer," recalls Solomon. "We just stumbled onto it." For example, someone would mention the suffering of Christ in his prayer. Then others would respond aloud, "Yes, Lord, it is also for me that you suffered, it is also for me." When people were touched by someone's prayer, everybody joined in.

Because there was no time to take turns praying, they prayed aloud at the same time after they had shared their prayer requests. As Gemechu Gebre, an evangelist at Wonji explained twenty years later, "There was not enough time for all of us to pour out our hearts to God if we simply prayed by turn as the missionaries did."

Individuals possessed by demons would scream when they came to the prayer meetings at the chapel. The group began casting out demons in the name of Jesus Christ. Attendance increased to several hundred. At the government high school, the students witnessed during recess and in the evening. The school directors became concerned and asked Solomon to stop preaching because they feared religious conflict. He agreed, but others started to preach. The number responding kept growing until a spiritual crisis emerged.

A disruption occurred at the chapel when a girl, believed to have been freed from demon possession, pretended to be filled by the Holy Spirit and prophesied falsely and spoke in tongues. The girl also instructed the leaders to report her prophecy about future events to the students and teachers at the high school, which they did. Arguments about the prophecy broke out, and the school was closed for a whole day.

Because of this disturbance, thirty leaders of the Semay Birhan group were suspended from school for one week and had to do a second week of labor. Several days later the leaders discovered that the girl had a deceiving spirit, and they had to tell the students that the prophecy was false. Many hundreds of students who had been enthusiastic about following Christ became discouraged and left the faith. The town leaders instructed parents not to let their children go to the chapel. Attendance dropped from hundreds to thirty.

The remnant participating in the Semay Birhan group continued and gradually picked up momentum, both in vitality and in numbers meeting at the chapel in Nazareth. They began to ask God how they could be a witness that would spread throughout the country, even the world. Each day they prayed for one of the countries of the world, one of the fourteen regions of Ethiopia, one hospital, one school, and one organization at work in the country. Soon they were meeting during the two-hour lunch break and praying instead of eating.

The group had genuine experiences of speaking in tongues and exercising other gifts. However, now they tested every experience with scrutiny and discernment to guard against another deception of the evil one. The group encountered a series of other deceiving spirits, but these were discerned immediately before causing confusion and problems. Demons were cast out. The students prayed for the sick and saw them healed.

Zeleke returned from Harar for Easter vacation and brought with him a friend, Assefa Alemu. They shared their

versity students who went to the Public Health College for their national service. Seven or eight students rented a house and started to preach every day after lunch. Many students came to the Lord, and many were baptized. By 1970, eighty students were in the fellowship.[2]

By 1966, the fervor at the Semay Birhan chapel in Nazareth was great, and the sounds coming from the rented chapel building were loud. MKC members began to wonder what would happen to this movement unless someone gave mature leadership. The elders of the MKC congregation on the hospital grounds met with the Semay Birhan leaders. They agreed jointly to appoint Gebreselassie Habtamu, who lived near the chapel, to participate occasionally in the students' meetings. Three years had passed since Eshleman's classes had begun.

The students trusted Gebreselassie; they found him to be a "good person" who encouraged them. They asked him sometimes to give the Bible teaching. They also told Gebreselassie that if he would allow them to pray for him, he too would receive the gift of tongues. The youth started to

Aster Debossie, Gebreselassie Habtamu, and Shiferaw Koyamo, long-time members of MKC. Aster and Gebreselassie were active in the renewal movement. *Jonathan Charles photo.*

pray; Gebreselassie fell to the floor and immediately started speaking in a new prayer language. In 1996, Gebreselassie said, "The Holy Spirit comes by praying. I often pray in tongues. I can pray for two hours and have no sense of the passing of time."[3]

Gebreselassie's preaching in the Nazareth congregation took on new power. His public prayers called on Jesus to drive back the devil and destroy his works. He continued to relate to the Semay Birhan group and assured the Nazareth congregation that they were brothers and sisters in the faith. When the police arrested the youth for their "unorthodox" gatherings, MKC members appeared at the prison, served as guarantors for them, and asked to have them released. The trust and family spirit built among them later made it easier for MKC to assimilate Pentecostal groups when the government outlawed their meetings in 1972.

MKC leaders urged Semay Birhan youth to declare their loyalty to MKC, but the group was reluctant to do so. "We feared we would lose our vitality," one of them recalled in 1996. From the Semay Birhan perspective, MKC members did not have the baptism of the Holy Spirit; they did not tithe, and they depended too much on funds allocated each year from the mission board in the States. Reported an MKC leader in 1996, one who was part of that student group, "We all tithed any income that we got, so we felt more righteous than they." He recalled that if his parents gave him a pair of trousers costing 20 birr, he would try to earn two birr to put in the offering at the chapel. With the money, they conducted conferences, invited speakers from other places, and bought books for the chapel.

For the most part, missionaries did not receive a Holy Spirit baptism in the same way as that experienced by the Semay Birhan group. However, they too had times of renewal. Their renewal was shaped somewhat by their contacts with missionaries in Tanzania who had experienced the East Africa Revival. At the annual missionary retreat in 1965, Don Jacobs, guest speaker from Kenya, urged the missionaries to experience cleansing like Naaman received when he bathed in the Jordan River. For days afterward, missionaries "walked on air," as one described it, and freely shared with Ethiopians their testimonies of renewal. The East Africa Revival as such never became a separate movement in Ethiopia.

Missionaries also were concerned about church growth. Once at a midweek prayer meeting, the mission director, Daniel Sensenig, asked God to "break me" if in any way he was a hindrance to the gospel. At their annual retreats, Dan's constant call for a deeper walk with the Lord challenged missionaries to pull together, refocus their priorities, and make new commitments.

An incident in 1966 helped push Semay Birhan closer to MKC. The Semay Birhan group had rented a cinema hall in Nazareth to hold its second spiritual life conference. Their first such conference used a tent on the hospital grounds. Now they invited their friends to attend, including many from neighboring towns. The police broke up their meeting because the local Orthodox Church asked them to do so. Orthodox leaders considered the propagation of religion to be their sole prerogative. To finish the conference, the group asked MKC leaders for permission to meet in the hospital chapel. The Nazareth elders granted them permission. After that, Semay Birhan conferences were held at the hospital, and MKC welcomed them. Such cooperative ventures helped allay suspicion and opened the way for Semay Birhan people to eventually join MKC.

While Semay Birhan was experiencing the flush of new-found faith, MKC was also active. Students from the Nazareth Bible Academy, especially Mamo Dula and Mekonnen Wendimu, rode bikes to Nazareth and assisted with services at the chapel on Saturday afternoons. Also, the Nazareth church elders repeatedly bailed the students out of prison when they were arrested. They stood alongside with counsel but tried not to thwart any work of the Holy Spirit.

One of these elders was Gemeda Baruda, who worked many years as a laboratory technician at the Nazareth Hospital. He and his wife, Aster Debossie, had migrated

from Kambatta to work at the hospital in the early 1950s.
They longed to see the people of Nazareth turn to the Lord as
they had witnessed it happening in their home area, in a
movement that had brought their own parents to faith.

Gemeda and Aster would climb to the hilltop west of
Nazareth, look over this dusty city of the Great Rift Valley,
and pray, "Lord, give us Nazareth." Their prayers also
included workers in the sugarcane fields at Wonji, six miles
south of Nazareth and also in view from their vantage point.
Gemeda went there every Sunday to encourage small groups
of believers who were coming together to form congregations.

Gemeda died in 1981. In 1997, Aster still exulted with
unspeakable joy over the evangelical congregations and the
Orthodox renewal groups established in Nazareth. When
special conferences are held, sponsored by any of the several
evangelical groups, people attend by the thousands.

Students leaving the Atse Gelawdeos High School in
Nazareth carried the new fervor to the higher educational
institutions and colleges in other parts of the country. Many
more persons received the power of the Holy Spirit and started to witness. The movement grew. People such as Mekuria
Mulugeta, Seyoum Gebretsadik, Kassa Agafari, Tadele
Legisso, and Wehibe Kebede were among those who played
significant and leading roles.

Membership in a particular church was not a big concern
of university students, although some often discussed the
idea of joining MKC. The main discussion about church
membership, however, took place at Nazareth, where a number of the students often went during weekends.

Solomon Kebede reminded the students that they could
not remain youth forever. He encouraged them to join MKC.
However, many thought that if they did so, they would lose
their enthusiasm. "Those who are with the Spirit will do the
work of God regardless of affiliation," Solomon told them.
He backed up his words by formally joining MKC in Addis
in 1973. Mulugeta Zewdie, in 1997 the acting general secretary of MKC, followed Solomon's example. By 1974 the

Women at prayer as worship service is in progress. Prayer groups are a vital part of MKC. After believers are baptized, the elders discern their gifts and assign them to a ministry. Some accept a special responsibility to pray. *Jonathan Charles photo.*

whole group decided to join.

Annual Christian Life conferences, begun at Nazareth by MKC, were later also held at Dire Dawa, Deder, and Bedeno so participants could avoid expensive travel. Teachers in the valley schools at Deder and Bedeno faced the hardships of rural life to teach Muslim children to read, sing gospel songs, and study the Bible. Students from the Nazareth Dresser School spent their vacations trekking the country, selling books, and preaching. MKC leaders emphasized that faith in Christ is the true motivation for educational, medical, and development work. Ethiopians were increasingly taking responsibility for the pastoral leadership of congregations.

The church grew among the sugarcane fields at Wonji-Gefarsa and Wonji-Shoa. Church buildings were crowded as Christians faithfully witnessed to their fellow employees and brought them into church membership. Many of these new members had previously experienced congregational life in the churches that developed out of SIM efforts begun in the 1930s among the Kambatta and Wolaytta people. Although scattered by relocation, they responded favorably to the congregational worship and teaching MKC provided. They were able to model congregational life for other MKC congregations.

Fifty miles downstream from the Wonji churches, other congregations were established among workers who had moved into an area where a third sugar factory operated in the lower Awash River Valley.

At Metahara, the first of these congregations, Ertero Erencho was a pioneer evangelist who experienced the filling of the Holy Spirit in a new way, including speaking with a new language. In an area where medical services were limited, Ertero prayed for sick people and many times saw them healed. In 1972 while showing visitors the church building, he said, "Everything you see here—the building, the benches, the paint for the walls—is a result of prayer."[4]

MKC had six congregations in the Awash Valley Region when the church was closed in 1982. By 1997, there were ten congregations with 3,500 members.

The MKC congregation at Nazareth grew in size. It could no longer be accommodated by the small chapel building on the hospital grounds, which did not allow for expansion. The congregation was able to buy land in 1964 and finally gained permission to build a meetinghouse, dedicated in February 1971. This enabled them to move their worship services out of the hospital buildings. It was a major breakthrough, because just fifteen years earlier, mission efforts were strictly limited

Ertero Erencho, evangelist for the churches in the Awash Valley for 25 years. *1973 photo.*

to the hospital grounds. Soon after the building was completed, someone tried to set it on fire at night. This was evidence that some in Nazareth did not welcome an evangelical movement in their town.

The 1964 Annual Report to EMM noted "times of rejoicing . . . when souls are added to the church, but large numbers have never yet characterized the growth of the MKC. New classes are now under instruction in every congregation, but leaders are crying to the Lord for the daily additions that characterized the church after Pentecost."[5]

Dagne Assefa, who had been a leader in Semay Birhan chapel at Nazareth, moved to Addis Ababa in 1973 as a full-time evangelist in the Bole (now Kebene) congregation. Dagne's coming to Bole became a turning point in the worship life of the congregation. He opened the way for a charismatic type of worship. Many with a Pentecostal experience found it easy to join the worship program. A group from Tsion (Zion) Pentecostal church started to worship at Bole because their small church was closed. Their choir was welcomed to sing regularly during Sunday worship. The worship style changed.

The singing of new songs and the rhythmic clapping of hands made old MKC members uncomfortable. The hymnbooks which the church had published were mostly ignored as new songs were composed and sung from memory. People carried notebooks to church to copy the words of songs they were hearing for the first time. Those with tape recorders sat on the front benches and held out microphones to record songs the choirs sang.

Many young people came to the Lord. Dagne scheduled every Wednesday to be a day of prayer, when people prayed aloud and in unison. Many newcomers received the baptism of the Holy Spirit during these prayer times.

Individuals in the Tsion group were invited to become members of MKC. After a while, Zelalem Tefera from the group became a member. The choir suddenly stopped serving in the Bole church and left the congregation. They later joined the Mulu Wengel Church.

The Tsion choir was immediately replaced by a new MKC choir, which became very popular. The choir still exists and is known as the MKC Addis Ababa Region choir. A number of Mulu Wengel members were also worshiping with the Bole congregation. Their church, too, had been closed. As a result, the Bole church became overcrowded and eventually needed to conduct three worship services on Sunday mornings.

Missionaries, remembering the Anabaptist persecution of the sixteenth century, encouraged MKC leaders to welcome the persecuted. Some MKC leaders, who had originally come to Christ through the influence of Semay Birhan, were able to help bridge the gap between the Mulu Wengel people and the traditional members.

In 1994, Million Belete, then serving as chairman of MKC, summed up the influence of charismatics: "Those from the charismatic stream have greatly benefited MKC—and vice versa."[6] Bible and discipleship teaching helped MKC survive through ten years of Marxist restrictions, when the church had to devise completely new ways to function in a hostile society.

Today MKC leaders emphasize that they want truly to be a New Testament church, obedient to the Lord who saved them. The expansion of the church in Ethiopia is evidence of God at work, ordering events far beyond the prayers of his people.

11

Revolution—
A Society in Upheaval

Evangelist Dagne Assefa was speaking to the Meserete Kristos Church (MKC) congregation at Bole in Addis Ababa one Sunday afternoon. He told worshipers that the Scriptures urge God's people to pray for their nation. It was July 1974, and Ethiopia needed prayer—fervent prayer. Dagne divided the congregation into groups, separating those who prayed aloud and in unison from those accustomed to pray silently and one at a time. The issues were too great to spend time discussing the relative value of different prayer styles. Dagne asked everyone to seek God in the way he or she chose.

Indeed the issues were great. Ethiopia was in turmoil. High school students and Addis Ababa University students repeatedly staged marching demonstrations, calling for a reform of the government. "Down with Feudalism" and "The Land to the Tiller," they shouted as they made their way through the streets of major towns. They saw the monarchy as outdated and criticized government officials, whom they saw as more interested in their own enrichment than in working for the progress of the country.

The army, at bases in the north and in the south of the country, had gone on strike for higher pay. In 1973, the Arab-Israeli conflict had greatly escalated the price of fuel. Taxi drivers in the major cities said they could no longer afford to drive. Teachers went on strike for better benefits. The government was forced to reduce the price of gasoline and to grant a pay increase to the military.

Then without notice, Haile Selassie's cabinet resigned because they no longer were able to control the situation. The new prime minister, Endalkachow Mekonnen, en route home for lunch one day, was surrounded by a threatening mob asking him to resign. As the summer of 1974 wore on, it became clear that His Majesty was no longer in control of his government. The army was ruling from the wings, and the changes that were taking place have been called "the creeping coup."

To make matters worse, a severe famine was developing in northern Ethiopia, a famine that would eventually take the lives of many thousands of people. Rains had been short for the preceding five years. Yet the government was reluctant to expose its plight to the rest of the world.

Students talked about the need for democracy. However, they had little understanding of the long road ahead if Ethiopia would undertake such drastic measures as reorganizing the government. Kings had ruled the country for three thousand years. Powerful nobles, the Orthodox Church, and the Crown controlled much of the land.

Landowners had mules and cars for transportation. Peasants always walked. They toiled in the fields and paid their landlords up to half their grain each harvest. The average annual income for an Ethiopian family was about $100 U.S. A few people lived well, even in luxury. Most were very poor.

The evangelical churches[1] throughout Ethiopia called for a day of prayer that July. Most people felt instinctively that rough days were ahead for their beloved nation. Yet no one seemed to know what could be done about it. Many youths took to the streets in protest. Others turned to evangelical churches for security and some protection from the coming doom. Young people filled the churches, and they sang and prayed and implored God to show them a meaningful future.

On Ethiopian New Year's Day, Meskerem 1 (Sept. 11, 1974), Ethiopian television presented films and commentary on the devastating famine in the northern part of the country

Kedir Delchume and Selamawit Ersa, MKC delegates on a visit to America, converse with Raymond Charles in 1978. Kedir was pastor of the Nazareth congregation and assistant chairman of MKC. He served as a traveling evangelist and encourager of the church during the underground years.

and contrasted it with the opulence of the king's court. The next day the military managed to take over the government. The emperor was accused of being "an expensive luxury." He was taken from his palace, pushed into the back of a small Volkswagen, and driven off to seclusion. Reportedly, he told his captors they would see the day when the Ethiopian people would refuse to live under their totalitarian regime. Haile Selassie I died August 25, 1975, after reigning 44 years.

People suggest various reasons why a Communist government was able to rule Ethiopia for seventeen years. Western journalists usually attribute this to the decision of Emperor Haile Selassie I to receive aid from the former Soviet Union. Negash Kebede was chairman of the church when it was officially closed by the Marxist government. He helped put into perspective the events leading up to the era of Col. Mengistu Haile Mariam, an avowed Marxist who ruled with an iron hand from 1977 to 1991:

The Italian occupation (1936-41) had forced Emperor Haile Selassie I into exile in Britain. During those years he observed European advancement and economic development achieved through modern education. To achieve his goals for Ethiopia, he recruited many teachers from abroad. As the cold war intensified, competition between the superpowers made Ethiopia one of the highest beneficiaries of U.S. aid in Africa. This came in the form of military aid, education, agriculture, and highway construction. Many observers believe that the greatest impact of U.S. aid was in the field of education.

Unfortunately, the expansion of education did not result as positively as Haile Selassie had expected. Rationalism, democracy, and materialism became the fashion of the day. Leaders were condemning and abandoning old values, both religious and cultural. The masses of uneducated people . . . expected the educated elite and the students to solve the problems of the country.

Although Haile Selassie received economic aid from the former Soviet Union, his allegiance was always to the West. The Soviet Union, for example, helped build a polytechnic institute in Bahir Dar and provided some of the teaching staff. However, all the Ethiopian staff members had secured their training in the United States. Foreign personnel in Addis Ababa University and other institutions were all from the West. As a result, students reacted by reading Marxist literature and embracing an extreme form of Communism. They accused Haile Selassie of being a puppet of the West, and attacked his inefficient bureaucratic government and the unfair land tenure system. Students staged demonstrations and riots. Finally, when the spirit of rebellion reached the army, the end came. Haile Selassie had lived too long, and whatever positive achievements he had made did not satisfy the new generation.

Actually the Soviet Union had given up spreading Communism in Ethiopia during the time of the emperor and had turned instead to Somalia. The Ethiopian army was expecting help from the United States, as in the days of the emperor. When this did not happen, the army learned Communism from the students and persuaded the Russians to change sides and come to Ethiopia. This is how the Ethiopian people began the long road to revolution and hardship.[2]

At first it appeared that the new government would bring progress to an ancient land, stifled by its traditions. Landowners had to surrender any land that they were not able to farm with their own hands. The peasant could farm the land on which he lived and no longer had to pay rent to a landlord.[3] Evangelical believers tried to be positive about anything that looked like genuine reform and tried to cooperate with government policy as well as they could.

Shawle Wehibe, an early MKC leader now living in the United States, visited Ethiopia in 1977 and reported,

> The burden of the Ethiopian peasant is being removed. It was customary for the tenant farmer to give one-third of the grain to his landlord, but in some areas of the country, landlords took as much as three-fourths. The farmer worked day and night for nothing. The relationship with his landlord was "master and servant." All this is no longer applicable to Ethiopia. The peasant is given land to farm and support his family and only pays a minimum land tax to the government.[4]

Carl Hansen, a missionary working in development, also praised the new government and called it "avowedly socialistic." However, "this does not mean it is going Communist," he wrote in 1975. "Socialism is immensely popular in Africa today. . . . Ethiopians are profoundly religious and are repelled by the atheism of Soviet Communism." Carl called for "respect [for] what has been achieved by the revolution . . . as a noble attempt of a brave people to do all at once what should have been done gradually by the former generation."[5]

The government began a crash literacy program. It ordered students to drop out of school and do two years of national service, teaching in rural areas. This project looked like a good thing. The literacy accomplishments of the Marxists outstripped the best efforts under the monarchy and the efforts of many other nations. Evangelical churches were happy about the emphasis put on literacy. However, when the government asked churches to make their buildings available for literacy classes, they usually demurred. Church leaders realized that it would be an easy step for the government to add classes in Marxist indoctrination under the name of literacy.

The uncertainties on the horizon caused evangelical Christians to pull together. In September 1976, about a thousand people—church leaders, pastors, evangelists—from a dozen denominations met at the Bible Academy in Nazareth "to discover their unity and affirm the lordship of Christ." The organizers tried to avoid publicity. Even so, they heard threats that political groups might try to cause a disturbance. The leaders committed the whole matter to the Lord, and trouble never came.

The meeting was the first of its kind. For many, this was a new experience, with Pentecostals and Lutherans sitting in the same meeting, or even sleeping in the same room. Though the atmosphere was tense at first, barriers came down. By the end of the conference, the participants were feeling that they were one in the Lord. Tesfatsion Dalellew, executive secretary of MKC, wrote to *Missionary Messenger* and called the meeting "a stepping-stone toward the unity of the churches in Ethiopia." As a result of that conference, nine denominations agreed to cooperate in a council of churches.[6]

Evangelical church leaders sometimes differed in their interpretation of the true identity of the revolution. Some wanted to cooperate as much as possible and felt that Christians should make every effort to avoid a confrontation with the government. These leaders documented the relief and development efforts and brought them to the government's attention. Others wanted to make it abundantly clear that Marxism was an evil system, and they refused to cooperate in any way. As with Mennonites in North America, opinions varied: some believers wanted as little involvement with the government as possible, and others thought the government desperately needed Christians.

The Nazareth congregation organized a team led by Seyoum Gebretsadik, current education secretary for MKC, and charged it with preparing printed material to help Christians keep their faith in the midst of Marxist philosophy and indoctrination. The team, hiding at the Nazareth Bible Academy, spent the whole of two summer vacations (1975-76) producing written material on Christianity and scientific socialism.

The studies carried the following titles: *Let Creation Speak. Shall We Deny? What Does the Bible Say? When You Witness. Christian Youth and Science.* These resources were used at seminars held at the Bible Academy for various denominational leaders during four summer vacations, 1975 to 1978.

MKC leaders were eager to know how a church could exist under a Marxist government. When Ethiopian representatives attended Mennonite World Conference in Wichita, Kansas, in 1978, they met Mennonites from the Soviet Union, who invited the Ethiopian believers to visit their country. Thus in early 1979, a delegation of six Ethiopians visited the Soviet Union: Tesfatsion Dalellew, Solomon Kebede, Bedru Hussein, Yohannes Germamo, Asrat Gebre, Tsega Woldemariam. Here they recognized a greater affinity with the Russian Baptist-Mennonite Union than with the traditional German Mennonites who had migrated into Russia two hundred years earlier.[7]

As a result of that visit, MKC asked EMM to send Harley

Wagler to Nazareth, Ethiopia. He was a Mennonite missionary serving in the former Yugoslavia, and they wanted him to conduct a seminar on Christianity and Marxism. Wagler brought a new approach by helping church leaders to understand Marxism before they developed a Christian response. He believed Christians would survive the difficulties if leaders were given direction.

MKC tried to understand Marxism before criticizing it. Teachers at the Bible Academy complied with the government order to teach Marxism in the classroom because they thought it best for Christians to be the ones who taught it. Some other churches and missions refused to comply with this order.

At the seminars, duplicated study materials were given to enrollees from various denominations, along with strict orders to keep them confidential. On one occasion the *kebele* leaders found someone who possessed study materials from the Bible Academy seminars, resources that clearly refuted Marxist ideology. The leaders insisted that the young man reveal where he had gotten these writings, but he refused to tell. As a result, they put him into prison for four years. Bedru says, "If he had told where the materials were produced, we leaders could well have been killed."[8]

Alemu Checole, teacher at the Bible Academy, recalled those days: "We prayed, leaving the entire matter in God's hands. The students would pray and then pass all the road checks on the way home without the guards finding the materials." Sometimes guards would give only body checks and not search their luggage. Some guards were illiterate and ignored printed materials because they did not want to betray their inability to read.

From time to time, Derg (the military government) officials would visit the Bible Academy and try to discover any students secretly involved with EPRP, an underground movement that threatened the Derg. The academy staff members feared that the officials might find the study materials on Christian faith and Marxism. They wrapped all of the apologetic papers in plastic bags and buried them at different

Alemu Checole, who as a child was a student at Merha Ewourran School (for the Blind) in Addis Ababa, taught for many years at the Bible Academy. He serves as a member of the MKC Executive Committee and as an elder in the Nazareth congregation. *Dale Gehman photo, 1990.*

places on the campus.

While the delegation was visiting in the Soviet Union in 1979, the Bible Academy staff feared that the government would search the campus. So a woman on the staff dug up the buried papers and burned them. Most of these files, however, have since been replaced by students who had kept their copies carefully hidden in their houses.

Meanwhile, MKC congregations continued to grow. In Addis Ababa, three worship services were held every Sunday, beginning at 6:00 a.m. Janet Kreider visited Ethiopia in 1981 and described the push of human bodies waiting for access to the Bole chapel when one service was dismissed and another began:[9]

> We entered the churchyard at 10:30 and stood near the door so we could get a seat for the eleven o'clock service. There had been a healing and prayer service at 6:00 a.m. and a worship service at 9:00. It was still going strong when we arrived.

> I looked over the crowd gathering in that churchyard and still couldn't believe what I saw. The majority of the people were young. Beside me, a girl sat with her head bowed in prayer. In a building to my right, I heard a strong, repetitious command and was told they were casting out a demon. People continued to gather. They stood silent and orderly, waiting.
>
> At last the doors opened and people filed out. When the building was emptied, the surge toward the door began. . . . That huge sea of persons literally propelled us in. I just had to be sure to lift my feet going up the steps and not to drop my Bible. There would have been no retrieving anything. . . . Soon the benches were packed full, and those who didn't get in, filled up the shelters on either side of the outside wall.

Physical healings frequently took place, healing from cancer, paralysis, blindness, asthma. Occasionally healings would extend to persons who had not made a profession of faith; this would result in their salvation and commitment to Christ. Daniel Mekonnen, MKC evangelist in Addis Ababa at the time, prayed for many people and described the healings as love healings—not faith healings. He believes that healings do not happen just as a result of the amount of one's faith but as a sovereign act of a God who is love.

Once a man with a painful leg, who claimed to be an atheist, came to a church with twenty of his friends. He planned to disturb the service. The speaker received a word of knowledge from the Holy Spirit and said, "The Lord wants to heal a young man in the audience with a painful leg." When the man heard his condition described, he was completely dumbfounded. His pain was so annoying that he could not sleep at night. So he went forward, received healing, and found the Lord.[10]

With the growing numbers attending services, the government increased its surveillance of Christian worship.

Government agents would infiltrate the meetings to see who attended and to observe everything that was done. Church leaders were careful to do everything openly and refrained from criticizing the government. In Nazareth, they encouraged people to attend the kebele meetings and even arranged to conduct their own worship services on Sunday afternoons rather than Sunday mornings.

Reporting on their decisions during the time of the Derg, leaders would frequently say, "It is not that we were so wise; the grace of God helped us." They often testified that after they prayed, God would lead them to do the proper thing. They also said that God protected them and enabled them to go about their work without fear. Shemelis Rega, evangelist in Dire Dawa, said, "We learned to depend on God for everything. We were like the Levites, who had no land, so they had to depend on God."[11]

Then, without warning, kebele leaders, over a period of seven months in 1982, appeared at the doors of each of the fourteen Meserete Kristos Church (MKC) congregations with a weighty order: "This church shall be closed, and it will be the property of the Ethiopian government."

The believers in these congregations, totaling about five thousand, were to learn in a still deeper way what it would mean to fully depend on God.

12

The Many Faces of Persecution

In 1978 the local *kebele* at Nazareth called Bible Academy students to their office for questioning. While still holding the students, they wanted to talk to the school director, missionary Herb Kraybill. The Ethiopian administrator of the academy, Alemayehu, reasoned that it was not fair to load political decisions onto an expatriate.

"I am an Ethiopian, and this is a problem I have to bear." Alemayehu stretched himself to his full six-foot-two height, seeming to relive those days in 1978 when he insisted that the kebele release the students. Eighteen years later, in 1996, he taped that experience for the record.[1]

Earlier the kebele had urged Alemayehu to serve as their leader, but he was disqualified because he had once bought a piece of land to develop before the Marxist Revolution. No former landowner was allowed to serve as a kebele leader.

Now the kebele wanted to indoctrinate students with Marxism, and Alemayehu had to speak for them. The Bible Academy staff insisted that students not be interrupted in their studies. The kebele was against all religion and set on destroying the values the academy was teaching. Kebele leaders did not understand academics because they had little chance at schooling themselves. Their work was to harass anyone whom they perceived as not supporting the revolution.

"They wanted to beat us and put us in prison," Alemayehu recalls. At times during meetings when they argued with academy staff members, kebele leaders would pick up their guns to intimidate the teachers.

Once the kebele called the students and asked them to take an oath denying their faith. Alemayehu, leaving Herb Kraybill behind, took other staff members with him and sat down to talk with the kebele leaders. The leaders insisted on seeing the director. Alemayehu said, "I represent the director." Next kebele leaders said they didn't want anyone else present when they talked to Alemayehu. He declared, "If you don't want to talk with my colleagues, then I don't want to talk with you, either."

This made the kebele leaders angry. Finally, after the leaders discussed the matter among themselves, they let the other teachers stay with Alemayehu. The session took four hours. Part of the time, the teachers were questioned by the political cadres, government appointees assigned to see that peopled followed true Marxist principles.

"We said, 'You can't force our minds. We will obey what does not go against our religion. But if you go against our religion, we will not obey you. We obey God. Our minds are God's property.' " Alemayehu and his colleagues would not budge.

The cadres said, "What we cannot settle around the table, we will settle with our guns."

The teachers answered, "Your guns are to protect us, not to kill us. But we are ready and happy to die for our faith."

The kebele released the teachers but continued to hold the students.

Three days later, the teachers met with another group of kebele leaders, who ruled that those who ordered the students to prison were wrong to do so. "This is not the time that we hold you and put students in prison or convince you by talking," they said as they let the students go.

The harassment, however, did not stop. Repeatedly the kebele called Alemayehu and attempted to give him directives of various kinds. Alemayehu remembers conversations he had with God at that time: "God, is it really this hard to follow you? Have our forefathers had this kind of problem?

God, shall I leave you? But where would I go? It's not my
wish to leave you, but the situation is pressing."

God gave Alemayehu peace: "You can endure this and
come through it to a better time. Just be patient," he heard the
Lord say.

Members of the Nazareth congregation were also put into
prison. Kebele leaders asked the believers to raise their left
hands, curse their enemies, and shout the slogan, "The revolution is above everything." The believers refused because
they firmly maintained that God is above all. They were kept
in prison for a few days and beaten in an attempt to force
them to say the slogan. Many considered it a privilege to suffer for the Lord and remained faithful through these ordeals.

Church leaders met twice a day to discuss what to do.
They appealed to town officials. Once they wrote letters to
twenty different kebeles in Nazareth, asking for the release of
prisoners.

In 1977, after a long meeting of church leaders, Gemede
Baruda (now deceased), Gebreselassie Habtamu, Solomon
Kebede, and Alemu Checole went with Alemayehu to make
an appeal to the Nazareth governor. They acknowledged that
if any of them were killed, they would meet in heaven.
Whatever happened, those remaining would not stop teaching the Word of God.

The five asked their questions forthrightly. "What is the
problem? What have we done to hurt our country? Is there
any evidence?" After a long conversation, the governor
promised that he would try to have the harassment stopped.
The leaders believed it was the work of God. The persecu-
tions ended, and yet there were restrictions. No one under
thirty years of age was supposed to attend church.

Alemayehu describes the feelings he had when asked to
be one of the six to go to the governor:

> Before we six leaders were nominated to make this
> approach to the governor, there was fear in my
> heart. I said, "God, don't let the leaders choose me:
> I am not ready to face this." But after I was chosen,

I felt strong; I felt happy. The fear went away. I said,
"Thank you, Lord, for the chance to die for you."
The idea did not come from my flesh. God put his
power in me. God puts his own power in people
when he uses them as an instrument.

Alemu Checole remembers 1977 and 1978 as the most
stressful and difficult years. The authorities would arrest the
young people under 30. Officials often refused to pay attention when people appealed for fair treatment of youths. So
girls in their late teens or 20s would wear their mothers' long
dresses and give the impression they were 30 or 40. Because
the youth choir had to disband, a new one formed that
included people above 30 as well as youths who dressed as
older people. Some of the church leaders put on choir gowns
and participated. Up to that time, choirs were always composed only of young people.[2]

Eventually one government official who had ordered
youths not to attend church, died suddenly from an auto

Bole Choir, 1977. Choirs began to develop in MKC in the early 1970s.
Young people began to write music and lyrics and copied the words in
notebooks for group singing.

accident. After that, other officials were not so strict.

During 1977 and 1978 the country also experienced the Red Terror. This was the determined effort of the government to stamp out the EPRP (Ethiopia Peoples' Revolutionary Party), a rival party that operated underground. They arrested or killed without trial anyone whom they suspected of being part of this movement. The population was almost paralyzed with fear.

However, even during this dreadful time, MKC invited church leaders from all over the country to attend seminars at the Bible Academy. There MKC resource persons taught church leaders the basic beliefs of Marxism and Christianity and contrasted creationism and evolution. Bedru Hussein, Solomon Kebede, Seyoum Gebretsadik, and Girma Mersha taught and directed these courses during the summer months. The students were able to withstand the strong opposition from Marxism and took it as a challenge to stand on their faith.

Also during the school vacation each year, large interdenominational conferences were held on the Bible Academy campus. World Vision funded some of these. In 1976, guest speakers were invited, such as Roy Clemens, a Baptist Britisher from Nairobi; Gotfried Osei Mensah, from Ghana; Bishop Festo Kivengere, from Uganda; and Samuel Kemaleson, from India. Once there were a thousand people on campus. The local kebeles could not begin to muster that kind of enthusiasm for the revolution. The Marxist threat, common to all churches, helped evangelicals affirm their Christian unity.

When the government asked to use the Nazareth church building for literacy classes, the church refused, pointing out that it was a place for worship. When refusing, the leaders reminded the government that it had not asked the Muslims for their mosques or the Orthodox for their churches. Therefore, MKC had the same right to decline. MKC was convinced that if the church gave permission for literacy classes to be held in their buildings, soon the kebele would use them for political meetings and indoctrination of Marxist ideology. No doubt, the kebele would call meetings on Sundays to interfere with worship services.

As an alternative, MKC offered to build classrooms on the kebele compound to use for literacy classes. The church kept its word by building four rooms. It didn't seem, however, to make relations smoother between the kebele and MKC.[3] Marxists often discredited such philanthropy from churches because it gave the lie to the Marxist line that religion is the opiate of the people.

The kebele continued to force young people to attend indoctrination classes. Everyone from ages thirteen to thirty had to attend the Communist meetings. Several afternoons a week, students would have to go directly from school to the kebele headquarters, where they heard droning lectures on the wonders of Marxism till ten at night. After about a year of training, some of them would have to trek to the countryside to teach country folk the essentials of Marxism.[4]

In Dire Dawa, 1976 was a difficult year. The war between Ethiopia and Somalis living in the southeast border areas was coming close. This situation created anxiety in the mixed population of Dire Dawa, where many Somalis live. The church was in difficulty, though it was not yet closed. Kebele leaders and Communist party members would try to get the people to beat up those attending the MKC congregation. The people, however, usually did not pay much attention to such harangues.

Solomon Kesete, a congregational elder at the time and now coordinator of the MKC Dire Dawa Region, faced many problems because of the Somali War, the Derg infighting, politics, propaganda against the believers, and Orthodox opposition. Once the Dire Dawa church leaders were put in prison for eleven months and finally released when a local magistrate said they could continue to conduct worship. The order to close the church in 1982 came as a blow because by then the leaders thought they had weathered the stormiest time.[5]

Political parties had developed, some wanting democratic socialism and others wanting a Communism more severe than the Derg practiced. When EPRP started assassinating

Hargewien Deneke, delivered from demonic oppression, witnessed by passing out tracts in the marketplace. *Jonathan Charles photo.*

Derg leaders, the Derg used a more vicious Red Terror in retaliating against what they called the White Terror. They arrested EPRP members or shot them at night, often leaving their corpses on street corners to terrify the people.

It was indeed a fearful time. The Western reader in a democratic society can hardly grasp the extent of the ridicule heaped on evangelical believers. Radio programs and newspaper articles constantly called them foreigners, CIA agents, antiprogress people, reactionary elements, even dogs. Their experiences were like those of the early Christians, as the apostle Paul said, "We have become the scum of the earth, the refuse of the world" (1 Cor. 4:13, NIV). Yet, like Paul, when believers were cursed, they blessed; when persecuted, they endured; when slandered, they answered kindly. "We were harassed in front of political meetings because of our faith," reported Kassa Agafari when he visited the U.S. in 1990. "We learned that the way to go up is down. We experienced the protection of the Lord."[6]

Evangelists and pastors focused their preaching on the uniqueness of Jesus, the power of the Holy Spirit as greater than any other forces, and the assurance of God's presence in difficult times. They did not refer to the political situation; but the people understood. In spite of the opposition, the church continued its work. Daniel Mekonen, an evangelist, had a healing ministry. People came from many areas and were healed. They would hear the name *Meserete Kristos* and set out to look for it.

Dr. Tesfatsion Dalellew, then national director of World Vision in Ethiopia and elder of the Addis Ababa congregation, tells the story of a woman who came for healing. Genet Lulseged Kumsa, a choir member in Mekane Yesus Church, was beaten until the nerves of her feet were damaged; the pain was excruciating, and she could not walk. At an MKC conference before the church was closed, evangelist Daniel Mekonnen told the people to put a hand on the spot of any ailment they had while he prayed for them. Genet fell down, convulsing and shaking. After he finished praying, Daniel said, "The lady with the injured feet is healed." Genet went to the front to testify that an electrical power had gone through her and that all her pain was gone.[7]

"When we fear persecution, the growth of the church is stunted," contended Ijigu Woldegebriel, evangelist at the Kebena congregation in Addis Ababa during the late 1970s. "When we are serious about preaching the gospel, there is a price to pay." He notes that a wholistic ministry is good, caring for soul and body, but the church must give proper emphasis to the proclamation of the gospel, even if that proclamation brings persecution.

Ijigu described his own prison experience:

> I had my turn in prison, put there by the kebele because I continued going to church against their order. They wanted me to come each week and sign that I would not go to church. I said, "No, I can't; this is my faith." Once they gathered a group of us together from our kebele to brainwash us because I had gone with the choir to Dilla. They kept us a week and tried to make us deny our faith. They would even quote Scripture to us and ask us how we could be disobedient. We answered that we accepted all the Scriptures and together they

give us guidance. They couldn't do anything with us so they released us.

The final time I was detained, they asked me to carry a gun and serve as a military guard in the area. When I got wind of this, I left home. So they put my father in prison and told him that unless I return, they would not release him. My sister sent word to me that my father was in prison. So I went and surrendered myself, and they released him. They wanted me to swear allegiance to the revolution. I told them I didn't have time for it along with my responsibilities. Finally, they asked for my identity card. They took off the photo and gave it to me, tore up the card, threw it in the wastebasket, and said, "From now on you are not a resident of this kebele. We don't know you; get out of here."

God took care of me. I had a student identification card that I did not show them. I tried to avoid places where I would be asked to show my kebele identification.[8]

When Mennonite audiences in North America hear stories from Ethiopia about persecution, they tend to think primarily of the six MKC leaders imprisoned when the church was closed in 1982. Actually, many people—not only leaders—had a prison experience, and many were beaten. Some were detained three days, others for a week, and still others for a month or more. Six months of detention was not uncommon. Some were detained repeatedly because they continued their witness.

Opposition, harassment, and prison were the experience of many evangelical Christians. Although the central government did not officially close evangelical churches larger than MKC, local authorities would often imprison pastors and forbid meetings, especially large conferences. Kebele leaders constantly criticized churches for not wholeheartedly supporting the Marxist Revolution. Students attending evangelical Christian schools were sometimes beaten or imprisoned for short periods for not taking the oath that stated the revolution to be supreme.

MKC members were primarily concerned about being faithful in their witness for the Lord. Although they tried not to antagonize the government, at the same time they did not restrict their activities out of fear that the church might be closed. Discussions centered more on how to extend the Christian message than on how to avoid being closed down. A few felt that it was only a matter of time until the church would be closed, but this did not seem to be a major worry. They were more concerned to find a Christian way of responding to a hostile government. Believers constantly sought guidance for their responses by studying the passages in the book of Acts that describe the opposition the first Christians faced.

When the government closed the church in January 1982, MKC believers knew they would find a way to survive.

13

Prison Life

Ethiopian prisons are austere. The theory is that criminals should not be provided with the comforts of life. Food supplied by the prison is inadequate, so family members have to take food daily to their relatives if they want them to eat properly. A person without a sympathetic family may go hungry, except that prisoners who receive food from their families usually share with fellow inmates. Security guards inspect the food to make sure that no weapons are concealed. The guards ram a stick through the bowls of food, carefully prepared by their families. Then all the food, from whatever household, is placed on large trays from which a dozen men eat in communal style.

Visiting is allowed only on Sundays, and the visitor has to stand behind a barrier and shout across a six-foot space to the prisoner, who stands behind another barrier. Because everyone is visiting at the same time, the visitor and the person he visits must shout loudly enough to be heard above the din of many voices. Guards walk back and forth between the barriers.

During the Marxist years in Ethiopia (1974-1991), there were great numbers of prisoners. The Derg often detained people for months at *kebele* headquarters, at police stations, or at the Central Investigation Department. Often they were put in warehouses ill equipped to give reasonable care. There were no beds. The prisoners themselves had to supply their own mattresses, which they spread on the floor each night in the same area where they lived during the day.

The six church leaders mentioned in chapter 1 were sep-

Worship is a vital part of MKC life. Whether in large congregations on Sunday or in small groups in homes during the week, believers express gratitude to God for his great salvation.

arated and crowded into rooms about thirteen feet square along with thirty other men. At night, they slept end to end on their sides, not having enough space to lie on their backs. If anyone wanted to turn in the night, he had to get the agreement of all the rest to turn at the same time. After twenty months of incarceration, they were transferred to the regular prison in Addis Ababa. Then Shamsudin Abdo remarked that having enough space to lie on his back at night was like checking into a five-star hotel.

The six Meserete Kristos Church (MKC) leaders were held at the Central Investigation Department, where a thirty-man cell had a single door. The only ventilation was an open space above the door. Breathing became almost impossible for anyone with the slightest asthma or congestion from a common cold. Shamsudin says that on one occasion they "lifted a prisoner above their heads to enable him to breathe from the open space."[1]

Wives and families of the prisoners were not allowed visits during the twenty months they were incarcerated at the Central Investigation Department. After they were moved to the main prison, wives could visit once a week under the circumstances mentioned above. Children were allowed only one visit a month. However, at the main prison the men could stroll around the courtyard. Two of them who happened to be in the same area of the prison would take a morning walk and discuss a passage of Scripture. The one who had criticized Shamsudin fifteen years earlier for not changing his Muslim name to a Christian name had adequate time to reflect upon his shortsightedness.

Tilahun had been released before this transfer. Here at the main prison, the five remaining leaders spent thirty more months, living under the anxiety that at any time they could be executed.

Apparently the Derg's intention was to close MKC, round up its leaders, and execute them. The orders were to have this matter dispatched quickly. However, police officers were delayed in rounding up the MKC leaders. Other responsibilities called them, and they did not carry through with the execution order. One official said, "If we had been able to round up you guys when we wanted to, it would have been a very short matter."

A recent change in government policy required some high official to give the order before anyone was executed. There was a time, especially during the Red Terror, when almost any local official could order an execution. When reporting these events, Negash Kebede commented, "We see the marvelous working of God in the timing of things and caring for his people." Indeed, God answered the prayers of his people in many parts of the world as they interceded for the safety of the Ethiopian prisoners.

When Negash did turn himself in, an official said, "So you have been trying to hide from us. You think you can get away and escape?" He spoke roughly. Negash answered, "Am I acting like someone trying to escape by coming here and turning myself in?" The question so disarmed the official that he didn't know what to reply.[2]

Eastern Mennonite Missions tried to be helpful. The overseas office asked Robert S. Kreider, formerly president of Bluffton College in Ohio, to visit Ethiopia and try to obtain release for the prisoners. Kreider had wide experience in relief distribution in Europe after World War II, and in setting up MCC's Teachers Abroad Program (TAP) for Africa in the 1960s. He had carried on dialogue with Marxists in eastern Europe. Thus he was well fitted for this task in Ethiopia.

Robert Kreider counseled with MKC leaders and offered his services. With Herb Kraybill and Beyene Mulatu, Robert visited many offices and talked to many officials, explaining the worldwide humanitarian involvements of Mennonites. He carefully pointed out that Mennonites were not a threat to governments. Officials repeatedly assured the three men that the matter of the church being closed was being investigated. However, no one made promises or took action to release the prisoners. Those negotiations did not bring the desired results.

Church leaders imprisoned for their faith, 1982-1986: **Top row:** Kelifa Ali, Kiros Bihon, Shamsudin Abdo. **Bottom row:** Negash Kebede, Abebe Gorfe, Tilahun Beyene (1982-83).

MKC leaders verified to Robert Kreider that the church still stood by its decision made three months previously, that no news reports be released to the press about the closing of the church. It was MKC's perception that such publicity would only put the prisoners in greater danger. Mennonite editors in North America, however, insisted that they should tell the story. They argued that greater visibility of this grave injustice against the church might help to restore its freedom. The editors were dissuaded with great difficulty.

EMM stood between MKC and the North American thirst for information, maintaining that the only way to relate to sister churches with integrity was to respect their wishes. MKC still believes that it was better for them to suffer in silence than to try to bring the pressure of world opinion to bear on the Marxist government. "God is our protector," MKC leaders said.

The late Paul Kraybill, at the time executive secretary of Mennonite World Conference (MWC), made a second attempt to have the prisoners released. He contacted a Derg leader in France during the 1984 MWC meeting held in Strasbourg that year. The Derg leader insisted that Ethiopia was not detaining anyone for religious reasons. When Paul said he knew of church leaders who were detained for their religious beliefs, the Derg representative asked for their names. Astutely, Paul declined to tell him. Today the former prisoners affirm that such wisdom was God's special direction to Paul.

There is only one way for persons to understand the dynamics that take place when a church is suddenly outlawed: that way is to go through the experience themselves. During 1996, we interviewed many people as part of the research for this book. We were asking questions that often seemed to stump our informants.

"Why were you put into prison?" We asked a man who as a youth, zealous for the Lord, spent eight months in an overcrowded warehouse, a make-do prison because so many people were being detained. The government was rounding up political dissidents as well as evangelical Christians whom they scathingly referred to as "Pente" (Pentecostals).

He replied, "Just because I wouldn't attend their kebele meetings, where they indoctrinated people on Communism." When we expressed amazement that such an act would merit detention, the man was puzzled. He stared at us for a moment as he tried to comprehend our naïveté. "Let me tell you that people were incarcerated for much lesser things, like coming to visit us or bringing us food in prison," he explained.[3]

While doing research for this book, we were impressed with the great numbers of people who had been detained by the kebele of their area for one month, two months, six months, or even a year. The Marxist government from 1974 to 1991 was indeed bent on stamping out evangelical Christians. Orthodox and Muslim persons were not liked either for their religious beliefs, but those blocks of the population were too large to attack, at least in the early years.

Workinesh Bantiwalu, whose conversion story was told in chapter 9, described the kind of harassment she faced in Nazareth:

> I am a woman of faith, and faith was not wanted in those days. But in truth, God protected me. Once I was accused of having a pistol. They came with four cars and took me to the kebele in one of them. They told me to turn over my arms. I said, "My only weapon is the Bible." They said, "We are not saying to turn over your weapon if you have a pistol; we are saying *that* you have one." I told them that I don't protect myself; God is the one who protects me.
>
> They said they would detain me and took me to the kebele headquarters, where many women were imprisoned. I spent the night with them in a dark room. We sat on mattresses. The next morning when their husbands came for them, they sent the women home and their husbands off to jail. I asked the Lord one thing: "Lord," I said, "the other

women here were exchanged for their husbands; I have no husband to be exchanged for. You are my husband, my exchanger, and for that I thank you." I praised the Lord and waited.

That evening people came to beat us. They asked about me, and I said that my answer was the same. I have no weapon. So the next morning, they had the remaining women sign and let them go. Only I remained. They came and said, "Aren't you going out?" Finally I went out without even signing. This is how much God looked after me. I was not asked about this again.[4]

Believers give numerous accounts of beatings when they refused to deny God or refused to put up their hand and repeat the Marxist slogan, "The revolution is above all." Their standard answer was that this was a matter of religious faith for them and therefore was a pledge they could not take. Believing prisoners considered it a privilege to suffer for their faith. They spent their time in prison witnessing to other prisoners.

In the previous chapter, we noted how the Marxist government from its takeover in 1974 gradually became more and more oppressive in its policies. Now in 1982, with the Red Terror over, tension seemed to be easing. MKC congregations thought they had weathered the worst, only to find that they were targeted for complete closure and confiscation of property. This was similar to what had happened to the Mulu Wengel Church ten years earlier.

Imprisonment of the six MKC leaders in 1982 made it clear immediately that a commitment to evangelical faith would be costly. Some people left the faith, not willing to risk imprisonment. Others stopped their church activities to minimize their risks. Still others continued to be actively involved, willing to take any consequence.[5]

About six months after the church closed, pastor Kedir Delchume shared his burden with elders of his congregation at Nazareth. He appealed for the church to come together, because all meetings for worship and administration had been stopped. They encouraged him to pursue his vision.

Kedir called together representatives from each of the congregations. Ten people attended and formed an evangelism committee to replace the former executive committee. The committee called all MKC members to a day of prayer, scheduled for the anniversary of the church's closing. Members were also asked to spend a day in fasting and prayer each month. In February 1983, one year after the church was closed, a General Church Council met, with twenty persons present. It continued to meet twice yearly in semisecrecy during the underground years.

At a meeting in March 1984 at the Catholic school in Dire Dawa, the council authorized the evangelism committee to consult with each congregation. The committee was assigned to see that elders were chosen where this had been postponed because of the difficulty of the times. The minutes of that meeting—handwritten in a spiral notebook—indicate that an elder in one of the congregations "went back to the world; he has not harmed us, although he knows all our secrets." The minutes referred to the Stateside mission board as "our sister church." In 1986, the Wollega and Gojam churches were accepted as members of MKC. In 1987, Tefera Gonfa, leader of the Wollega churches, was appointed as assistant coordinator of MKC. Kedir was overall coordinator.

The minutes of those first meetings of the evangelism committee and General Church Council indicate that house fellowships should be limited to five people each. Evangelists were to work from their own homes.[6]

Evangelists needed Bible study helps for these cell groups to nurture themselves. Therefore, the church set a priority on duplicating materials produced before it was officially closed. Someone typed the stencils. Someone else took the stencils to Herb and Sharon Kraybill, former teachers at the Bible Academy, who now worked at the ALERT (All Africa Leprosy and Rehabilitation Training) Centre in Addis Ababa.

Herb had reconditioned an old Gestetner duplicating

machine he secured from the American Embassy. Late at night, hoping the neighbors would not ask questions about the thumping noise in their house, he duplicated thousands of Bible study sheets for distribution through the underground. A concealed chain of people conveyed the materials from Kraybill's home to the hundreds of cell groups in the church areas. No one knew the total networking of this system. Each person knew only the one segment for which he or she was responsible.

Women became active during the underground. In fact, more women than men were leading cell groups. They taught Sunday school and served as elders. The government usually paid little attention to women. In a patriarchal society, officials considered a woman's influence to be insignificant.

In 1979, church leaders in Addis had organized a women's fellowship to train jobless women for employment, to nurture their spiritual lives, and to provide assistance to families at times of weddings and funerals. When the church was closed in 1982, a group of women prayed all night, seeking God's direction. In a word of prophecy, the Lord told them to continue their work and trust him for protection.

The women's committee was composed of Tenfaylish Yigezu, Tsehay Abebe, Wodinesh Burka, Mulu Yelala, Elene Assefa, Yeshareg Bekele, and Tewabech. They organized women in groups of ten. Often short of taxi fare, some of them walked across the city from Bole to Mexico Square and to the *merkato* (bazaar, mostly outdoors), organizing the groups and arranging for evangelists to teach them.

Because the groups were many and the evangelists few, women were encouraged to serve as lay ministers. When the kebeles started to threaten the women for holding meetings, the church leaders told the women to discontinue them. When the women reminded the leaders that God had led them to minister in this way, the church leaders allowed them to continue and recommended that the groups be limited to six persons. Then the elders started to work with the women's committee, assigning men also to the groups.

Women served as watchers, elders, and teachers, and they participated equally in ministry with the men.[7]

In April 1986, God answered the prayers of many people who had pleaded for the release of the prisoners. One morning Negash Kebede heard his name called, and he was told to go to the prison office. There he met Kiros Bihon, Shamsudin Abdo, Abebe Gorfe, and Kelifa Ali. They had also been called, but no one would tell them why. Eventually they were transferred to the maximum security prison without being told why they were going.

All five were apprehensive. Were they being called for release or for execution? They had heard names called before. Although their means of getting news was extremely limited in the prison, rumor had it that a summons to "come to the office" usually resulted in execution. Finally, in the late afternoon the men were released and told to find their own transportation home. That was a night of great celebration for the church and for the five families. They wept for joy and thanked God for this reunion.

To report the release to American Mennonites, someone sent a telex bearing only the Scripture reference "2 Cor. 1:8-11." The readers were able to guess that they should change the word *Asia* to *Ethiopia*. Thus they had a complete message describing the ordeal the prisoners had come through:

> We do not want you to be uninformed, brothers [and sisters], about the hardships we suffered in the province of Asia. We were under great pressure, far beyond our ability to endure, so that we despaired even of life. Indeed, in our hearts we felt the sentence of death. But this happened that we might not rely on ourselves but on God, who raises the dead. He has delivered us from such a deadly peril, and he will deliver us. On him we have set our hope that he will continue to deliver us, as you help us by your prayers. Then many will give thanks on our behalf for the gracious favor granted us in answer to the prayers of many. (NIV)

However, the church was still closed and would remain so for five more years, until the Marxists would be driven out of the country. The men who had been released kept a low profile in those first months. They did not want to give the impression that they were taking up leadership in the church again.

New leaders were in place, and the church was fully organized as an underground church. A new evangelism committee, chosen in 1983 in place of an executive committee, was now giving leadership to the underground. As the government became more and more preoccupied with the war in the north, there was a general relaxation of religious persecution.

MKC members gradually became more bold and functioned more openly, allowing larger numbers than the prescribed five or seven people to meet in a home. Administrative meetings were not as secretive, and General Church Council, first held in February 1983, could be more relaxed in the late 1980s.

14

Regrouping to Survive

The Meserete Kristos Church (MKC) was not totally unprepared for its churches to be closed. Church leaders had anticipated that this might happen, given the large crowds gathering for multiple services each Sunday in Addis Ababa.

Marxists could tell that church life was more interesting and more exciting than listening to the promises the revolution had to offer. They saw that people came to the kebele meetings reluctantly. However, people flocked to the churches, arriving early to assure themselves a seat. Kebele meetings were also held on Sunday mornings, to wean people from the churches. So families sometimes sent one of their members to the kebele meetings to satisfy the minimum requirements, while the rest of the family went to worship.

Ijigu Woldegebriel, evangelist in the Addis Ababa Kebena congregation, said that during 1979 and 1980, the Spirit impressed upon him that the church would be closed:

> I went from place to place and gathered believers to pray about this. Because of my youth, I was not listened to very much, but the Spirit seemed to be telling me I must take a more active role as in the days of Esther. If I failed to do as God was telling me to do, salvation would come from other quarters. I was frightened by the call of God.[1]

Ijigu talked with Solomon Kebede about his concern.

Eventually the church elders approved a budget of 500 birr to start a Bible study course.

This was the beginning of a training program in Addis Ababa. A three-day seminar for forty people was planned to be held at the Mekane Yesus Seminary. So many people begged to attend that eventually seventy-nine were enrolled. A committee was formed to give direction to cell groups: Meseret Endeshow, Yerusalem Teshome, Firew Mukuria, Alemayehu Mekuria, and Ijigu. The committee chair was Meseret, who had learned inductive Bible study at Hesston College in Kansas, and she believed it to be a good method to use in the house fellowships.

As they were meeting to organize leaders for the house fellowships, police came into the classrooms at the Bole chapel in Addis and took many of them off to jail. Some of them were in prison for six months. Ijigu escaped because he was attending a program at his high school. The committee continued organizing cell groups as well as they could, using the remaining leaders. By the time the church was closed, about twenty groups were meeting. These became the model

Taye Solomon with MKC printer that was used during the underground years and is now used to produce Bible study materials. *Jonathan Charles photo.*

for organizing the whole congregation in Addis after church closure.

Also at Nazareth before the church was closed, the elders had divided members of the congregation into zones for holding prayer meetings. The elders circulated among the groups, leading the Bible studies. Negash Kebede tells of attending such a meeting soon after his arrival from a two-year stay in the States. Forgetting to be careful, he taught with an open Bible. He was greatly surprised when five guards appeared and ordered the group to the kebele head-quarters for questioning.

Negash argued with the guards, insisting on his right to teach the Bible; his brothers frantically tried to keep him quiet. "It is not wise to argue with the guards," they said. A higher official eventually released the group, explaining that "a new ruling now allows people to carry Bibles." Such incidents proved to church leaders that restrictions on evangelicals could be imposed at any moment.

Church life was successful among evangelicals. When anything drew so many people, Marxists could interpret it only as being subversive. They assumed that, hidden within the large crowds on Sunday mornings, there were political elements intent on overthrowing the government. Suspicious of everyone, the Marxists were either unable or unwilling to see that Christians who keep their word and work conscientiously are the best assets any government can have.

It took several months after the church closure for MKC members to ponder what had happened and develop ideas on how to regroup. The leaders who had not gone to prison tried to be careful to avoid offending kebele leaders, so they maintained a low profile. They knew, however, that they must find a way to encourage each other.

Meanwhile, women's groups started to meet in homes and sent word to MKC leaders that they should take the risk to do the same. Slowly the men emerged. "God gave us the idea to have cell groups," one elder recalled in 1996. Women were meeting and praying that God would give courage to the men.

The men, without the opportunity to meet together freely, tried to find a way to move. They didn't know whom to trust. Doubts and fear were rampant. Under Marxism, everyone was suspect. However, when church leadership was provided through the underground system, people regained trust and started to gather.

Meeting places were chosen. Five people were assigned to each group, except for holidays, when larger groups could gather under the guise of celebrating the holiday. To keep the underground system secret, no group knew about the functioning of any other group. Only a few leaders were in the know. These leaders kept information from the people so they could honestly say that they did not know about other functions of the church, if they were called by the kebele for questioning. In Nazareth, persons attending meetings in Gebreselassie Habtamu's house did not know the people meeting next door in Beyene Mulatu's house. Meeting locations were constantly changed. Groups never discussed what other groups were doing.

In Addis Ababa, groups sometimes were as large as ten or twelve. When rumors spread about new government crackdowns, the groups would quickly divide and reduce their numbers. Larger groups would gather for birthday celebrations. During the holidays of Christmas or Epiphany, forty or fifty people would meet together. They celebrated Christmas as the birthday of Jesus, with a large cake. If government officials questioned them, they reported that they were celebrating a birthday.

For these larger meetings, the group had to obtain permission from the house owners so they could reckon with the chance of a government search. Church leaders made decisions about the reorganization of groups, sometimes assigning people to a house fellowship some distance away, where they were not likely to know other participants. Leaders also prepared Bible study outlines so that all groups were studying the same material. The total number of members was never known precisely, except that the leaders knew the number of house fellowships and could multiply by five or seven to make an estimate.

Kassa Agafari explained on a visit to the States in 1990 that five to seven people formed a cell group, and that two to four of these groups (up to twenty people) formed a house fellowship. Cell groups meet weekly; house fellowships meet monthly to celebrate the Lord's Supper.[2]

New members were added to the groups through individual witness. Special evangelists discipled such persons from six months to a year. When it was clear that their confession of faith was genuine, they would be introduced to a group. Each group had a mixture of older and younger people.

"It was a special movement of God, something that we had not seen before," says Beyene Mulatu, who has served in church institutions for thirty-five years. "Before this, believers were few, and it was hard work to get people to accept the gospel and to keep them following on with the Lord. Now it seems that things just happened."

Beyene continued: "When I think back, I realize we tried to shape our church by writing a constitution, so our church would appear proper, having a clear administrative structure that we could show to anybody and say, 'This is what we have.' " Beyene chuckled. "But God didn't want it that way; he did it his own way, and we are thankful for that. We had to forget all our paperwork."[3]

During the difficult underground years, God called a number of leaders to devote themselves to minister to the house fellowships. One was Kedir Delchume, pastor at the Nazareth congregation. He shared with the elders his call to carry on an itinerant ministry and received their blessing. The MKC Executive Committee and General Church Council did not continue in the early days of the underground. So the Nazareth congregation chose one of their evangelists and four of their elders to form a committee that would give leadership. Although illegal, it was relatively easy for five to meet. No one was afraid.[4]

At Kedir's direction an elder came from each of five churches, Addis, Mojo, Wonji, Shoa, and Nazareth. To avoid the risk of a large meeting, they agreed that the Rift Valley church leaders and the Dire Dawa leaders should meet in their own areas.

Kedir then visited the Dire Dawa and Rift Valley churches, nine in all, and proposed that the General Council meet on Yekatit 13, 1975 (February 1983), with one representative from each of the fourteen churches. This was one year after MKC had closed. The men did not even discuss these plans with their wives. Because the Nazareth elders were uncomfortable with such a large meeting, the group met in Addis Ababa, in pastor Kassa Agafari's home.

Ten of the churches each sent a representative, making a total of eleven, counting Kedir. It was the first underground General Church Council meeting, and it continued to meet twice annually during the underground years. A new Evangelism Committee was chosen, which appointed a committee for training leaders from 1984 onward.

Kedir says he took these initiatives because he had a burden to do so. He ran great risks in traveling to many communities and nurturing the home groups. Kedir secured a letter from Herb Kraybill, director of Mennonite Mission, saying he was employed as a purchaser for the mission. He never had to show it during the ten years the church was underground. When he stayed in hotels, he would write on the register that he was employed by Mennonite Mission.

The Marxist government set up a compulsory service program, known as *Zemecha.* It assigned teachers and students to teach in government schools or open adult literacy classes, especially in rural areas. Christians serving in this program shared the gospel and immediately began to organize congregations wherever they went. This was a new thing. Even though MKC members previously had gone to many communities to serve as dressers and teachers, they didn't usually plant new congregations. One exception was Million Belete, who started fellowships in Mekele and Bahir Dar in the 1960s. In the 1980s, God gave his people a new vision for the *Derg* years.

According to Kedir, Daniel Mekonnen, an evangelist with

the gift of healing, helped the church have its own identity through the revival meetings he held four years before the closure of the church. Wherever members traveled, they now would say, "We are MKC people." This had meaning because reports of healings had made the church widely known. Thus it was easier to establish new fellowships under the MKC name. Before 1978, persons who believed as the result of MKC's traveling preachers would join whatever evangelical group happened to be in their community.

When the church had to go underground, Kedir had a vision and a burden for new believers. In 1984, he visited four or five new believers in Jimma who had gone there from Nazareth. He stayed a week, serving the church affiliated with the Philadelphia Church Mission (Heywet Birhan), which was also underground. In addition, he contacted Freheywet Alebachew, a member from MKC in Dire Dawa; Fikru Zeleke, assigned by the government as registrar of the Jimma Agricultural College; and Emebet Mekonnen, a high school biology teacher. He asked them which church they would like to join, Mulu Wengel or Heywet Birhan. "Neither," they replied. "They have their own programs, and if we join either one, we will not feel comfortable."

So Kedir laid hands on Fikru and Birhanu Zewdie, a

Emebet Mekonnen, dean of Meserete Kristos College, was a founding member of the Jimma congregation during the underground years. *Jonathan Charles photo.*

World Vision employee who visited Jimma once a month, and prayed for them. Before he left, Kedir gave them Matthew 28:18-19 as the mandate for their ministry. They wondered why they were given the text since neither of them were church leaders.

Fikru took this charge seriously. He witnessed and instructed new believers in the faith. Along with Freheywet, he continued to witness, and people kept on being added to the group. Soon officials began to watch what Fikru did and where he went. The security department checked his mail. So Fikru instructed believers as he took walks with them, giving them a few verses he had written out on slips of paper. Sometimes he met believers at a table in a hotel dining room frequented by town officials. Here they prayed with their eyes open and passed around handwritten Scripture passages.

Once in 1985, with the help of traveling evangelist Getaneh Ayele, Fikru baptized eighteen new believers in a government hotel while Communist officials were drinking on the porch. The believers came and left two at a time, at twenty-minute intervals.

Not more than five believers met in each house fellowship; more than that was illegal. The groups did not know about each other. Fikru moved among the groups, teaching new believers and training leaders. When believers went or were transferred to other towns for employment, Fikru would visit them and encourage them to start new fellowships.

Reflecting on those days, Fikru commented that such intense activity under an antagonistic government could not have happened by the efforts of flesh and blood. "The grace of God and the power of the Holy Spirit exceed all other things," he said.

In November 1985, a guard from the security department came to Fikru's office. He handed him a summons to appear for questioning. Pulling out a pistol, the guard ordered Fikru into a closed van. At the regional security office, he accused Fikru of spreading the faith of the forbidden MKC, a religion that had been outlawed. The officer had a pistol lying on the table; several secretaries were writing.

"From the time I entered the man's presence, a special power came upon me which was not of my own—something I had not experienced before. So I began to dispute with him. I told him I'm preaching a permitted gospel and that I have permission to do so." The officer cited the number of the government order for the closing of MKC and pronounced Fikru a criminal.

Fikru replied, "I have permission from the King of kings." When asked to show his permission, Fikru pulled a small Bible from his pocket and read from Matthew 28:18-19. "All authority in heaven and on earth has been given to me. Therefore go and make disciples of all nations" (NIV).

Becoming angry, the guard slapped Fikru on the face. They debated for ten hours, from 10:00 a.m. to 8:00 p.m. Finally Fikru was released after he promised not to invite people into his home for teaching. However, he made it clear that he would teach anyone who came to his house on their own, without an invitation. Later the officer himself was imprisoned for some reason and eventually received the Lord.

"It is the power of the Spirit that sends people forth with the gospel. This I have learned. It was the power of the Spirit that enabled me to dispute with that officer," Fikru testified.

Thus an MKC congregation was formed in Jimma, not because it was planned, but because "it was the leading of the Lord." Today the Jimma District is a major church center, with more than six thousand members in eight congregations and forty-two church plantings.

The underground church found ways to carry on its ministry against great odds, including the gathering and distribution of tithes and offerings. Financial support for Kedir and other evangelists continued even though there were no regular offerings or bank accounts. For six years (1983 to 1988), Kedir served as general coordinator for MKC and as evangelist for the Nazareth church. He received support from the central treasury for any work outside his congregation. Kedir received money from individuals and kept records.

Once someone asked Kedir whether he feared that he might be ordered to turn over his records to the kebele. He replied, "You have to trust the Lord; there is no other way." The head office of the MKC was in his bedroom. Kedir admitted that the security people knew many things, and it would have been a simple matter for them to investigate his activities. "But," he emphasized again, "no one was allowed by the Lord to contact me; it was the protection of the Lord, and we thank him for it. It was not safe to serve the Lord at that time unless you trusted him fully."

Trust and keep secrets, there was no other way. Kedir didn't even share with his wife what he did. It would have been dangerous for family members to be in the know.

Hailu Cherenet, an evangelist, began in 1990 to serve house fellowships in Addis Ababa. He told about caring for the money contributions:

> Trusted brothers and sisters were chosen to handle the finances. We divided Addis into different *keftenyas,* using the same terms the government used for political divisions. In my area, I was responsible for three keftenyas, which included twenty-some kebeles, about eight hundred members at that time. In each keftenya, we had eight or nine trusted people who would bring the offerings and tithes to the most trusted people. We had a big book, and we wrote their names and amounts.
>
> The deacons would verify the records and transfer the funds to the treasurer, who was one of the elders. We used the same treasurer for eight or nine years because it was difficult to change treasurers. It was risky, of course, but we were praying at the same time. We kept two sets of books, stored them at different places, and moved them to a different home every week.

That treasurer was a merchant, so that when he was seen counting money or depositing it in the bank, people would not think that he was keeping church money. The church money was kept in a different bank from the one he used for his business deposits. He would take the money and deposit it. Then the bank account records would be kept in another elder's house. So when we needed money two people would withdraw it, the one who kept the account and the one who was collecting and depositing the money.[5]

However, the sudden shutdown was still a surprise to some congregations. "It took us two months to decide how we could organize house fellowships," recalled Yohannis Germamo, a church leader at Wonji near Nazareth. While the men were trying to find a way to have planning sessions without being detected, the women started to have *mahiber* meetings, associations native to the culture, which arranged for feeding people at funerals and weddings.

Tenfaylish Yigezu, the leader of this approach in Addis Ababa, told the women, "If the security people check on us, we will simply put our Bibles away, pick up our coffee cups, and tell them we are having a *mahiber* meeting." With this approach, they dared to move beyond the five or seven people which the church had recommended as the maximum number who should meet in a house fellowship.

By mid-March, six weeks after the church closing, the Addis Ababa congregation of two thousand people were meeting in a hundred homes throughout the city. One by one they came as dusk settled over the capital at 6:00 p.m. Two or three hours later, they left the same way, to avoid detection. A meeting held on Monday evening at a believer's home was moved to another house and held on Tuesday evening the next week. Thus believers encouraged each other as they sang softly, shared their testimonies, and searched the Scriptures for guidance in such a time of duress.

In Wonji, leaders also devised strategies for meeting.

Yohannis Germamo held meetings for leaders in his car as they drove through the cane fields of the sugar estate. Two persons would ride their bicycles together and make plans as they rode. For several years, the government posted guards on six-hour shifts around the clock at Yohannis' house to assure that he did not carry on any religious activity. He had signed a pledge that he would not preach openly. However, they were unable to get evidence against him about his many underground activities. Yohannis testified about God's protection during those years: "The Lord helped us."[6]

Getaneh Ayele, called by "a voice" to go to the Meserete Kristos Church in Addis Ababa and accept the Lord, was a zealous evangelist during the underground period. He would go from group to group in Addis, encouraging and teaching them and preparing new believers for baptism. About eight months after the church was closed, he arranged a baptism for about forty new believers on a single day, using the large home of a believer. Most MKC leaders in Addis were present. No one anticipated that the friends of baptismal candidates would accompany them, swelling the number to about eighty people. When Kassa Agafari and Yeshitela Mengistu saw every corner of the house packed, they were aghast at the risky nature of the celebration. They quickly told Getaneh that it was not wise to give such visibility to a baptism.

Getaneh replied, "The people are not afraid; so don't you scare them." The baptisms began in the bathtub. Halfway through, they drained the tub to start again with clean water. Then they discovered that the water would not flow. Volunteers went to nearby homes with pails to fetch more water. Neighbors, thinking there must be a fire, knocked on the door to offer their help. By this time, the homeowner, already embarrassed by hosting such a large group, was sweating profusely as he tried to give the neighbors excuses for the unusual activity. After this, church leaders agreed that seven persons should be the maximum number meeting at any one time in a house fellowship, and that no more than one church leader should be among them.

However, risky operations were commonplace for Getaneh. He left the highways and traveled on foot, to reach towns in the countryside. There he evangelized and instructed people in the faith. He baptized people in the hotels where he put up for the night. His many miles of walking permanently damaged his legs.

Getaneh also worked with the Addis Ababa elders in dividing the city into five areas: north, east, south, west, and central. Thus elders could localize responsibilities of shepherding the house fellowships and avoid having anyone travel a long distance for Christian nurture. This agreement was reached after considerable discussion, because some wished to keep activity at a minimum during the time the government was maintaining sharp surveillance. Eventually the elders agreed to map out suitable divisions.[7] Today a congregation exists in each of these sections, and other daughter congregations were established as well. By 1997, there were seventeen congregations in Addis Ababa and its suburbs.

Missionaries did not attend the house fellowships, although sometimes they went to larger gatherings held on holidays when it seemed safe to have a family or community event. Believers were careful to disguise their worship and Christian nurture meetings as typical holiday celebrations. Funerals provided an excellent opportunity for evangelicals to gather in large numbers. As part of the funeral service, the gospel was preached openly, clearly, and with great fervor. During the next few days, people quietly let it be known that they had been touched by the service and were ready to make a faith commitment.

When persons accepted the Lord through someone's witness, that believer instructed them or put them in touch with a teacher who monitored their spiritual growth and prepared them for baptism. After baptism, which might be a year after their first decision, they were introduced to a house fellowship where they could relate with others. This way the church avoided persons who might join a house fellowship just to spy for the government. Even so, believers were on constant guard. One night a dream revealed a spy to an evangelist. The next day, he recognized that same man in a group meeting. So the evangelist dismissed the meeting and said they would meet some other time.

Evangelists continued their rounds, encouraging the house fellowships for ten years, from 1982-91. They had no work permits, since Bible teaching was not considered a valid job. Often they risked imprisonment because they didn't carry proper identification papers. Frequently they carried study materials in quantity, which would be confiscated if found. Kassa Agafari, a pastor who traveled extensively during the underground, says that often at checkpoints, God apparently blinded the eyes of the inspector so he did not see the materials. Sometimes an inspector might be secretly sympathizing with the evangelical movement. The stories from the underground days have a recurring motif about God's intervention in miraculous ways.[8]

In 1986 Kassa Agafari summarized the lessons from the underground: "When we were dispossessed of material things, we began to reach for spiritual realities. We used to go to church in the hope of gaining material things. Now there is none of that. We try to use the wisdom God gives us in planning for meetings, but we live by faith that God will care for us."

Then Kassa concluded with a comment to the missionaries that is touching for its great humility: "We realize now that we could have learned much more from you when you were here, but we were then in our childhood."[9]

So many people were suffering for their Christian witness that the imprisonment of the six leaders did not become a preoccupation for the church. Because the political situation was so tense, it was not considered wise to make an appeal to the government for their release. Once when Paul G. Landis, president of Eastern Mennonite Missions, visited Ethiopia, he assured the families of the detained leaders that the church in North America was praying diligently for the release of the men. The families' response overwhelmed him: "We appreciate your prayers, but we have not been praying for their release; we pray instead that God will enable them to faithfully witness in the prison."

MKC members living in large houses willingly volunteered the use of their homes for house fellowship meetings. They took the risk to do this, knowing that at any time the cadres from the kebele could come and search or ransack their houses, and even take them to prison. Mersha Sahele hosted fellowships in his home through the underground years. He said, "When we gave our home for an underground church, we were ready to suffer the consequences. We locked all the doors and went ahead. God actually gave us a cover, and I was not afraid." Although believers used caution, they did not live in fear or allow fear to paralyze them. "We were with the Lord, and the Lord was constantly teaching us," said Mersha's wife, Metasebiya Ayele.[10]

The MKC continued to train persons to serve as cell leaders during the underground period, but everyone was always cautious. If it seemed too risky, meetings would be discontinued. When committees met, the members arrived alone and never with another person. They never shook hands or gave greetings in a doorway. If there was a back door, some would use that. Believers took special precautions if they thought someone was following them.

The Marxist pressure, with its political and atheistic teachings, led some MKC members to go astray. Yet the turbulent times also brought many to the church in search of meaning for

Metasebiya Ayele, a nurse, assisted in organizing house fellowships after the church was closed in 1982.
Arlene Hege photo.

their lives. Gradually leaders developed a system for discipling the seekers in each congregation. The methods were found to be so effective that they are still used today.

Each new believer would pass through several screenings before being recommended for baptism. Even so, a few agents slipped through the grid, saying and doing all the "right" things so they could gather information about the church's activities. During intense prayer meetings, as believers prayed fervently for the defeat of Satan, sometimes those who came without sincerity would cry out and actually become converted. Sometimes believers prayed for God to cast out evil spirits.

Today, house fellowships still function in a similar manner. New believers are discipled by evangelists and elders. After about six months, they are recommended for baptism—if they have not missed any of their instruction classes on following Jesus and the doctrines of the church. At this point, cell group leaders in a pastoral care committee discern the gifts and needs of baptized members and assign them to a fellowship that meets near their home. Every member is engaged in some type of ministry. To equip them for their ministries, the believers attend weekly classes after baptism for another six months on the subjects of discipleship, forgiveness, and spiritual authority.

Each congregation has ten committees to see that all aspects of Christian nurture are supplied: great commission, prayer, women's, deacons', youth and choir, Sunday school, Bible study, marriage counseling, education, training, and pulpit. People who show themselves reliable and qualified are chosen to serve with greater responsibility as evangelists, administrators, and pastors.

The life of the church is in the house fellowship. "A member may miss the large gatherings on Sundays, but none should miss the Bible studies and prayer times in the small groups," remarked Hailu Cherenet, currently a student at Eastern Mennonite Seminary. While addressing a meeting of stateside Mennonites, he said the day of "spectator Christianity" is over. In the MKC, every member must carry some kind of responsibility.

The house fellowship is a basic element in MKC life today, even though the church is free to meet openly since the overthrow of the Marxist government in 1991. The small group is a way to cope with discipling some twenty thousand new people joining the church each year. Hailu said we should never think of the church as totally free. Satan is always trying to defeat the elect, and constant vigilance and prayer are needed to keep the evil one at bay.

One evangelist saw the underground days as strengthening the church. "If we had not been closed, if we had not suffered persecution, we would still be a small church and not have grown as we have today," he said. Some leaders, however, said that growth was already significant before the church closure. They attribute the rapid expansion to prayer, inspired and empowered by the Holy Spirit.

The pressure brought on the church by the Derg taught the church to be self-reliant and independent. Tithing became an important part of church membership. Teaching on tithing often stressed Malachi 3:8, "Will a man rob God?" The people responded generously, saying, "We don't want to be thieves; please take our tithes." The church was able to hire many full-time workers.

After the church was closed, it continued to have sufficient funds to support many evangelists, and all this without the use of banks or central bookkeeping records. "There was a great deal of trust among us," one treasurer remarked. This was highly unusual, because during the days of the Derg, it was commonly assumed that no one could be trusted.

When the church was officially opened again, EMM, MBM, and MCC helped raise funds above budget to assist MKC congregations in building church buildings. Between 1992 and 1996, these contributions amounted to $400,000 U.S., a small fraction of the total amounts members themselves raised. The central office allocated amounts for construction after assessing a congregation's own ability to raise funds.

MKC congregations contributed over $300,000 U.S. in

1996, 20 percent of which they sent to the central office for general administration, education of leaders, and church plantings. The rest they used to support local leaders and for outreach in their own areas. Funds for church buildings were raised by congregations who put on special drives in addition to the tithes and offerings they gave on a regular basis.

Meserete Kristos Church in its first twenty-five years developed fourteen congregations in two regions of the country, Shoa and Hararge. No one could have predicted that the Marxist Revolution would be a factor in moving this church into all fourteen regions of the country. MKC members "were scattered abroad," as the Scriptures say of the early church, and they established house fellowships wherever they went.

15

Into Every Region

Samuel Bateno set out on September 27, 1989, for Addis Ababa, about two hundred miles north, to search for the Meserete Kristos Church (MKC). He was sent by sixteen evangelical believers who had been ostracized by their own church in Shone, fifty miles southwest of Sheshemane. That rejection came because of their intense search for a deeper spiritual life and their practice of the charismatic gifts.

This group of sixteen wanted renewal in the church and committed themselves to long hours of prayer. They were rebuked by the elders for kneeling for prayer in the church and for their charismatic expressions during the service. The atmosphere became tense when the elders tried to physically push the young people out of the church building.

The sixteen had fasted and prayed that God would lead them to a church that would shepherd them and give them guidance. They knew MKC only as a name, but they listed it along with four other possibilities and took a vote by secret ballot. All sixteen of them chose MKC. So they prepared a letter for Samuel to carry and sent him off with 30 birr they had gathered for bus fare. Samuel stashed what he thought would be enough *dabo* (Ethiopian bread baked with spices) in his bag to last a week. He had only 10 birr left after buying his bus ticket. That evening he looked for lodging for two birr in a city of three million people, where he had seldom been before. He was looking for the Meserete Kristos Church, which at the time had no office or address. Its leaders were scattered, and its people were meeting in small groups in homes underground.

In some areas MKC members bring grain to church for their tithes. Here evangelist Debebe from Mojo displays grain stored in an offering house beside the church. *Jonathan Charles photo.*

Samuel had no names of MKC leaders in Addis. The only clue, which he could not interpret, was that one of their group had received a vision of someone washing their feet. (The Shone group did not know that MKC practiced foot washing as an ordinance.) Samuel kept asking people whom he recognized whether they knew of MKC. After searching for a week, he contacted Belay Mengesha and sister Senait Abebe, a nurse, who promised to take his petition to MKC leaders. Samuel returned home.

Today among the Hadiya people of the Shone Region are 19 MKC congregations (and 12 outreach fellowships) with 9,000 members. They have grown from the 16 committed believers who were troubled by their church not accepting their charismatic expression.

MKC leaders in Addis contacted the denominational leaders of the other church about the conflict at Shone. Finally it was mutually agreed that the group was free to join MKC.

Many towns in southern Ethiopia previously associated with other evangelical groups now also have MKC congregations: Abuka, Arba Mench, Jarso, Shone, Welayta Sodo, and Durame are a few of these. In addition to reaching many of the Hadiya people, God has enabled the churches of the Shone Region to bring Muslims to the Lord through the healings of several of their children. Also in 1996, about 150 members of a Mormon Church in the area said they had been deceived by their Mormon teachers. They applied for membership in MKC. Another special blessing of the Lord has come through the reconciliation of the MKC group at Shone with the group they left. They now worship in each other's churches.

An elder at Shone, in reporting this story, says that finding MKC was like finding a home in comparison to what they had been through.[1] Today the two denominations at one location at least have meetinghouses within sight of each other. They have made peace, and members from each church attend the special conferences and holiday service celebrations of the other. Christians have formed a joint committee that coordinates the work of five denominations in the area: MKC, KHC, Mulu Wengel, Mekane Yesus, and Birhane Heywet.

The Hadiya people are industrious and resourceful. In addition to farming their land and pasturing their cattle, they spend weeks carefully preparing food from the false banana plant by scraping, washing, and curing it. They make a staple product which can be stored in the earth for a year or more, to carry them through times when the rains fail and grain is in short supply.

Giving to the Lord is part of their faith. Though unemployment is high and many do not really operate within the cash economy, on Sundays they bring their tithes and offerings to support the outreach of their churches. All tithes and offerings go for evangelism, and extra drives are made to raise money for erecting church buildings. Tithes are expected. A receipt is given for them; they are not put in the Sunday morning offering.[2]

Although the people's mother tongue is Hadiya, they have chosen Amharic as their official language so they can communicate with other ethnic groups in the area. The Bible is not yet available in the Hadiya language.

At the Bulgita congregation, two elderly men, with keen recollections of the Italian occupation 1936-41, compared the church now with the church then. Those were the early days, when only a few people believed as a result of SIM efforts in southern Shoa Region, dating from 1927. Persecution came from Orthodox believers and from the Italian occupation troops. The elders recalled how complete their renewal was. They were not tempted by the wealth of others when the Italians, on the eve of their ouster, opened the bank and told anyone to come take whatever money he wanted. One elder asked, "Would the youth of today have such restraint?" Without answering his own question, this saint for sixty years praised God for pouring out his Spirit on this generation, bringing a renewal equal to if not exceeding that of those early years.[3]

In addition to the Shone churches, fourteen congregations make up the Middle Rift Valley Region and are located around Sheshemane and the lake region and north along the road toward Addis. Some of these are Awasa, Butajira, Adamitulu, Zway, Wenlencho, Meki, and Alem Tena. The Middle Rift Valley congregations also have twenty-three outreach fellowships.

Many of the congregations in the Rift Valley developed during the Marxist years as an outreach from Nazareth. Each district now has developed a systematic plan for outreach and nurture. They set goals; they know what they hope to accomplish this year and next. They keep thinking ahead. They disciple the new believers and constantly train new leaders.

Nazareth, often considered the mother church of the MKC, is also located in the Rift Valley; however, it is part of the Nazareth District of sixteen churches, including four in Nazareth city and four in Wonji. Here fifty new believers are receiving instruction at any given time. They are divided into

Ready to distribute MKC's magazine, *Misikir*. From left: Million Gelelcha, Wariso Fura, Bezuayehu, Berhanu Wakene, Solomon Gebreyes (editor), Showangezaw Zenebe, Ketema Bedaso. *Jonathan Charles photo.*

three or four groups. Teachers receive special training by the pastors to disciple new believers. Some classes meet on Sunday mornings before the worship service. Others meet during the week. Much of this teaching, as well as teaching children in the Sunday school, is done by lay leaders, so the burden of discipling does not fall on full-time church workers.

In 1996, three of the four congregations at Nazareth met for Sunday worship at the location of the first church. As additional shelters are erected, they will move to other areas of the city. Although they meet together on Sundays, they function as four different congregations and are called Nazareth North, Nazareth South, Nazareth East, and Nazareth West. Nazareth South moved out in 1995, but the first church house is still packed each Sunday.

In 1996, Nazareth South, was meeting in a shelter erected beside a rented house. They had to stop their meetings because neighbors complained of too much traffic in a residential area. Apparently the next-door neighbor wanted to sell his house and believed the many people coming and going would make it difficult for him to find a buyer. So the meetings had to be suspended.

Any of the two hundred Mennonite missionaries and MCC workers who served in Ethiopia through the 1950s, 60s, and 70s would be truly amazed if they were to visit the country and see how God has accomplished greater things than they dared to pray for.

Kedir Delchume, pastor at Nazareth, commented on this phenomenon: "We, too, are amazed; we didn't expect it. We were just praying for our survival, and God did something more. Even when we heard the Lord speaking, we had no faith to believe him. Yet he heard us. Yes, we are seeing things we did not expect to see."[4]

MKC has a total of 192 congregations and 310 outreach fellowships where worship is held at least once a week. The map (at the back; see Contents) shows the regions and their congregations as of 1997.

Any church planting may apply for status as a congregation when it has twenty-five members and enough trained leaders to serve as elders, and is able to be financially self-supporting. The central office reviews the proposal and visits the location, then makes a recommendation to the Executive Committee. The fifteen districts average about twelve congregations each, and each congregation has one or more outreach fellowships, many of which are currently in the process of becoming congregations. In the late 1990s, MKC membership was increasing at the rate of 20 percent annually.

North American Christians ask how it is possible for the church in Ethiopia to grow so rapidly. They want to know the secret for such growth in the hope that by following the same patterns, churches in North America will also grow. But can the work of God be put into a formula?

Before Ethiopians will comment on that question, they typically say, "Let's give glory to God; no one can take credit for what has happened." Ijigu Woldegebriel, however, did reflect on an MKC response that God used to bless the churches:

> When the charismatic movement began to expand and various differences arose between Protestant groups, Mennonites were concerned about peace instead of debate. Missionaries would remind us that our chief concern is the spread of the gospel, and that methods are secondary. They had open spirits. The Ethiopian church leaders had the same openness. They profited from the emphasis that charismatic groups placed on the Holy Spirit and were open to what the Spirit wanted to teach the church. Early Mennonites knew persecution, so they accept others who are persecuted. And because we of MKC have been persecuted, we know how to receive those who are persecuted. Persecution has caused many to give themselves to God. We were concerned about what the Bible says rather than putting emphasis on a particular doctrine.[5]

However, the practices of MKC members in the 1980s went beyond the teaching of missionaries. Prayer and fasting were important dimensions of the house fellowship groups. Each Wednesday was set aside for prayer. Sometimes youths would meet for three days of prayer and fasting. People were filled with the Holy Spirit. Some were healed. Many also went out to witness. Evangelists reported that as they prayed, people came. God brought them. The times were ripe for God to work.

The significance of persecution is that it scattered people who then preached wherever they went, as in the early church (Acts 8:4). When the church in Addis closed, it was one congregation. When freedom was given to worship publicly, there were six. Today Addis, including the suburbs, has

Meazu Abebe served in the "One Year for Christ" program. She is secretary at the Mehal congregation in Addis Ababa.
Jonathan Charles photo.

seventeen congregations. The same thing happened in rural areas because Christians were scattered.

However, the new freedoms were slow in coming. Kassa Agafari reported in 1990 on a visit to U.S. that burial plots were hard to get. "We are waging war against the power of darkness. People are open to the gospel because Communism did not give them what they wanted. Most laypeople are involved in ministry," he said.[6]

Even after freedom was given for people to worship openly, the harassment did not stop. When one congregation rented a large hall for meetings, Orthodox priests stirred up the people so that the rental contract had to be suspended. Undaunted, the group began using a high school classroom instead. "We believe that one million people will come to the Lord," Kassa predicted in 1990.

On the eve of the Marxist ouster, MKC members began to meet at six places in Addis for public worship. David Shenk, conducting a seminar in Addis Ababa in 1991, described the great exhilaration when the seminar group decided to risk opening the windows and singing lustily for the first time in ten years. The 1992 video, *Against Great Odds,* described the new freedom as the church emerged into the light of day.

The congregation at Nazareth celebrated the return of their building in a special service on September 1, 1991. *Missionary Messenger* reports the event:

> Two thousand people walked several blocks from the first house fellowship which began when the church was closed. Singing as they marched, they entered the "new" building with continuous joy cries (*ililta*). More than half the audience had to be seated in a tent adjoining the church. . . . Armed guards assured that no one would hinder the celebration. Twenty-nine people responded to an altar call to accept Christ. . . . The leader of the service, overcome by emotion, put his face in his hands and wept. The church building had been closed over nine years.[7]

However, buildings were in short supply. The original ones, even if returned by the government, were completely inadequate to house the members who had multiplied tenfold during the underground. So congregations rented the same halls the government once used for Marxist indoctrination and began to worship in large numbers. Immediately they started to raise money to build and asked North American Mennonites to put up matching funds.

The first buildings were actually shelters, tin roofs on eucalyptus poles to shelter worshipers from sun and rain. Congregations supplemented these with tents pitched alongside for the constantly increasing crowds. Worship was animated, ecstatic, and filled with frequent joy cries. Choirs practiced with new enthusiasm and wrote songs to celebrate their freedom.

16

Expansion to Wollega

Tefera Gonfa sat still on the center of the cornstalk raft as swimmers pushed him across the Blue Nile. His food, secured in a dishlike wooden box, hung on his shoulder. He clutched his Oromo Bible to his chest. If he made a careless move, he could end up in deep water, his mission thwarted. Tefera was taking the evangelical gospel to Gojjam, a stronghold of Ethiopian Orthodoxy for more than a thousand years. He had seen God do a mighty work among the Oromo of Wollega Region, and he believed the people of Gojjam should also hear the gospel.[1]

In the past, most efforts of missionaries to evangelize in Gojjam had ended in failure. Before the Italian occupation of Ethiopia in 1934, Dr. Thomas Lambie of the SIM had attempted to open a mission station in Lalibella, the place of the famous rock-hewn churches built by Emperor Lalibella in the twelfth century. However, it was a mission short-lived. Through the years, the people of Gojjam have followed Orthodox tradition so devotedly that any teaching of a different interpretation of the Bible was always a threat they could not tolerate.

Even as recently as the early 1960s, after Million Belete had built a small chapel in Bahir Dar on Lake Tana, the town rioted and completely destroyed the building. Earlier, Million had succeeded in opening a small bookshop in Mekele. Yet he was constantly at odds with local Orthodox leaders, who would manage to find "heretical" statements in the books he sold.

Tefera Gonfa was a student in the fifth grade at Obora

Tefera Gonfa and Tadesse Negewo (shown here with the author in a recent photo) were pioneers in evangelism in the Wollega Region during the early 1970s. Tefera was ordained pastor by MKC in 1986 and in 1997 oversees 30,000 people in 47 churches. *Arlene Hege photo.*

when he met Mekuria Mulugeta, originally from the Semay Birhan chapel in Nazareth. In 1966, after Mekuria had graduated from the Harrar Teacher Training Institute, the government sent him to teach in Wollega Region. His subjects included morals. Mekuria was not just a teacher; he was also an evangelist who lost no time in instructing interested students in his house during the evenings and urging them to make a commitment of faith in Christ. Tefera was one of those who made that commitment in 1968 at age sixteen. At the age of eighteen, he felt God's call to evangelize his own people.

Tefera left his studies and joined Mekuria and Taddese Negawo, a committed Christian brother who came from Nazareth a year later to teach in the same school with Mekuria. Together they traveled about, preaching the gospel and baptizing people. A great persecution arose against them. All of them were put into prison for four months, accused of being Pentecostals and defiling the faith of the Orthodox Church.

Tefera was still quite young. People said, "What does this kid, in prison with Mekuria and Taddese, know about what he is teaching?" They thought that because of his youth, he had been bought off with candy. Tefera told them that he was not bought with candy but with the precious blood of Jesus Christ.

After he was released from prison, Tefera was not able to teach openly because of the persecution. So he worked in the lowlands, where bandits abounded. By avoiding the main roads and using the secret paths the bandits used, Tefera was able to carry on his ministry. Many times he was seized by the landowners and detained for two or three days. Tefera was still single at this time.

The people in the areas where Tefera worked were either nominal Orthodox or followers of African traditional religions. When they heard that Jesus was able to free them from the fear of Satan, they started to listen. Much of their time and energy was spent in trying to appease evil spirits so their herds would be protected, so their babies would live, and so they could be healed of their ailments.

When Haile Selassie's government fell in 1974, the evangelists enjoyed about two years of respite from harassment. During this time, many grass houses were built for worship. Then the Marxist Derg started to persecute evangelicals and drove them from one area to another. Believers were often imprisoned by the kebeles. In 1977, the country was in turmoil as the new Marxist government tried to organize the people into communes and made things difficult for evangelical Christians.

The burden to evangelize was so strong that Tefera traveled long distances from home. A two-day, three-day, or even a four-day journey one way was not uncommon. For seven or eight hours a day, he walked. At first there were no organized churches; he would preach to the people, spend the night with them, and go on to another village the next day. If he failed to find lodging, he'd sleep in the woods. When working in the area of the Blue Nile, he might cross the river three times in one trip because of the bends in the river.

The Blue Nile flows in a deep gorge three thousand feet below the surrounding plateau. Here at midday, temperatures reach a hundred degrees Fahrenheit in the shade. The canyon sides support only small scrub trees. The valley floor is barren. Sometimes to get to the Oromo people, Tefera crossed through territory of the Shankila, known for fierceness and hostility toward anyone they suspected of being an intruder. Because of their reputation, Tefera feared for his life. Frequently at night, far from the river, tired and hungry, Tefera would spread leaves and sleep under a tree.

Evangelism in Gojam was especially difficult. Tefera was soon marked as an evangelical preacher. Government leaders passed the word around that anyone could kill him without having to answer for the slaying. So Tefera moved from village to village, disguised one day as a tramp, the next as a farmer, the next as a merchant. Sometimes he shouldered a rifle to make it appear he was part of government security forces. He taught, and he moved on.

Once when his life was in special danger, he lived in the forest for a month as people came to him for teaching. He encouraged them not to leave the Lord. He gathered them in a cave and taught them a Bible course. Often he was hungry and thirsty and extremely weary from his many travels on foot. There were no proper roads and no public transportation in the area. The believers brought him food. After three months, he returned home.

How could Tefera face the obstacles? What kept him going? In his own words, "The Holy Spirit kept me going; otherwise there was no hope. There was no money or anyone to give me money. It was only the Holy Spirit who helped me."

At one point, Tefera heard a rumor that the authorities were coming to kill him. A man, though not a believer, took a liking to Tefera and warned him to flee before the police came. Tefera escaped, but many believers, including women, were beaten in the marketplace as officials pressured them to deny their faith. The place was Galisa in Gojam.

In 1968, Mekuria Mulugeta, Taddese Negawo, and other teachers joined with a few of the early believers and announced a conference to be held in Hagamsa, where Jesus would be present. The people took them literally, expecting to see Jesus in person, and over two thousand of them flocked together from a large area. They met under a massive fig tree, the favorite place where local religious leaders held meetings to make sacrifices to Satan or pray for the rains to return. It was the beginning of a great revival.

Many people responded to the invitation to accept Christ. They were encouraged to tell others immediately about the release from fear they experienced. Haga Hirpha, a layman, remembered that he knew nothing of Christian doctrine, but he told others that Jesus had freed him from the fear of Satan, and that Jesus would do the same for them.

Those first believers took faith seriously and suffered many hardships. One brother, Sekata Gelata, tells of his ordeal with government officials who tried to make him drink *araki,* a strong alcoholic beverage which evangelicals refused to touch after they became Christians. The officials beat him mercilessly to break his will. The torture was so revolting that community people gathered round, begging him at least to taste the stuff so the beatings would stop. Sekata was steadfast and spent a few days in prison, where he faithfully witnessed.[2] People noticed the determination of the believers to be faithful to the Lord and the joy of their testimonies. Thereby they attracted hundreds to embrace the Jesus who had set believers free from the fear of evil and would do the same for them.

As Mekuria and Taddese taught, many demons were cast out, many people were healed, and many people were released from idolatrous and satanic worship. This brought a measure of freedom for preaching the gospel, although officially such preaching was outlawed.

In the *weredas* (districts) of Obora, Shambo, Fincha Af, Gediayana, Hinde, and Limu Werede, a powerful revival broke out, and many people came to the Lord. Mekuria and

Taddese traveled around during school breaks, and people came from a distance carrying their food to attend meetings and stay for several days.

Those first believers called themselves the Holy Spirit Believers Renewal Church, but they had no affiliation with anyone else. Mulu Wengel (Full Gospel) was the name of a church he often heard about at the time, but Tefera didn't even know that Mekuria and Taddese related to MKC. When both of them returned to Addis Ababa in 1970, Tefera continued serving alone. Persecution and hardships mounted, but he continued praying. In 1971, Taddese returned to Wollega and served with Tefera for three months.

There were, of course, other brothers who helped with leadership. As they continued in the work of evangelism with Tefera, the Lord enabled them to mature. Since they were not related to any church, they discussed with Taddese and suggested the name *Andinet Amleko Betachristian* (the church which worships in unity). They had a stamp made with that name and started to train evangelists.

During those early years, the church had no policies to follow. Elders were appointed in every congregation, and the leaders used the Bible for guidance in administration. They sent out evangelists; they gathered tithes. As persecution became more severe, a sense of loneliness overwhelmed Tefera, and he realized that they needed to relate to some larger church.

They had heard from Taddese about the Semay Birhan group at Nazareth, who related to Mennonite missionaries. Their investigation led them to MKC, to which they applied for membership. After discussion and prayer, MKC in 1986 received into membership the Wollega churches, with about 2,500 people, even though MKC was operating underground at the time.

Today Tefera oversees 30,000 people in 43 congregations in 4 districts (*kilel*): Sembo, 19 congregations; Degem, 15; Dengeb, 5; and Shambu, 4. He coordinates elders and evangelists as they make plans for growth. When MKC accepted the Wollega group into membership, they ordained Tefera as a pastor (*megabi*) and sent him back to the Wollega Region as the leader of his people.

As churches develop, they put leaders in place, such as deacons and elders, and choose volunteers to serve in the One-Year-for-Christ program. About eighty elders from Wollega, two from each congregation, attended the biennial meeting of the General Church Council in Addis Ababa in February 10-11, 1996. Most of them knew some Amharic, but discussion items leading up to a decision had to be translated into the Oromo language, Oromigna. During the next decade, the MKC is facing a great challenge of working to integrate the Oromo of Wollega into the Meserete Kristos Church so that they feel comfortable.

In the MKC, diverse peoples of Ethiopia can gather in one meeting, working together on the decisions of the church. This shows fulfillment of Paul's teaching in Ephesians about walls being broken down. To facilitate this integration, MKC is preparing instructional materials in Oromigna. The Oromo Bible, which formerly was only available in the Amharic script, is to be printed in the Latin script, which the new generation will accept. The New Testament is already available in the new script. MKC has asked Globe Publishing House to prepare Sunday school materials also in Oromigna, using the Latin script.

In Wollega, the church is giving priority to leadership training. Tefera knew that he alone could not be overseer of so many people. He is arranging for others to be trained to help him.

Like the apostle Paul, Tefera knew plenty and hunger, trouble and persecution, the lack of clothing and a house to live in. But today he calls himself rich because he is the father of nine children. He has a house and a modest salary from the MKC central office.

The Christians in Wollega are still poor, but in comparison to their lives before they found Christ, they are better off now. Tefera said that God blesses the farmers as they plow and plant, and they are able to support themselves. Instead of spending money for alcohol or ceremonies to ward off evil, they teach their children about the Lord, and they give their tithes.

"We don't want to be dependent on anyone. We don't want to live by asking for help from others, because we have lived until now by looking to God. We have experienced the blessings which come from giving what we have in our hands." Tefera spoke with conviction.

Two students, Negash Gerbi and Teferi Mekonnen, recently graduated from the Mennonite Theological College of Eastern Africa in Musoma, Tanzania, and have returned to Wollega. Tefera planned to send five students to the certificate course at the Meserete Kristos College in Addis Ababa in 1996, and the following year send five more. Tefera hopes eventually to have a Bible school in Wollega where students can study in the Oromo language. He would like American Mennonites to partner with them in this endeavor.

The signs and wonders referred to in the book of Acts happen today in Wollega. In the early days, many people believed when they saw Satan cast out and people healed. People left their idol worship and threw away their charms.

Negash Gerbi and Teferi Mekonnen trained at the Mennonite Theological College of Eastern Africa in Musoma, Tanzania, and serve as leadership trainers among the churches in the Wollega Region. *Jonathan Charles photo.*

Today, the sick come to church, are prayed for, and are healed, but their faith is not founded on miracles.

Mekuria visited the Bible Institute in Addis once while Tefera was there, but Tefera would like him to visit Wollega again. "He is my father. I was a child. Now I've grown up," Tefera said. Mekuria works for *Living Hope*, an Amharic radio program in Nairobi which is aired over the Sychelles station.

As he matured in his faith, Tefera came to new understandings of God's grace. He explained how the Holy Spirit gave him new insights:

> I once felt that if I don't suffer hardships, if I'm not imprisoned, if I'm not persecuted, I will not know salvation. I felt that one's salvation was assured by these things, for the apostle Paul says, "Don't be amazed at persecution, for it is a sign of salvation." However, I came to understand that imprisonment is not a goal. I realized that I must carry on my witness. So after that, I moved swiftly from area to area and tried hard to escape those who were searching for me. God often delivered me. God has helped us. We preach, we teach, we go by foot, we go without food. But the Lord helps us.

The Wollega story and the blessings that have come through the faith of this new people group will continue to enlarge the vision of MKC for years to come.

17

Facing Tomorrow

More than 1200 people gathered at the Meserete Kristos Church (MKC) pavilion in Dire Dawa for a spiritual life conference in March 1996. Five denominations, sitting for two days in sessions five hours long, sang and prayed and listened to the Word preached with a concentration and reverence seldom seen among churches in North America. Pastors from the five denominations took turns leading the services.

At the end of each session, an altar call was given, inviting any who would accept Christ for the first time to come forward. By the end of the conference, eighty-six people had answered this call, among them a few who were clearly dressed in Muslim garb.

Temesgen Doche (left) and Tewodros Desta (right) were two of the first graduates of Meserete Kristos College, April 1996. Solomon Kebebe (center) is chairman of MKC. *Arlene Hege photo.*

This response is typical of most evangelical services in Ethiopia. Every Sunday morning a call is given. People who respond are put into classes for discipleship training. Anyone observing this phenomena would immediately think of the Scripture in Acts 2:47: "The Lord added to their number daily those who were being saved" (NIV).

Yet one can hardly call it popular to be an evangelical Christian in Ethiopia today. When persons break from traditional religion and practice, they have to face opposition and ridicule from Orthodox people and the resistance of some families. Such experiences are commonly reported. Nevertheless, today it is much easier to be an evangelical believer than twenty years ago. One can participate with a thousand others in worship and declare oneself a member of one of the evangelical bodies that have gained some respect with the government and the community. The new government even contacted churches and invited them to be legally registered with the Ministry of Internal Affairs.

In 1990, MKC presented copies of its organizational structure and its constitution to the Ministry of Internal Affairs and was registered as a *mahiber* (association), a registration renewable every year.

MKC has made copies of the registration for every local church. The Ministry of Internal Affairs sent copies to the local government of every region, to the Ministry of Information, and to the Commercial Bank. The document is necessary to open a bank account, which each MKC district has in its local area.[1]

Registration with the government in 1990 marked the end of a 25-year effort by MKC to find some way to operate legally in its own country. During all those years, the church had to use the name Mennonite Mission in Ethiopia for any transactions requiring legal documents. However, no one was troubled about it, because church leaders knew that the authority of the church comes from God. It does not depend upon the state for its existence. Leaders also knew that the first Christian churches established by the apostle Paul survived and grew for 300 years without government recognition.

Hailu Cherenet, a teacher at Meserete Kristos College, Addis Ababa. *Arlene Hege photo.*

A new day is dawning in Ethiopia as churches learn to live under a government that does not support any particular religion. The government now gives freedom for all groups to choose their burial plots. Families are becoming more tolerant as they allow family members freedom to choose a church for themselves. Hotels, even in rural areas, are more likely to list meat dishes on their menus during the Lenten fast of fifty-six days.

There are social forces that help move people toward the evangelical churches. One of these is unemployment, which affects many people living in the cities. It is common to find high school graduates who have been looking for work for five, six, or seven years. Congregations work hard to meet the needs of all their members. Unemployed members try to engage in meaningful activities, even if there is little pay. Prayer is seen as the most important work.

One reason the church can carry on an intensive program of instruction classes and seminars is that many members do not go to a job on a regular basis. Also, many retired people volunteer their services to the church. Because the legal retirement age is fifty-five, retirees who manage to live on their retirement income are available to instruct new believers and encourage and pray for the younger people.

Much of the praying, after periods of praise and adoration, is asking God to supply basic needs, to show job opportunities, or to heal the sick. Most congregations have a midweek meeting they call a healing service. When believers do find employment, they continue to spend many volunteer hours serving the church. Tithing is taught and expected from all members.

Singing is a significant part of worship. The congregation does not have songbooks, but with much repetition and frequently the help of a synthesizer or guitar, they learn many songs and choruses. Even small children join in the singing and clapping. A choir usually ministers at each service. Each church usually has at least one choir with its own color of robes. The choirs in their robes are beautiful, but the quality and depth of their original music outshine their robes.

Choir members must commit themselves to pray, to attend practice times, and to ask God for inspiration to write songs and compose music. Most choirs write their own music and prepare for a music ministry to many congregations and across denominational lines. Discipline of delinquent members actually happens, and the group is able to discern which reasons make absences legitimate.

The A choir of twenty-five members in Dire Dawa, for example, survived the Marxist years by meeting for practice at the Catholic church and then singing in homes and at funerals. "We would check the landscape first, then go; we were considered 'harmless children,' " said Johni Teklu, the choir's leader. The A Choir travels to all the churches of the Dire Dawa district and sometimes ministers in churches of other denominations. They have 194 songs in their repertoire, written and composed by their own members. The choir studies the new songs, sings and evaluates them, and then either selects or rejects each one by a vote. In 1994, the choir produced a cassette tape of a dozen songs and netted 1,700 birr on the sale of 5,000 copies. "It was the grace of God that made it happen; we prayed about it a lot," Johni said.[2]

Prayer undergirds their ministry. Twice a month the choir

spends all night in prayer, Bible study, and practice, 9:00 p.m. till 6:00 a.m. "God keeps us awake; God gives us strength, and we love each other. God mysteriously provides in a way which cannot be explained in human terms," says Girum Tadesse, secretary for the A Choir. The Dire Dawa congregations also have three other choirs: B Choir, Agape, and Rehobote.[3]

Erecting church buildings is important for MKC, not only to use for Sunday worship, but to use all week long for instruction classes, prayer meetings, choir practice, and activities for youth and for women. Seldom would a visitor find a church building empty and closed on any day of the week. Local governments in rural areas will often grant plots of land as building sites for congregations, providing the church promises to be involved in social activities such as running kindergartens and clinics. In urban areas where the price of land is high, congregations often rent a dwelling and build a shelter on the plot. Walls and a concrete floor may be added as the people are able to raise the funds.

During the underground years, women played a prominent part in organizing house fellowships. MKC estimates that 70 percent of the small groups were led by women during those years. A few served as elders.

Today the church is discussing the question of women in leadership. As of 1997, women do not serve as pastors or elders. Yet they do minister as evangelists, deaconesses, Sunday school teachers, prayer group leaders, and Bible study group leaders. One woman is a member of the development board at the national level, and five serve on an executive committee to lead women's activities at the national level.

MKC believes its stance in relation to women is progressive. In a male-dominated society, it is only in evangelical circles that women are treated equally. In the Ethiopian Orthodox Church, women do not usually have leadership positions.

The MKC is not bent on developing its own identity in isolation from other Christian groups. Its leaders regularly serve in executive positions of the Evangelical Fellowship of Ethiopia, an association which coordinates the work of most evangelical bodies in the country. Members of a church have opportunities to serve; one has to have a home base, commented one leader. Leaders do not want to be restricted by one denomination but to fellowship with members of Jesus Christ, from whatever denomination, and to serve in their churches as well. MKC leaders are constantly called on by other denominations to preach and to hold seminars on various subjects.

MKC sees it as important to be a reconciling presence among the various denominations of the country, encouraging peaceful cooperation instead of competition. When renewal groups emerge, they may come for counsel and Bible study materials or even to ask for teaching on how to interpret the Scriptures—if they are assured that MKC will not steal their members. One leader said, "We pray for renewal groups, for the guidance of the Holy Spirit, and for their protection. We do not try to take their members."[4] MKC encourages the cooperation of all groups in evangelizing Ethiopia and in mission beyond her borders. As the beginning of its foreign outreach, there is a congregation in Djibouti and one in Eritrea.

The new move of the Holy Spirit in Ethiopia, which started over thirty years ago, was not the beginning of a new denomination. Instead, it was a student movement that came to the already-established churches and has affected almost every denomination in the country.[5]

Today Orthodox people are experiencing renewal as the evangelical churches experienced it a generation ago. Bedru Hussein described his vision for the future: "As renewal spreads throughout the land, I believe Christians will develop a new compassion to reach out to Muslims."

MKC is more interested in seeing the Orthodox Church experience renewal than to oppose its teachings. As far as possible, MKC encourages newly converted Orthodox to return to their church and serve there. Although some in the renewal movement want to stay in the Orthodox Church as

Church elders and evangelist at the Nazareth East congregation, 1995. From left, standing: Tegestu Sahele, Zeleke Dadie, Germa Tema, Yaekob Lumbamo, Shewangezaw Tafesse. Seated: Fekadu Argaw, Tefera Tagesse, Kifle Denboba. *Jonathan Charles photo.*

long as possible, others are keen to leave it. Staying in the church is difficult, for as soon as the renewed ones begin teaching, they are known to be different. Some Orthodox leaders make it clear that people making an evangelical profession are not welcome in their churches. In spite of opposition, many faithfully carry on a witness that results in still others coming to evangelical faith.

MKC wants to be available to minister to any group. The Bible College in Addis Ababa and the regular seminars and courses that are constantly offered at the regional level— these are open to all groups, including Orthodox members. MKC wants to live in peaceful coexistence with the Orthodox Church.

Meserete Kristos Church, now comprising close to one-tenth of Mennonites worldwide, is a member of Mennonite World Conference (MWC) and actively participates in those meetings held every six years. At its thirteenth meeting, held in Calcutta in 1997, Bedru Hussein, executive secretary of MKC, was elected vice president of MWC. Million Belete, currently vice chairman of MKC, was chairman of the world body from 1972 to 1978.

MKC encourages the expression of charismatic gifts, and most of its members know little about Anabaptist history. However, leaders express great appreciation for the teaching they have received from Mennonite missionaries like Calvin Shenk, on church history and the systematic study of the Bible. Leaders believe that God has poured out his Spirit in a special way on the church and has brought life to the dryness they sometimes experience when relating to Mennonite groups outside Ethiopia. This new life, coupled with an emphasis on solid Bible training, gives MKC a unique role among Ethiopian evangelicals. Others come to them for counsel about church structure and discipleship training.

Children worship along with adults, clapping and singing the songs from memory. *Jonathan Charles photo.*

MKC leaders readily admit that they had to rediscover the early Anabaptist emphasis on evangelism. They believe evangelism is a neglected teaching in typical North American Mennonite communities. As they studied church history more deeply, they discovered that Anabaptists of the sixteenth century were quite active in evangelism. That trait was lost or muffled in later years. MKC could well ask North American Mennonites if they are faithful in practicing the evangelistic outreach of their forebears.

Richard Showalter, president of EMM, commented on MKC's evangelism: "They are in the middle of what some missiologists would call a series of people movements to Christ. In this position, they are not only experiencing tremendous growth but also laying important spiritual foundations and organizational structures which may critically influence the vitality of the church for generations to come. As a young movement, they are vulnerable. Let's give thanks, but let us also pray earnestly, both for them and for us in our relationship to them. We have gifts to share, but we also have much to learn." MKC has few pastors, but 140 people have been commissioned as evangelists.

Traditional Mennonite values are also readily apparent in the lives of MKC members. The Mennonite understanding of community is closer to the African experience than it probably ever was to the wider culture in North America. MKC members share to help those in need with greater abandon than most North Americans know. The hope shown on the faces of worshipers in Ethiopia, a hope which refuses to be intimidated by threats or changing political systems, is a model for Mennonites on any continent. The leaders work to help evangelical denominations work together; such efforts show that they understand peacemaking. The MKC is a church concerned about true Christian doctrine. They have a deep concern to identify error in Christian teaching and to present Christ as the only way of salvation. The MKC letterhead carries Menno Simons' favorite verse in both Amharic and English: "No one can lay any foundation other than the one already laid, which is Jesus Christ" (1 Cor. 3:11, NIV).

The book of Acts in the New Testament describes the first Christian church and thus sets a standard for all churches. Acts 2:42-47 lists many characteristics of MKC today. Here we note attention given to doctrine, fellowship, prayer, and sharing the Lord's Supper with joy. People are filled with awe, and they witness signs and wonders. They share with those in need. Believers worship both in homes and in the temple or church building, and new members are added daily.

Any visitor who spends several months among the Meserete Kristos churches will discover an authentic New Testament church intent on faithfulness to the Lord. Observers see their dependence on the Holy Spirit for guidance and power, their awe and reverence in worship, their joy and sharing with each other, the miracles that bring unbelievers to faith, the perpetual courses and seminars for instruction, and the gatherings in both large groups and small. North American Christians are humbled by the fact that God is indeed pouring out a blessing on Ethiopia that

MKC office secretaries, Addis Ababa. From left: Tigist Alamerew, Birhanech Wolde, Tewabech Deita. *Jonathan Charles photo.*

the Western world will do well to covet for themselves.

Will MKC continue to grow? Part of that answer lies in the sovereignty of God. Part may depend on whether the 900,000 other Mennonites in the world are faithful enough to pray along with their Ethiopian brothers and sisters for growth and spiritual nurture of believers to continue.

The outreach into Gojjam and Gondar in the north, for example, marks a new day for evangelical witness in a strong Orthodox area. The vision of the Bahir Dar Region, now with nine congregations and many church plantings, is evidence that MKC is not reluctant to face difficult tasks. In a pamphlet telling its history, one district leader quotes the prayer of Jabez in 1 Chronicles 4:10, "Oh, that you would bless me and enlarge my territory" (NIV). Then he comments, "We strongly believe that God is leading us to fulfill the work he has entrusted into our hand. We are confident that God, who saw us through every circumstance and brought us this far with signs and with an outstretched arm, will continue to make us a *living witness* to draw many to the Kingdom of Light."

Ethiopian Christians worldwide have a vision for evangelism. They establish congregations wherever they go. Currently there are about a hundred Ethiopian congregations in the United States and Canada worshiping in the Amharic, Oromo, and Tigrai languages. The largest, with over a thousand members, is located in Washington, D.C., where an estimated sixty thousand Ethiopians live.

No missionary or foreign church body dare take credit for the church growth in Ethiopia. It is a work of God for which Christians everywhere can rejoice and give thanks. MKC is not playing the numbers game, interested only in adding churches to their list. Each number represents a person, and daily additions to the church are considered normal, just as recorded in the book of Acts.

The worshiping community in Meserete Kristos churches today numbers about 114,000, including those baptized, those under instruction for baptism, and the children of Christian parents. MKC leaders project that number to grow to one million in the next decade. We need to thank God for a people with that kind of vision. Tilahun Beyene, who is currently writing this same story in Amharic, commented, "When God decrees, he is very efficient; in contrast, man's plans are cumbersome. God allows us to do things our way for awhile; then he takes over to show us the limitations of our wisdom."

As this book goes to press, other books are in the making, being written by Ethiopians called of God to describe their part in a second Reformation happening in the world today.

Epilogue

Meserete Kristos Church (MKC) holds an equal place in our lives with the Lancaster Mennonite Conference. We, Nathan and Arlene Hege, have spent an equal number of years serving in each.

Kind and courteous Ethiopians helped us as immature missionaries to cope with a new culture and language. Ethiopians praised us for each step of progress we made in learning Amharic. They celebrated our wedding in 1951 and rejoiced at the birth of each of our four children. At the birth of our firstborn, we were no longer Mr. and Mrs. Hege; we became the father and mother of John.

When we left Ethiopia in 1974, the General Church Council commissioned Arlene and me to be their missionaries to the stateside church. MKC understands fellowship and the significance of resources and blessings running in both directions.

In the various responsibilities MKC assigned us to do, church leaders constantly insisted that they were selecting persons fitted for the task regardless of their country of origin. We truly felt adopted.

Today, looking back over fifty years, we delight in great memories and thank God for the privilege of having experiences with depth and meaning that we could never have orchestrated ourselves.

The tie between Mennonites of Ethiopia and Mennonites of North America is strong. Through the Marxist years, the church in America prayed daily that God would keep MKC faithful amid persecution. To our surprise, we learned during

a visit to Ethiopia in 1986 that MKC members pray constantly that their brothers and sisters in America would continue
faithful to the Lord in a materialistic and affluent society.

When the MKC asked me to write this book, I counted it
to be a gesture of confidence far beyond anything I deserve.
Arlene and I had the opportunity of returning to Ethiopia,
doing the research, hearing firsthand the many stories of
faith, and observing God's marvelous work in church
growth, now reaching into every region of the country. This
was a unique privilege, reminding us that we are truly
blessed.

We ask forgiveness if at any point in this book we have
misinterpreted information given us. We are conscious of the
book's shortcomings, and we especially regret that we could
not include many notable stories of faithful people. We trust
that the ones selected are representative of many other stories which one day will be published, to better round out the
MKC story.

Ethiopian reviewers of the manuscript urged that this
book not be preoccupied with the faults of either the Marxist
government or the Orthodox Church, although evangelicals
have suffered at the hands of both. They say it is more important to emphasize what God by his grace has done in bringing renewal to many churches throughout the country:
Protestant, Catholic, and Orthodox. MKC calls on Christians
everywhere to praise God for the fulfillment of Scripture.
Ethiopia indeed is stretching out her hands to God (Ps. 68:31,
KJV).[1]

The missionaries to Ethiopia sometimes ask themselves,
"What should we have done differently? Should we have
tried to work within the Orthodox Church, as the Bible
Churchmen's Missionary Society did, following their practice of working for renewal within the Anglican Church of
England?" We had no background to consider this as an
option. Ever since Anabaptists were pushed out of the established churches in Europe, they have taken a dim view of trying to reform such churches from within.

However, in the 1950s missionaries did pray for renewal

in the Orthodox Church. Apparently those prayers are now being answered. Reform groups within Orthodoxy are emerging frequently enough to alarm the mother church. At present there seems to be no way for evangelicals to have meaningful dialogue with the Orthodox. In 1994, leaders of the Evangelical Fellowship of Ethiopia proposed talks with the Orthodox patriarch in an effort to open dialogue. The Orthodox replied, "*We* are the church in Ethiopia, and we have no reason to dialogue with evangelicals."

We reflect upon the lessons which the Ethiopia experience taught North American Mennonites. We learned not to assume that cultural expressions can or should be transferred from one country to another. We came to realize that local believers need the freedom to select, adapt, and create expressions of faith. This was a hard lesson for North American Mennonites, and it took more than a decade to learn it. Early missionaries did work at dynamic equivalents in proposing church polity. That strategy indicates some awareness of cultural problems. But about twenty years had passed before the stateside church began to talk of lessons coming from Africa that could inform the meaning of Christian commitment in North America.

One of the lessons from Ethiopia is cited by the apostle Paul in 1 Corinthians 3:6, "I planted the seed, Apollos watered it, but God made it grow" (NIV). There was no reliable way to evaluate the evangelistic effectiveness of the schools and hospitals while they were functioning in the heyday of their operation. But after these institutions were either given to or taken over by the government, the church had more energy to focus on evangelism.

When the Marxists began to monitor evangelical church activities in 1977, church growth increased. When MKC was officially shut down in 1982, house churches flourished and membership increased tenfold in ten years. Spurred on by the uncertainty of the times, people looked to evangelical Christians for guidance. Evangelism strategies were hardly necessary because the Holy Spirit was bringing people to faith. Church leaders had to put their efforts into nurturing the new believers. God gave an increase far exceeding any-one's projections.

Another lesson coming from MKC is the conviction that these are the last days, the time when God wants to pour out his Spirit on all people (Acts 2:17). Miraculous things happen in the lives of believers, bringing prophecies and healings. Others are awakened to new faith when they see Christian faith becoming relevant to life's questions, and when they see that the change in believers' lives is genuine.

The people experienced difficult times that purified their faith as they fasted and prayed and depended solely on the Lord to direct their steps. The revival during the Marxist years affected all evangelical churches and also brought stir-rings of renewal within the Orthodox Church.

MKC has learned the significance of prayer, that fervent prayer opens the way for the Holy Spirit to work in the lives of people. The MKC members also developed a new aware-ness of the power of evil and the need to resist evil forces with constant prayer. Ethiopian church leaders who visit North America observe that Western Christians do not seem fully convinced that evil forces must be driven back so that people can embrace the gospel. In the counsel of these Ethiopian leaders, North American Christians depend too much on programs and organizational structure. They think too much about working *for* God rather than placing them-selves in the flow of the Holy Spirit and aligning themselves *with* God in work he is already doing.

Reverence for God's Word written is also evident today in MKC leaders' strong emphasis on biblical preaching and teaching. Ethiopians frequently refer to the emphasis Mennonite missionaries placed on the Scriptures. Likewise, MKC puts high priority on the instruction of new believers before and after baptism. Bible instruction courses are con-stantly offered at various levels by the congregations and dis-tricts.

The goal of MKC is to identify some responsibility for every member. Members study the Bible with serious intent. They know that sooner or later they will need to instruct others with the material they learn. A constant request by MKC pastors and evangelists is for study Bibles, Bible dictionaries, concordances, and commentaries.

Dependence on God and fearlessness in the face of opposition is an important lesson that comes to us from the MKC. Church leaders, unable to consult with each other freely during the underground years, had to depend on the Holy Spirit's direction to carry out their ministry. They also depended on the Lord for protection. Although they took reasonable precautions, leaders testify that they often could pass checkpoints without being arrested, even though they were carrying Bibles and Christian literature. Total dependence on the Lord included the surrender of the welfare of the church to the Lord's keeping. "When men usurp authority from the Lord, the church becomes a human organization," one leader commented.

Reflecting on how God has blessed in the past, MKC challenges us to pray that their numbers will increase to one million within ten years. We anticipate rejoicing with them when this goal is reached.

Regions of the
Meserete Kristos Church

SUDAN

Red Sea

ERITREA

YEMEN ARAB REPUBLIC

Blue Nile

ETHIOPIA

Bahir Dar 9 — Lake Tana

Dessie 4

DJIBOUTI REPUBLIC

Gulf of Ade

Dengeb 5

Degem 18
Sembo 20
Shambu 4

Addis Ababa 17

Dire Dawa 9

SOMALILAND

Awash Valley 10

Welliso 4

Nazareth 22

Jimma 9

Hosanna 18

Middle Rift Valley 14

Shone 17

Lake Turkana

SOMALIA

UGANDA

KENYA

Lake Victoria

Meserete Kristos Church has 180 congregations in 15 regions, 12 additional scattered congregations, and 310 outreach fellowships. MKC, with a Christian community of 114,000 people, comprises 2% of the evangelical church membership in a country of 56 million people. July 1997.

Historical Highlights, 1945-1998

1945   Mennonite Board of Missions suggests Eastern
        Mennonite Missions begin a mission in Ethiopia.

1946   EMM authorizes a mission to be opened in Ethiopia.

1947   Daniel, Blanche, and Janice Sensenig, first EMM mis-
        sionaries to arrive in Ethiopia.

1948   Ethiopian government gives permission to EMM to
        open a mission.

1949   Daniel Sensenig and Clinton Ferster begin building
        at Deder.

1950   First annual missionary conference held at Dire
        Dawa; Deder school opened.

1951   Mennonite Relief Committee transfers Nazareth
        Hospital program to EMM; Bedeno school opened;
        first believers baptized.

1952   School for the Blind opened, Addis Ababa; Dresser
        Bible School opened, Nazareth.

1953   Ellen Keener Eshleman passes away.

1954   Girls' boarding school opened at Deder.

1955   Leprosy clinic opened at Deder.

1957   Two Muslims baptized.

1958   Counselors chosen by each congregation to make up
        General Church Council.

1959   The Meserete Kristos Church name chosen; Bible
        Academy opened in Nazareth; Menno Bookstore
        opened in Addis Ababa.

1960   EMM recognized General Church Council of MKC,
        with Daniel Sensenig as chairman; Wonji church
        building built; Good Shepherd School opened.

1961   *Foundation of Faith, Instruction to Beginners in Christian Life,* and *God's Great Salvation,* published in Amharic; 1,000 enrolled in Bible correspondence course.

1962   First General Church Council meets; *Christian Family Living* published in Amharic.

1963   Clinic opened in Awash.

1964   Million Belete, first Ethiopian MKC chairman and first ordained MKC Ethiopian pastor.

1966   MKC applies for government registration; not approved.

1967   Globe Publishing House formed by MKC and Baptist General Conference Mission.

1968   Shamsudin Abdo, first Ethiopian MKC administrator.

1970   MKC organizes evangelism board to plan for reaching new areas.

1971   New buildings at Bible Academy with funds from the government of Holland. Nazareth congregation dedicates a new church building off the hospital compound.

1972   New hospital constructed at Nazareth with funds from Bread for the World, in Germany. Agricultural development project begins at Bedeno.

1973   Public health program launched among Afar people of Awash Valley; MKC with 800 members in eight congregations has a full team of national leaders.

1974   Revolution breaks out and Emperor Haile Selassie deposed. MKC distributes grain from MCC in drought-stricken Awash Valley.

1975   MKC organizes a development board to oversee relief, agricultural, and community development programs.

1976   Deder congregation moves into a new building

away from the mission compound. Leaders from a dozen denominations meet in a unity conference at the Bible Academy in Nazareth; 1,000 people attend.

1978   Nazareth Hospital management transferred to Ethiopian government. MKC opens relief and development project among displaced people in Bale Region.

1979   MKC sends delegation to visit Mennonite and Baptist churches in the Soviet Union.

1980   MKC and MCC begin a reforestation project near Nazareth.

1982   MKC buildings and all its programs closed by government order. Strict publicity ban imposed by MKC.

1983   Evangelism committee formed in lieu of executive committee. First underground General Church Council meeting held in February. MCC negotiates a new contract with the government for development work and appoints five expatriate workers.

1986   Church leaders released after spending four years in prison. A body of believers officially accepted into MKC membership from Horro Guduru, Wollega.

1987   The leadership of MKC transferred from the Evangelism Board to the Executive Committee. MKC constitution revised and amended to fit the underground church.

1988   Kelifa Ali becomes executive secretary for MKC.

1989   Policy on provident fund for full-time MKC workers reinstated.

1990   MKC lifts publicity ban and reports membership statistics to Mennonite press. Believers in Shone Region accepted into MKC membership. Kelifa Ali, executive secretary of MKC, dies at age 41.

1991   Marxist government overthrown. MKC churches begin to worship openly.

1992   Most of MKC administration decentralized to nine regions. Bedru Hussein becomes executive secretary. The video of the MKC story, *Against Great Odds*, filmed in Ethiopia.

1993   One-Year-for-Christ training program begun. MKC constitution revised and amended, reflecting the church's move from underground into the open.

1994   MKC officially registered with Ministry of Internal Affairs of the Ethiopian government.

1995   Bible Institute offering two years of postsecondary studies, opened in Addis Ababa.

1996   About 275 delegates meet in the biennial General Church Council assembly in Addis Ababa.

1997   Bible Institute upgraded to a four-year college offering a degree.

1998   Publication of MKC's 50-year history.

Meserete Kristos Executive Committee Members

(in chronological order of service, 1962-97)

Million Belete
Beyene Mulatu
Desta Alemu
Chester Wenger
Daniel Sensenig
Gemeda Baruda
Negussie Ayele
Haile Woldemichael
Kiros Bihon
Nevin Horst
Shamsudin Abdo
Daniel Lemma
Paul Gingrich
Nathan Hege
Muluneh Bachore
Fissiha Wondimagenghu
Michael Alemayehu
Beyene Chichaïbelu
Calvin Shenk
Paul T. Yoder
Negash Kebede
Teferi Orjino
Tesfatsion Dalellew
Yohannes Germamo
Tilahun Beyene
Solomon Kebede
Birhanu Zewdie
Bedru Hussein
Alemayehu Assefa
Kassa Agafari
Mamo Tekele
Bayessa Wakoya
Goitom Gebreselassie
Kedir Delchume
Solomon Kesete
Haile Gelan
Tesfaye Desta
Tadesse Doyao
Alemu Chekole
Gemechu Gebre
Seyoum Gebretsadik
Mulugeta Zewdie
Negussie Worku

Yeshitela Mengistu
Girma Tekelu
Simon Badi
Kena Dulla
Tsega Wakjera
Aga Hirppa
Zelalem Teferra
Tadele Lejiso
Fikru Zeleke
Demisse Yadetta
Beyene Gutema
Teferi Eshetu
Mekonnen Assefaw
Dawit Kidane
Tefera Bekere
Tefera Gonfa
Zina Tuke
Tesfaye Alemu
Dr. Samson Estifanos
Gemechu Debele
Haile Welebo
Olana Bajra
Negussie Tiruneh
Tadesse Chaka
Tilahun Alemu
Tsegaye Hailemichael

Executive Secretaries

(in chronological order of service, 1965-98)

Nevin Horst
Shamsudin Abdo
Tesfatsion Dalellew
Asrat Gebre
Solomon Kebede
Kelifa Ali
Kedir Delchume
Bedru Hussein
Mulugeta Zewdie

Workers in Ethiopia with MRC, MCC, and EMM

Name	Address in 1997	Years,19xx	Position
Amstutz, Florence	Goshen IN	71-72	Registered Nurse
Amstutz, H. Clair	Deceased	71-72	Doctor
Atkinson, Evelyn	Quakertown PA	74-77	Guesthouse Manager
Bauer, Cheryl	Crossville TN	75-76	Registered Nurse
Bauer, Edward	Crossville TN	75-76	Development
Bauman, Ruth	Goshen IN	50-51	Teacher
Beachy, Dwight	Mylo ND	63-71	Secondary Education
Beachy, Verna Rohrer	Mylo ND	64-71	Bookstore/Homemaker
Beachy, Vivian	Harrisonburg VA	73-75	Education
Becker, Esther	Lititz PA	54-90	Education
Bedford, Marian Newswanger	Muncy PA	70-73	Registered Nurse
Block, Arlene	Kathmandu, Nepal	74-77	Medical Technician
Block, Peter	Kathmandu, Nepal	74-77	Doctor
Bock, Diane	Lone Tree IA	75-78	Registered Nurse
Bock, Marcus	Lone Tree IA	75-78	Education
Boettger, Dennis	Mclennan AB	72-74, 77-79	Doctor
Boettger, Lucille	Mclennan AB	72-74, 77-79	Registered Nurse
Bomberger, Elton	Corning NY	53- 55	Maintenance
Brubaker, Carley	Scottdale PA	72-74	Registered Nurse
Brubaker, James	Scottdale PA	72-74	Doctor
Buckwalter, Betty Lou	Fulks Run VA	75-77	Registered Nurse
Buckwalter, Robert, Jr.	Fulks Run VA	75-77	Development
Buckwalter, Judy	Wellsville NY	88-91	Registered Nurse
Buckwalter, John	Alfred Station NY	76-79	Education
Buckwalter, Laurel	Alfred Station NY	76-79	Education
Burkholder, Helen	St Catharines ON	49-52, 56-67	Registered Nurse
Burkholder, Joseph	St Catharines ON	54-67	Doctor
Byer, Mary	Deceased	47-63	Registered Nurse
Byler, Allen	Belleville PA	50-65	Construction
Byler, Eunice Hartman	Belleville PA	50-65	Education/Homemaker
Chupp, Delilah	Sturgis MI	49-51	Homemaker
Chupp, Menno	Sturgis MI	48-51	Builder
Clemens, Jacob	Deceased	46-48	Hospital Administration
Clemens, Miriam	Lansdale PA	46-48	Hostess
Conrad, Laura	Deceased	48-50	Education
Conrad, Nancy Hernley	Scottdale PA	45-48	Nurse
Conrad, Paul	Scottdale PA	45-48	Doctor
Diener, Truman	Hillsboro KS	46-48	Maintenance
Dula, Mary Ellen Groff	Landisville PA	55-66	Registered Nurse
Eby, Alma	New Holland PA	58-61	Education
Eby, Kathryn Weaver	Lancaster PA	59-62	Homemaker (see Weaver)
Engle, Peg Groff	Harrisonburg VA	68-90	Nursing Instructor

Eshleman, D. Rohrer	Landisville PA	50-69	Doctor
Eshleman, Ellen	Deceased	50-53	Homemaker
Eshleman, Mabel Horst	Landisville PA	53-69	Registered Nurse
Friesen, Geneva Alexander	Henderson NE	46-48	Technician
Fretz, Tim	Washington DC	86-90	Development
Funk, Marian Landis	Rosthern SK	76-79	Education
Gamber, Henry	Harrisonburg VA	57-78	Evangelism/Development
Gamber, Pearl	Harrisonburg VA	57-78	Education
Garber, Alta	Lititz PA	52-75	Ministry to Women
Garber, Robert	Lititz PA	52-75	Education
Gehman, Orpha	Mohnton PA	71-74	Registered Nurse
Gingrich, Ann	Elkhart IN	54-70	Ministry to Women
Gingrich, Paul	Elkhart IN	54-70	Education
Grasse, A. Meryl	Calico Rock AR	48-50	Doctor
Greaser, Frances Bontrager	Goshen IN	50-52	Registered Nurse
Greenman, Jacqueline	Anchorage AK	76-77	Registered Nurse
Grosh, Ann King	Addis Ababa, Ethiopia	85-	Registered Nurse
Grosh, Jerry	Addis Ababa, Ethiopia	85-	Development
Grove, Erma	Goshen IN	49-51	Education
Gullman, David	Broadway VA	91-93	Development
Gullman, Debra Yoder	Broadway, VA	91-93	Registered Nurse
Hahn, Lois Marks	Wakarusa IN	50-63	Education
Haile, Grace Keeport	Elizabethtown PA	67-70	Registered Nurse
Haile, Tesfaye	Addis Ababa, Ethiopia	93-94	Internship
Hansen, Carl	Addis Ababa, Ethiopia	67-75, 96-	Education/Development
Hansen, Vera	Addis Ababa, Ethiopia	67-75, 96-	Homemaker/Business
Harnish, Kathryn	Deceased	53-58	Registered Nurse
Hege, Arlene Landis	Landisville PA	50-74	Education/Literature
Hege, Nathan	Landisville PA	50-74	Education/Literature
Hertzler, Donald	West Liberty OH	76-77	Bookstore
Hertzler, Evelyn	West Liberty OH	76-77	Education
Hooley, Paul	West Liberty OH	45-46	Mission Scout/Const.
Hooley-Gingrich, Joyce	Greenville NC	80-82	Education
Hooley-Gingrich, Robert	Greenville NC	80-82	Education
Horst, Blanche	Ephrata PA	54-70, 74-76	Homemaker/Teacher
Horst, Nevin	Ephrata PA	54-70, 74-76	Education/Bookstore
Hostetler, Leona Yoder	Deceased	49-51, 69-73	Elementary Education
Hostetter, Elizabeth	Harrisonburg VA	60-81	Bookstore
Housman, Harold	Lancaster PA	68-74	Doctor
Housman, Miriam	Lancaster PA	68-74	Homemaker
Hovde, Linda	Normal IL	83-88	Homemaker
Hovde, Robert	Normal IL	83-88	Administration
Kauffman, Lois Garber	Lititz PA	50-56	Education
Kauffman, Richard	Columbia PA	85-86	Development
Kauffman, Sharon	Columbia PA	85-86	Registered Nurse
Kebede, Janet Shertzer	Addis Ababa, Ethiopia	60-63, 68-72	Education
Keener, Clayton	Deceased	50-60	Administration
Keener, Martha	Deceased	50-60	Education
Keener, Dale	Centreville VA	60-63	Secondary Education
Kling, Nelson	Lancaster PA	70-73	Bookstore
Kopp, Ruth Ann Sensenig	Durham NC	67-70	Bookstore
Kratz, Elizabeth	Sellersville PA	64-69	Education
Kratz, Vernon	Sellersville PA	64-68	Doctor
Kraybill, Esther	Lebanon PA	70-72	Homemaker
Kraybill, Harold	Lebanon PA	70-72	Doctor

Kraybill, Herb	Lancaster PA	68-84	Education
Kraybill, Sharon	Lancaster PA	68-84	Education
Kreider, Arlene	Lancaster PA	67-90	Bookstore/Education
Kuhns, James	Harrisonburg VA	49-51	Administration
Kuhns, Olive	Harrisonburg VA	49-51	Registered Nurse
Landis, Vida	Coatesville PA	76-78	Registered Nurse
Leaman, Harold	Lancaster PA	71-73	Education
Leaman, Patricia	Lancaster PA	71-73	Registered Nurse
Lehman, Cora	Chambersburg PA	72-76	Registered Nurse
Lehman, G. Irvin	Harrisonburg VA	45-47	Administration
Lehman, Erma	Newport News VA	64-73	Houseparent
Lehman, Paul	Newport News VA	64-73	Houseparent
Lehman, John E.	Elkhart IN	48-50	Administration
Lehman, Margaret	Elkhart IN	48-50	Homemaker
Litwiller, Kenneth	Goshen IN	86-95	Development
Litwiller, Laura	Goshen IN	86-95	Development
Ludwig, Martha Wikerd	Ephrata PA	50-54	Education
Martens, Eleanor	Winnipeg MB	72-75	Registered Nurse
Martens, Raymond	Winnipeg MB	72-75	Doctor
Mayer, Loretta	Sarasota, FL	48-50	Hostess
Mellinger, Alta Zimmerman	Ephrata PA	60-63	Registered Nurse
Metzler, Laura	Columbiana OH	50-52	Office
Miller, Anna	Conestoga PA	51-67, 70-73	Registered Nurse
Miller, Lois Landis	Greenwood DE	51-67	Registered Nurse
Miller, Samuel	Merion PA	71-74	Education
Mishler, Dorsa	Goshen IN	46-48	Education
Mishler, Mary	Goshen IN	46-48	Homemaker
Mullet, Mildred Heistand	Goshen IN	50-67	Education
Nacht, Hedwig	Bern, Switzerland	72-72	Registered Nurse
Nafziger, Kenneth	Mount Wolf PA	72-75	Education
Nafziger, Phoebe	Mount Wolf PA	72-75	Education
Nafziger, Lois	Lansdale PA	71-74	Education
Neer, Charlene	Upsilanti MI	83-86	Registered Nurse
Ness, Daniel	Lancaster PA	67-73	Bookstore/Business Mgr.
Ness, Mary Ellen Umble	Lancaster PA	63-73	Bookkeeper
Newswanger, Betty Hershey	Lancaster PA	66-69	GSS Teacher
Nissley, J. Marlin	Lewisburg PA	69-72	Doctor
Nissley, Martha	Lewisburg PA	69-72	Homemaker
Ondine, A. Lois Graybill	Cicero IL	64-67	Bookstore
Payne, James	Heathsville VA	52-55, 61-62	Construction/Education
Payne, Marian	Heathsville VA	61-62	Homemaker
Pfahler, Karl	Duisburg, Germany	87-90	Development
Pfahler, Ruth	Duisburg, Germany	87-90	Homemaker
Reimer, Bert	Morden MB	88-94	Administration
Reimer, Evelyn	Morden MB	88-94	Homemaker
Reinford, Cleta	Kulpsville PA	79-80	Homemaker
Reinford, Daniel	Kulpsville PA	79-80	Education
Rempel, Eric	Niverville MB	76-80	Development
Rempel, Mary	Niverville MB	76-80	Homemaker
Ressler, Everett	Lancaster PA	74-75	Development
Ressler, Phyllis	Lancaster PA	74-75	Homemaker
Rohrer, Martha Hartzler	Dayton VA	56-76	Registered Nurse
Rush, Sara	Deceased	48-50, 54-57, 60-79	Nurse/Hostess
Schaffer, Anna M. Graybill	Manheim PA	51-56	Registered Nurse

Schlabach, Mae	Deceased	49-54, 77-78	Registered Nurse
Schlabach, Walter	Deceased	49-54, 77-78	Doctor
Sensenich, Dorothy	Neffsville PA	68-75	Registered Nurse
Sensenig, Blanche	Lititz PA	47-70	Guesthouse Hostess
Sensenig, Daniel	Deceased	47-70	Administration
Sensenig, Gary	Millersville PA	68-69	GSS Teacher
Sensenig, Joanne	Millersville PA	68-69	Registered Nurse
Sensenig, Janice	Lancaster PA	61-69	GSS Teacher
Shenk, Calvin	Harrisonburg VA	61-75	Education
Shenk, Marie	Harrisonburg VA	61-75	Business Education
Shetler, Jan	Dove Creek CO	80-83	Education
Shetler, Peter	Dove Creek CO	80-83	Development
Showalter, Ada	Deceased	46-48	Dietician
Snyder, Alice	Lititz PA	53-71	Bookstore
Stoner, Elaine	Deceased	65-68	Registered Nurse
Stoner, Gerald	Bainbridge PA	65-68	Education
Strickler, Larry	Lititz PA	56-59	Const./Home Repair
Strubar, Margaret Ulrich	Eureka IL	48-50	Education
Taylor, Marie Peifer	Hyattsville MD	67-70	Registered Nurse
Thomas, Marian Landis	Landisville PA	68-69	Secretary/Receptionist
Thomas, Marie	Lancaster PA	71-74	Homemaker
Thomas, Melvin	Lancaster PA	71-74	Administration
Weaver, Ed	Deceased	48-50	Education
Weaver, J. Irvin	Deceased	59-62	Bookstore
Weaver, Kathryn	Lancaster PA	59-62	Homemaker (now Eby)
Wehibe, Mary Jane Zimmerman	Elizabethtown PA	60-65	Registered Nurse
Wenger, Chester	Lancaster PA	49-66	Education
Wenger, Sara Jane	Lancaster PA	49-66	Homemaker
Wenger, Martha	Waynesboro VA	64-66	Education
Wenger, Paul	Deceased	64-66	Education
Wert, Esther	Sayre PA	67-70	Homemaker
Wert, Roy	Sayre PA	67-70	Doctor
Wiens, Linda	Vancouver BC	80-83	Registered Nurse
Williams, Alice J. Russell	Galeton CO	81-86	Development
Wolgemuth, Dale	Manheim PA	76-78	Registered Nurse
Wolgemuth, Lois	Manheim PA	76-78	Registered Nurse
Wonderly, Norma Dick	Deceased	63-67	Registered Nurse
Yoder, Daisy	Harrisonburg VA	56-77	Ministry to Women
Yoder, Paul T.	Harrisonburg VA	56-77	Doctor
Yoder, Leo	Baton Rouge LA	74-78	Doctor
Yoder, Mary	Baton Rouge LA	74-78	Homemaker
Yoder, Samuel A.	Deceased	48-51	Mission Scout
Zimmerman, Ruth	Lititz PA	48-51	Lab Technician

Notes

1. The Day the Church Was Closed

1. *Kebeles* were neighborhood associations, governing units of small local areas set up by the Marxists to maintain close control over the population.
2. Arlene Kreider, interview, Lancaster, Pa., Oct. 24, 1995. References to Kreider throughout this chapter are based on this interview.
3. Clusters of kebeles were organized under a head kebele or keftenya.
4. Yakuta Abdo, interview, Salunga, Pa., Aug. 31, 1996.
5. Abebe Gorfe, interview, Washington, D.C., Oct. 24, 1996.
6. Ibid.
7. Shamsudin Abdo, interview, Addis Ababa, Mar. 17, 1996.
8. Tilahun Beyene, interview, Landisville, Pa., Dec. 22, 1995.
9. Bedru Hussein, interview, Addis Ababa, Mar. 3, 1996.
10. Tesfatsion Dalellew, letter, Dec. 1996.

2. How Christianity Came to Ethiopia

1. *Ililta* is the joy cry that Ethiopians use at the birth of a baby and at weddings. Now it is used at high points of worship such as the dedication of babies and baptism of believers. Orthodox Christians give this joy cry when the Ark of the Covenant is brought out of the church on special days.
2. Calvin E. Shenk, "The Development of the Ethiopian Orthodox Church and Its Relationship with the Ethiopian Government from 1930 to 1970," unpublished manuscript, 22.
3. Graham Hancock, *The Sign and the Seal* (New York: Crown Pub. Group, 1992), 419-464.
4. Shenk, 21.
5. Edward Ullendorff, *The Ethiopians: An Introduction to Country and People* (London: Oxford Univ. Press, 1960), 77-78. Mohammed Gragn, a Muslim leader who persecuted the Orthodox Church, invaded from the south and west and reached as far as Tigre in the north. The Portuguese helped overthrow Gragn, who was killed in 1543.
6. Shenk, 25.
7. Gustav Aren, *Evangelical Pioneers in Ethiopia* (Stockholm: S. F. E. Press, 1978), 15, 130-134.
8. For the complete Sudan Interior Mission (SIM) story, see F. Peter Cotterell, *Born at Midnight* (Chicago: Moody Press, 1973).
9. J. Spencer Trimingham, *The Christian Church and Missions in Ethiopia* (London: World Dominion Press, 1950), 27.

10. Evangelical missions in Ethiopia in the 1950s were mainly Presbyterians, Anglicans, Sudan Interior Mission, Mennonites, and Lutheran groups from Germany, Norway, Sweden, and Denmark.

3. Mennonites—Called to Ethiopia

1. Information on the Daniel S. Sensenig family in this chapter is from Blanche Sensenig, interview, Lititz, Pa., Nov. 12, 1996.
2. Paul Erb, Orie O. Miller, *The Story of a Man and an Era* (Scottdale, Pa.: Herald Press, 1969), 188.
3. C. Gordon Becham, quoted in *Missionary Messenger* (*MM*), Nov. 1946, 15.
4. Jacob R. Clemens, diary, Dec. 28, 1947.
5. *Negarit Gazeta,* 1944, 161.
6. Dorsa Mishler, letter, Feb. 24, 1948.
7. Paul N. Kraybill, ed., *God Led Us to Ethiopia* (Salunga, Pa.: Eastern Mennonite Board of Missions and Charities [EMBMC], 1956), 49.
8. Ibid, 51-52.

4. Missionaries and Culture

1. Walter Schlabach, *MM,* "Prayer Letter Suppl.," Feb. 1954, 7.
2. Robert Garber, ibid., 6.
3. Lois Garber, *MM,* "Prayer Letter Suppl.," June 1953, 7.

5. Education—A Hunger to Learn

1. "EMBMC Annual Report," 1958, 62.
2. Harold Housman, M.D., interview, Salunga, Pa., July 26, 1996.
3. Lois Garber, *MM,* 1953. "Prayer Letter Suppl.," Dec. 1953, 9.
4. J. R. Clemens, diary, Aug. 30, 1947.
5. Information about the Nazareth Dresser Bible School is from articles Chester L. Wenger wrote in *MM,* 1952 to 1954.
6. "EMBMC Annual Reports," 1958, 63.
7. Ibid., 1959, 44.
8. The first Ethiopian to direct the Nazareth Bible Academy was Daniel Lemma, who served as director during Chester Wenger's home leave in 1962 to 1963.
9. Leona Yoder, *MM,* Jan. 1970, 19.
10. Evie Hertzler, *MM,* Sept. 1977, 20.

6. Medicine Opens Doors for Mission

1. Walter and Mae Schlabach served again in Ethiopia during 1977-78, just before the transfer of HMMM Hospital at Nazareth to the government.
2. Walter Schlabach, *MM,* "Prayer Letter Suppl.," Oct. 1952, 5-6.
3. Rohrer Eshleman, ibid., 5.

4. Joe and Helen Burkholder, interview, St. Catherines, Ont., Canada, June 24, 1996.

5. P. T. and Daisy Yoder, interview, Harrisonburg, Va., July 20, 1996.

6. Paul Gingrich, letter, *MM*, July 1968, 20.

7. Nevin Horst, letter to author, Feb. 1997.

8. Nathan Hege, "Retooling for the Future," *MM*, Aug. 1966, 9.

9. Nevin Horst, letter to author, Jan. 19, 1997.

10. Negash Kebede, "The Role of Institutions," unpublished paper, July 31, 1997.

7. Development—An Urgent Need

1. Carl Hansen, interview, Addis Ababa, Mar. 8, 1996.

2. Robert Garber, interview, Lititz, Pa., Jan. 7, 1997.

3. Henry and Pearl Gamber, letter, *MM*, Jan. 1976, 19.

4. Nathan Hege, "Agricultural Development Program Grows in Bedeno," *MM*, Jan. 1973, 9.

5. "Helping to Bring Relief in Ethiopia," *MM*, Aug. 1974, 12-13.

6. David Thomas, "When Brothers Meet," *MM*, June 1977, 14.

7. "Ethiopian Church Builds Development Effort," MCC News, *MM*, Jan. 1977, 20.

8. *MM*, May 1980, 22.

9. Picture story in *MM*, May 1975, 13.

10. Bernie Bayless, "Ethiopian Mennonites and MCC Help Restore Forests," *MM*, May 1981, 7.

11. "Food Aid Airlifted to Ethiopia," *MM*, Jan. 1985, 9; Peter M. Michael, "Ethiopia's Agony," May 1985, 12; "Grain Airdrop in Ethiopia," Nov. 1985, 20.

12. "Ethiopians Build Food Warehouse in Wukro," MCC News, *MM*, Jan. 1986, 21.

13. "MCC to Fund Development Project in Ethiopia," MCC News, *MM*, July 1986, 19.

14. Carl Hansen, reporting in "Zemedkun Bikeda Story," unpublished manuscript, 5.

15. Jerry Grosh, interview, Addis Ababa, Apr. 4, 1996.

16. Zemedkun Bikeda, interview, Addis Ababa, Feb. 29, 1996.

17. Mekonnen Desalyn, interview, Addis Ababa, March 1, 1996.

18. Carl Hansen, message to MKC General Church Council, Addis Ababa, Feb. 11, 1996.

19. Carl Hansen, interview, Addis Ababa, Mar. 8, 1996.

8. Opening the Holy Book

1. Bati Insermo, "My Greatest Joy," *MM*, Sept. 1961, 3.

2. Anna Mae Graybill, letter in *MM*, "Prayer Letter Suppl.," Aug. 1952, 6.

3. Lois Marks, *MM*, "Prayer Letter Suppl.," Feb. 1953, 7.

4. Lois Garber, *MM*, "Prayer Letter Suppl.," June 1955, 5.

5. Daisy Yoder, interview, Harrisonburg, Va., July 20, 1996.

6. Ann Gingrich, *MM*, "Prayer Letter Suppl.," June 1956, 6.

7. Daniel Sensenig, *MM*, February 1957, 14.

8. Paul Gingrich, *MM*, "Prayer Letter Suppl.," Feb. 1957, 4.

9. Ibid, Aug. 1957, 5.

10. Lois Marks, *MM*, "Prayer Letter Suppl.," Aug. 1955, 3.

9. Believers Form a New Church

1. Arlene Hege, diary, June 16, 1951.

2. Ethiopians, however, are not strangers to foot washing. When guests came to a home, the host traditionally washed the guests' feet, although the duty always fell on the youngest but able member of the family.

3. Workinesh Bantiwalu, interview, Nazareth, Apr. 2, 1996.

4. Minutes of First Inter-Mission-Station Brotherhood Conference, Jan. 17-19, 1959. Also, Chester L. Wenger, letter, Nov. 15, 1959. Observers at this meeting were Asfaw Bachore, Asfaw Biratu, Beyene Chichaibelu, Desalegne, Gebreselassie Habtamu, Haile Orficho, Tafesse Gerbi, and Nathan Hege.

5. Daniel Sensenig, "1958 Annual Report," in 1959 *Missions Yearbook*, 60.

6. EMBMC Executive Committee meeting minutes, June 13, 1962, 7.

7. Memo of Understanding, Exhibit A, EMBMC Minutes, Feb. 6, 1964.

8. "EMBMC Annual Reports," 1962, p. 40.

9. "EMBMC Annual Reports," 1963, p. 43.

10. "EMBMC Annual Report," 1964, p. 43.

11. Seyoum Gebretsadik, interview, Addis Ababa, Apr. 10, 1996.

12. Memo of understanding, Exhibit A, EMBMC Minutes, Feb. 6, 1964.

13. Negash Kebede, "Expansion and Church Organization," unpublished paper, July 31, 1997.

10. A Fresh Move of the Spirit

1. Much of the material in this chapter is based on an interview with Solomon Kebede, Addis Ababa, Mar. 21, 1996.

2. Bedru Hussein interview, Addis Ababa, Mar. 19, 1996.

3. Gebreselassie Habtamu interview, Nazareth, Apr. 2, 1996.

4. Arlene Hege, "Everything Is a Result of Prayer," *MM*, May 1974, 5.

5. *MM*, May 1965, 10.

6. Million Belete, *MM*, July 1995, 4.

11. Revolution—A Society in Upheaval

1. The main evangelical churches in Ethiopia are Mekane Yesus (Lutheran and Presbyterian), Kale Heywet (SIM), Birhane Heywet (Baptist), Mulu Wengel, and Meserete Kristos (Mennonite). MKC makes up only 2 percent of this membership, now estimated to be six million.

2. Negash Kebede, letter, Aug. 28, 1997.

3. Carl Hansen, "Reflections on Development in Ethiopia," *MM,* Nov. 1975, 8.

4. Shawle Wehibe, "Visit in Ethiopia," *MM,* May 1977, 7.

5. Carl Hansen, *MM,* Sept. 1975, 16.

6. Tesfatsion Dalellew, "One in the Spirit in Ethiopia," *MM,* Sept. 1977, 14-15.

7. Asrat Gebre, "Ethiopian MKC Delegation Visits USSR, *MM,* Nov. 1979, 11.

8. Bedru Hussein, interview, Addis Ababa, Mar. 19, 1996.

9. Janet Kreider, "A Vision Fulfilled," editorial, *MM,* Oct. 1981, 24.

10. Marian Landis, "Love Healing in Ethiopia," *MM,* May 1979, 2-4.

11. Shemelis Rega, interview, Dire Dawa, Mar. 22, 1996, referring to Josh. 13:14, 33; 14:3-4; yet see Josh. 21, assigning Levites to places among other tribes.

12. The Many Faces of Persecution

1. Alemayehu Assefa, interview, Nazareth, Feb. 29, 1996. The references to Alemayehu in this chapter are based on this interview.

2. Alemu Checole, interview, Nazareth, Apr. 2, 1996.

3. Ibid.

4. Arlene Hege, "Prisoner for Christ," *MM,* July 1996, 8.

5. Solomon Kesete, interview, Dire Dawa, Mar. 25, 1996.

6. Kassa Agafari, speaking in a chapel devotional for EMM staff, Salunga, Pa., Apr. 1990.

7. Tesfatsion Dalellew, letter to author, Nov. 1996.

8. Ijigu Woldegebriel, interview, Addis Ababa, Feb. 16, 1996.

13. Prison Life

1. Shamsudin Abdo, in *Against Great Odds* video, Gateway Films, 1991.

2. Negash Kebede, interview, Addis Ababa, Apr. 1996.

3. Belayneh Gebrehanna, interview, Addis Ababa, Feb. 15, 1996.

4. Worknesh Bantiwalu, interview, Nazareth, Apr. 2, 1996.

5. Kedir Delchume, interview, Nazareth, Apr. 2, 1996.

6. From MKC minutes of 1983 and 1984.

7. Senait Abebe, correspondence, July 17, 1997.

14. Regrouping to Survive

1. Ijigu Woldegebriel, interview, Addis Ababa, Feb. 16, 1996.

2. Kassa Agafari, *The Mennonite,* June 12, 1990, 250.

3. Beyene Mulatu, interview, Addis Ababa, Jan. 19, 1996.

4. Kedir Delchume, interview, Nazareth, Apr. 2, 1996. Material ascribed to Kedir Delchume in this chapter is from this interview.

5. Hailu Cherenet, interview, Addis Ababa, Apr. 11, 1996.

6. Yohannis Germamo, interview, Addis Ababa, Feb. 2, 1996.
7. Getaneh Ayele, interview, Addis Ababa, Feb. 15, 1996.
8. Kassa Agafari, interview, Nairobi, Kenya, Jan. 8, 1986.
9. Ibid.
10. Mersha Sahele and Metasebiya Ayele, interview, Addis Ababa, May 7, 1996.

15. Into Every Region

1. Haile Wolebo, coordinator for the Shone District, interview at Shone, Apr. 7, 1996.
2. David Shenk, interview, Salunga, Pa., Sept. 1996.
3. Delemo Bassa, interview, Shone, Apr. 7, 1996.
4. Kedir Delchume, interview, Nazareth, Apr. 2, 1996.
5. Ijigu Woldegebriel, interview, Addis Ababa, Feb. 16, 1996.
6. Kassa Agafari, interview, Salunga, Pa., Apr. 1990.
7. "Church Buildings Returned to MKC," *MM*, Nov. 1991, 20.

16. Expansion to Wollega

1. Tefera Gonfa, pastor of the three districts in Wollega, supplied much of the information in this chapter during interviews in Addis Ababa, Jan. 26 and Feb. 16, 1996.
2. Sekata Gelata, interview, Hagamsa, Apr. 19, 1996.

17. Facing Tomorrow

1. Bedru Hussein, interview, Addis Ababa, Mar. 19, 1996.
2. Johni Teklu, interview, Dire Dawa, Mar. 28, 1996.
3. Girum Tadesse, interview, Dire Dawa, Mar. 28, 1996.
4. Kedir Delchume, interview, Nazareth, Apr. 2, 1996.
5. Bedru Hussein, interview, Addis Ababa, Mar. 19, 1996.

Epilogue

1. Also see Ps. 87:4; Amos 9:7; Acts 8:27-39.

Glossary and Abbreviations

Addis	The common abbreviation for Addis Ababa, the capital city of Ethiopia.
ALERT	All Africa Leprosy Rehabilitation Training Centre, at Addis Ababa.
araki	A strong, homemade alcoholic drink.
Ato	Mr. For example, Germa Mekonnen is called Ato Germa—not Ato Mekonnen, which is the name of Germa's father.
BCMS	Bible Churchmen's Missionary Society, a mission from England that is working in Ethiopia, now known as Cross Links.
birr	Monetary unit used in Ethiopia. 6.80 birr = one U.S. dollar in 1997.
chat	Leaf of a narcotic plant that is chewed to produce euphoria.
dabo	Ethiopian bread baked with spices.
DBS	The Dresser Bible School trained health assistants at the Haile Mariam Mamo Memorial Hospital, Nazareth, Ethiopia.
Derg	Literally "a committee of equals," the name used to refer to the military government in charge during the revolutionary years, 1974-1991.
dresser	Health assistant trained to give basic care to hospital patients and operate rural clinics. Dressers are not registered nurses (RNs).
EMBMC	Eastern Mennonite Board of Missions and Charities, Salunga, Pa., is the official name of the Lancaster Mennonite Conference mission board organized in 1914.
EMM	Eastern Mennonite Missions, a shorter form of EMBMC, used since 1992.
EPRP	Ethiopia People's Revolutionary Party
GSS	Good Shepherd School was built for missionary children and international students.
HMMM	Haile Mariam Mamo Memorial Hospital, at Nazareth.
ililta	Joy cries in worship.
injera	Large flat pancake made with *tef* flour and eaten with *wat*.
kebele	A neighborhood association for administering affairs in the smallest district at the local level; a "higher" *kebele* (*keftenya*) would administer many "lower" *kebeles*.
kilel	Church district.

keftenya	A head *kebele* administering a cluster of kebeles.
KHC	Kale Heywet Church (Word of Life Church), which grew out of the missionary work of SIM.
LMC	Lancaster Mennonite Conference, in eastern Pennsylvania, has 220 congregations with a total of 20,000 members. LMC is one of 22 conferences of the Mennonite Church.
mahiber	An association of people who help each other in times of need, such as preparing for funerals and weddings.
MBMC	Mennonite Board of Missions and Charities, Elkhart, Ind., the denominational mission board of the Mennonite Church; later, MBM.
MCC	Mennonite Central Committee, Akron, Pa., is a relief and development agency of Mennonite and Brethren in Christ denominations.
MEDA	Mennonite Economic Development Associates.
megabi	Pastor.
meno	Food served in prisons; a small portion.
merkato	Bazaar, marketplace, much of it outdoors.
MKC	Meserete Kristos Church (Christ Foundation Church), the Ethiopian Mennonite Church, organized in 1960.
MM	*Missionary Messenger*
MME	The Mennonite Mission in Ethiopia, the official body registered with the Ethiopian government to carry on mission and development activities. EMM has maintained this registration at the request of MKC, to facilitate activities when MKC registration was not possible.
MRC	Mennonite Relief and Service Committee administered relief efforts of the Mennonite Board of Missions, Elkhart, Ind., during the 1940s.
MWC	Mennonite World Conference.
MYC	Mekane Yesus Church, the name of the Ethiopian church that grew out of missionary work by Lutherans from Europe and North America. The Presbyterians are a separate Bethel Synod of MYC.
Pente	An abbreviation of Pentecostal, used as a derogatory term for Christians not in the Orthodox Church.
shash	A scarf tied over the hair, worn by many Ethiopian women.
SIM	Originally Sudan Interior Mission, now SIM Missions, an interdenominational mission board operating worldwide.
tabot	The ark of the covenant (Exod. 25-26); a replica is kept in every Orthodox Church.
tef	A small cereal grain peculiar to Ethiopia, used in making *injera*.
wat	Food, often highly spiced, served with *injera*.

Weizero   Mrs. For example, Aster Bekele is addressed as Weizero (W/o) Aster—not W/o Bekele, which is her father's first name. Her name is not changed with marriage. Weizerit (Wt.) refers to an unmarried woman.

werede   A small political division similar to a township in Pennsylvania.

Zemecha   A campaign for development set up by the Derg, conscripting young people to do literacy teaching and Marxist indoctrination throughout Ethiopia.

zigba   A tree whose wood is similar to that of a pine tree in North America.

Persons Interviewed

Abebe Gorfe
Abebech Watche
Alemayehu Assefa
Alemayehu Jabang
Alemu Chekole
Alice Snyder
Almaz Assefa
Amanuel
Ann Gingrich
Ann King Grosh
Arlene Kreider
Ashene Getachew
Aster Debossie
Aster Kassa
Bedru Hussein
Beyene Chichaibelu
Beyene Mulatu
Birhanech Wolde
Blanche Sensenig
Carl Hansen
Chester Wenger
Colin Mansell
Daisy Yoder
Daniel Ness
Eyob Shugute
Eyoel Woldegebriel
Fikru Zeleke
Fissiha Wondemagenghu
Fufa Semo
Gabriel Chane
Gebreselassie Habtamu
Gemechu Gebre
Getahun Assefa
Getaneh Ayele
Haga Hirpha
Hailu Cherenet
Hailu Wolebo
Hana Asheber
Helen Burkholder
Henry Gamber
Ijigu Woldegebriel
Janet Kebede
Jerry Grosh
Joseph Burkholder
Kedir Delchume
Kefyalew Cherinet

Kelemwerk Tessema
Mabel Eshleman
Mae Schlabach
Mary Ellen Ness
Mekonnen Asfaw
Mekonnen Desalyn
Menbere Wobi
Mersha Sahele
Meshel Shibera
Metasebiya Ayele
Million Belete
Mulugeta Zewdie
Muluwerk Mekuria
Negash Kebede
Nevin Horst
Paul Gingrich
Paul T. Yoder
Pearl Gamber
Peg Groff Engle
Rahael Asheber
Rasme Gelatis
Regassa Wirtu
Rohrer Eshleman
Samuel Bateno
Sara Jane Wenger
Sehene Dejene
Sekata Gelata
Seyoum Gebretsadik
Tilahun Beyene
Walter Schlabach
Wedeneh Hapteyesus
Wegayehu Debebe
Wehibe Kebede
Werknesh Bantiwalu
Yednekachow Kelile
Yeshitela Mengistu
Yohannis Germamo
Yonas Bachore
Zemedkun Bikeda
Zerihun Teseme
Zina Tuke

Bibliography

Abraham, Emanuel. *Emanuel Abraham: Reminiscences of My Life.* Oslo, Norway: Lunde Forlag, 1995.

Aren, Gustav. *Evangelical Pioneers in Ethiopia.* Stockholm: S. F. E. Press, 1978.

Brant, Albert E. *In the Wake of Martyrs.* Langley, B.C.: Omega Publications, 1982.

Cotterell, F. P. *Born at Midnight.* Chicago: Moody Press, 1973.

Cumbers, John. *Count It All Joy: Testimonies from a Persecuted Church.* Kearney, Neb.: Morris Publishing, 1996.

David, R. J. *Fire on the Mountains.* Grand Rapids: Zondervan, 1966.

Erb, Paul, *Orie O. Miller: The Story of a Man and an Era.* Scottdale, Pa.: Herald Press, 1969.

Hancock, Graham. *The Sign and the Seal.* New York: Crown Pub. Group, 1992.

Kraybill, Paul N., ed. *Called to Be Sent.* Scottdale, Pa.: Herald Press, 1964.

_____, ed. *God Led Us to Ethiopia.* Salunga, Pa.: Eastern Mennonite Board of Missions and Charities, 1956.

Lipsky, George A. *Ethiopia: Its People, Its Society, Its Culture.* New Haven: HRAFP Press, 1962.

Shenk, Calvin E. "The Development of the Ethiopian Orthodox Church and Its Relationship with the Ethiopian Government from 1930 to 1970." Unpublished manuscript, 1972.

Trimingham, J. Spencer. *The Christian Church and Missions in Ethiopia.* London: World Dominion Press, 1950.

Ullendorff, Edward. *The Ethiopians: An Introduction to Country and People.* London: Oxford Univ. Press, 1960.

Willmott, Helen M. *The Doors Were Opened.* London: SIM, 1960.

Yoder, Samuel A. *Middle-East Sojourn.* Scottdale, Pa.: Herald Press, 1951.

Index

The Author

Nathan B. Hege was born in Hagerstown, Maryland, to parents who prayed that he would become a missionary. With his family, he served in Ethiopia from 1950-74, in teaching and church-planting assignments with Eastern Mennonite Missions (EMM) and Meserete Kristos Church (MKC).

After Hege trained in literacy journalism at Syracuse University in 1963, he returned to Ethiopia and worked at producing Christian education materials in the Amharic language.

Since 1974, Hege's responsibilities have included editing *Missionary Messenger*, EMM's periodical, pastoring in his home congregation at Willow Street, in Lancaster, Pennsylvania, and giving oversight to the seven churches of the Willow Street-Strasburg District of Lancaster Mennonite Conference.

Now retired, Nathan Hege lives with his wife, Arlene, at Landisville, Pennsylvania. They are members of Willow Street Mennonite Church and the parents of four children, three still living, and grandparents of eight.